DEATH, DYING AND THE LAW

Titles in the Series:

A Patient's Right to Know: Information Disclosure, the Doctor and the Law
Sheila A.M. McLean, University of Glasgow

New Reproductive Techniques: A Legal Perspective
Douglas J. Cusine, University of Aberdeen

Medico-Legal Aspects of Reproduction and Parenthood
J.K. Mason, University of Edinburgh

Law Reform and Human Reproduction
Edited by *Sheila A.M. McLean*, University of Glasgow

Legal and Ethical Issues in the Management of the Dementing Elderly
Mary Gilhooly, University of Glasgow

Legal Issues in Human Reproduction
Edited by *Sheila A.M. McLean*, University of Glasgow

Mental Illness: Prejudice, Discrimination and the Law
Tom Campbell, Australian National University, Canberra and
Chris Heginbotham, Riverside Mental Health Trust, London

Pregnancy at Work
Noreen Burrows, University of Glasgow

Changing People: The Law and Ethics of Behaviour Modification
Alexander McCall Smith, University of Edinburgh

Health Resources and the Law: Who Gets What and Why
Robert G. Lee, Hammond Suddards, Leeds and *Frances H. Miller*, University of Boston

Surrogacy and the Moral Economy
Derek Morgan, Cardiff Law School

Family Planning Practice and the Law
Kenneth McK. Norrie, University of Strathclyde

Mental Health Law in Context: Doctors' Orders?
Michael Cavadino, University of Sheffield

Artificial Reproduction and Reproductive Rights
Athena Liu, University of Hong Kong

Medicine, Law and Social Change
Leanna Darvall, La Trobe University

Abortion Regimes
Kerry A. Petersen, La Trobe University

Human In Vitro Fertilization: A Case Study in the Regulation of Medical Innovation
Jennifer Gunning, Agricultural and Food Research Council and
Veronica English, Human Fertilisation and Embryology Authority

Law Reform and Medical Injury Litigation
Edited by *Sheila A.M. McLean*, University of Glasgow

Medical Negligence Law
Andrew Philips, University of Strathclyde

Competence to Consent to Medical Treatment
John Devereux, Griffith University

Contemporary Issues in Law, Medicine and Ethics
Edited by *Sheila A.M. McLean*, University of Glasgow

**The Contractual Reallocation of Procreative Resources and Parental Rights:
The Natural Endowment Critique**
William Joseph Wagner, The Catholic University of America

Clinical Resource Allocation
Christopher Heginbotham, Riverside Mental Health Trust, London and
Peter Mumford, King's Fund College, London

Designer Babies
Robert Lee, Hammond Suddards, Leeds and *Derek Morgan*, Cardiff Law School

Legal Issues in Obstetrics
Vivienne Harpwood, Cardiff Law School

All titles are provisional

Death, Dying and the Law

Edited by
SHEILA A.M. McLEAN

Dartmouth
Aldershot • Brookfield USA • Singapore • Sydney

Published by
Dartmouth Publishing Company Limited
Gower House
Croft Road
Aldershot
Hants GU11 3HR
England

Dartmouth Publishing Company
Old Post Road
Brookfield
Vermont 05036
USA

British Library Cataloguing in Publication Data
Death, Dying and the Law. - (Medico-Legal
Series)
 I. McLean, Sheila A.M.   II. Series
 344.1044197

Library of Congress Cataloguing-in-Publication Data
Death, dying, and the law / edited by Sheila A.M. McLean.
        p.   cm.— (Medico-legal series)
    ISBN 1-85521-657-4
    1. Right to die—Law and legislation—Great Britain.
 2. Terminally ill—Legal status, laws, etc.—Great Britain.
 3. Euthanasia—Great Britain.   4. Assisted suicide—Great Britain.
 5. Medical ethics—Great Britain.   I. McLean, Sheila.   II. Series.
 KD3410.E88D415   1995
 344.41'04197—dc20
 [344.1044197]   95-34897
                                                                        CIP

ISBN 1 85521 657 4

Typeset by Manton Typesetters, 5–7 Eastfield Road, Louth, Lincolnshire LN11 7AJ, UK
Printed and bound in Great Britain by Biddles Limited, Guildford and King's Lynn

Contents

List of Contributors

Pieter Admiraal is now retired. Dr. Admiraal was an anaesthetist in Delft for over 30 years. During this period he was extensively involved in pain treatment, terminal care and euthanasia. Amongst his many awards was the 1992 Humanist Award. Pieter Admiraal is a member of the Academy of Humanism.

Christopher Docker is Executive Secretary, Voluntary Euthanasia Society of Scotland.

Bryan Jennett is Professor Emeritus of Neurosurgery, University of Glasgow.

Barbara J. Logue is Senior Demographer, Center for Policy Research and Planning, Mississippi Institutions of Higher Learning. She is the author of *Last Rights: Death Control and the Elderly in America* (Macmillan 1993).

Sheila A.M. McLean, the General Editor of this series, is the International Bar Association Professor of Law and Ethics in Medicine and the Director of the Institute of Law and Ethics in Medicine at Glasgow University.

J.K. Mason is Professor (Emeritus) of Forensic Medicine in the University of Edinburgh. He is currently working and teaching medical jurisprudence in the Faculty of Law at that University.

Nicholas A. Pace is Consultant Anaesthetist, Western Infirmary, Glasgow. He is co-editor of *Ethics and the Law in Intensive Care*.

Cheryl K. Smith is Legal Services Director, Oregon Rehabilitation Association. She was the primary drafter of the Oregon Death with Dignity Act.

Ann Sommerville is advisor on medical ethics to the British Medical Association and has been involved in many of its recent publications, including the code of practice *Advance Statements about Medical Treatment* (1995). She wrote the BMA's ethics handbook for doctors *Medical Ethics Today* (1993). Her previous background was in the field of human rights and civil liberties.

Introduction

Few issues have so grasped the public and academic imagination in recent years than that which concerns the extent to which it is right, lawful or acceptable that people should control the time, manner and means of their own death. We accept readily that people should have control over their lives, but seem less confident in confronting that same control when it comes to death and the dying process. Moreover, it is only recently that courts and legislatures throughout the Western world have been expected to address significant numbers and types of situations in which the concept of human rights has been inextricably linked with choices about health care provision and/or death itself.

Although these issues have been considered sporadically in the past, concern about their implications has now reached a peak of intensity which has seen governments and their agents and courts challenged as never before. This book deals with some of the most topical dilemmas confronting societies, individuals and states in this most fundamental of areas.

For reasons which should be obvious, the book is divided into two Parts. Part I examines the situation in the United Kingdom in the light of the House of Lords Select Committee on Medical Ethics and a number of watershed legal decisions. Although the manuscript was completed before the Law Commission issued its Report on Mentally Incapacitated Adults, and before the publication of the British Medical Association Report on Advance Directives, I believe that the arguments contained in the book do not suffer significantly because of this. Indeed, it is interesting to note the extent to which these same arguments have found some fruit in what these august bodies have themselves concluded. Part II takes a more international perspective, looking both at some of the more notable legal changes in other parts of the world and also at alternative perspectives on the issues raised.

The variety of backgrounds of the contributors shows that issues about the end of life are human issues and not the exclusive province of one discipline or one jurisdiction. Indeed, this book was conceived with an underpinning intention not to medicalize or overlegalize these matters. It is sometimes too tempting for one discipline or one country to assume that they have the answer and that all will be well if the rest of us simply fall into line. This book postulates no 'right' answers or systems; it makes no assumptions about the appropriateness or otherwise of legalizing euthanasia, physician-assisted suicide or advance directives. Rather, it explores, in the light of what has already been achieved and what may yet come to pass, these complex, emotional and sometimes distressing questions. Because of this, there is no universal agreement within the chapters as to the correct or desirable way forward.

I am, of course, profoundly grateful to all the distinguished contributors to this volume, who have put in so much effort to produce stimulating chapters. I am also happy to acknowledge the contribution made by the staff at Dartmouth, and the friends, loved ones and colleagues of myself and all of the contributors. I must also express my gratitude to the Dean of the Faculty of Medicine at Glasgow University, Professor Brian Whiting, for his financial contribution to the meeting at which the idea of this book was born. I am also grateful to the School of Law at Glasgow University, and in particular to the Dean of the Faculty of Law and Financial Studies, Professor John Grant, for his continued – and much appreciated – support of the Institute of Law and Ethics in Medicine under whose auspices the meeting was held.

It is with pleasure that I again dedicate this book to my parents, both of whom continue to be vigorous, healthy, supportive and loving. Long may this continue!

Sheila A.M. McLean
Glasgow
February 1995

PART I

1 Law and Ethics at the End of Life: The Practitioner's View

DR NICHOLAS A. PACE, MB, ChB, FRCA,
MRCP, MPhil
Consultant Anaesthetist, Western Infirmary, Glasgow

Advances in medical technology have led to situations where doctors are unclear about their ethical and legal obligations to particular patients. Many of the dilemmas that doctors have to face in their everyday practice can be illustrated by referring to the following case history of a patient recently admitted to the Intensive Care Unit (ICU) at the Western Infirmary in Glasgow.[1]

Case history: A 72 year-old man was admitted with multiple injuries after crashing his car into a wall. He was concussed and had a flail chest. After bilateral chest drains were inserted, controlled ventilation was commenced and he was transferred to the ICU. Exploratory laparotomy for a possible ruptured spleen was contemplated but, at this point, his son refused consent, stating: 'My father will not thank you for saving his life.' The patient had previously complained to his relatives that his quality of life had become extremely poor because of severe chronic obstructive airways disease. He was almost chairbound and had frequently stated that he no longer wished to live.

We contacted his general practitioner (GP) to confirm his past history. The patient had visited her two days prior to the accident but, despite being extremely unwell, had declined hospital admission. The GP thought that the crash was probably a suicide attempt, but nevertheless felt that, rather than being depressed, the patient had a realistic view of his condition and future. The ICU staff, with the full support of the family, therefore decided to withdraw the life-supporting measures previously instituted. Inotropic support was stopped and supplemental oxygen discontinued. Ventilation was decreased and analgesic drugs were continued to ensure that the patient remained pain-free and peaceful. He died one hour later.

At first sight, this case history appears uncontroversial and straightforward, and most people would agree with the course of action taken. Closer examination, however, illustrates many of the everyday dilemmas faced by ICU staff. Indeed, the subject is so extensive this chapter affords the scope for only minimal examination, and many issues, such as those of dealing with minors, informed consent, research or organ donation, will have to be omitted.

Consent

Of prime importance is the ethical principle of patient autonomy. While there is little doubt that competent patients have the ethical and legal authority to make decisions about their medical treatment, because most patients in the ICU are unconscious or heavily sedated they cannot be directly involved in the decision-making process. On the other hand, if a patient is to be admitted to the ICU electively following an operation, the staff have a duty to discuss the various treatment options available and to ascertain the patient's preferences beforehand.

In the above case history, the son refused consent for his father's operation. As already stated, since many patients in the ICU are incompetent, doctors frequently ask relatives to give consent instead. But, how much weight should doctors place on the relatives' 'consent'? After all, there may be other reasons – quite apart from the best interests of the patient – that may enter into the decision-making process of individual family members. For instance, in the above case history, should the staff have discussed with the son his relationship with his father, including the possibility of any financial gain should his father die? In such a life-or-death situation, there may be insufficient time to enter into detailed discussions with relatives about the possible benefits of the patient's death. Moreover it is doubtful whether hospital staff have the right to ask these types of questions. Further problems arise where the family is divided about the best course of action to take or where there is disagreement between the hospital staff and the relatives. In the latter case, the usual scenario is that of the ICU staff wishing to stop treatment while the relatives insist on all available treatment being administered. This can usually be resolved by creating time-limited objectives.

What happens if one member of staff disagrees with the proposed plan of action? The nature of many of these situations is such that unanimous agreement is the exception rather than the rule. Should the decision be taken only by a few (for example, the consultants involved) or should all staff members have their say? The greater the number of people involved, the more difficult it is to achieve consensus.

Despite these problems, in the UK the vast majority of decisions appear to be made by consensus between the ICU staff and family. However, it must be emphasized that at present, legally, no-one, perhaps not even the courts, can give consent on behalf of an unconscious adult.[2] In these circumstances doctors who treat patients rely on the 'defence of necessity' test – that is, that it was necessary to treat the patient without consent because it was in the best interests of the patient and necessary to save 'life or limb'. For this defence to be valid the need for such treatment must be urgent and unable to be delayed until the patient regains consciousness.

Thus, for example, the legality of treating attempted suicides is not as clear-cut as some doctors may believe. Suppose that the patient in the case history had left a note stating that he did not wish to be resuscitated. Would the hospital staff then have had the legal or ethical authority to proceed with treatment? What if the note had been found after treatment had started and, in a case other than this, was very likely to be successful? Should such treatment then be stopped? In such circumstances there is a likelihood of a subsequent action against the hospital staff, especially if that treatment has led to a diminished quality of life, although the chances of such an action being successful are felt to be remote.[3]

Clearly there is a huge legal hiatus around which health-care staff and families have to work. Since competent patients clearly have the right to refuse treatment, the fact that they have become incompetent does not mean that their right to autonomy can be disregarded. There is little doubt that the majority of people would choose to avoid continuing their existence in certain medical conditions, such as the persistent vegetative state, and would rather die. People are rightly concerned about the inappropriate use of medical technology. This problem can be easily resolved by a competent patient since he or she could then refuse treatment such as fluid or food. Unfortunately, the medical conditions which most people would choose to avoid are those in which the patient is incompetent and therefore unable to participate in the decision-making process.

Clearly, the public will lose faith in the medical profession unless doctors not only recognize the needs of their patients but also respect their wishes, even if these are contrary to the doctor's advice. In principle the vast majority of doctors profess to reject paternalism, even though in reality they may not always practise what they preach. Doctors also believe that they always act in the best interests of their patients. Unfortunately, this does not necessarily mean they are always right.

Death is perceived by some medical staff as a failure of their skills. If, however, they merely prolong the inevitable and the patient is not allowed to die with dignity, they are clearly not acting in the best interests of the patient. Often a fresh view may offer a better appreciation of where the patient's best interests lie.[4]

In the case history above, the GP knew the patient and, at first sight, appears to be the logical person to consult when a patient is incompetent. However, the GP's view of what the patient may have wanted is not necessarily accurate. Furthermore, since the average GP consultation takes about three minutes, how much can the GP truly know about a particular patient's circumstances and family relationships?

These difficulties in dealing with incompetent patients have led to the recent interest in the establishment of advance directives or 'living wills'.[5] In principle, advance directives protect patients' autonomy by giving them the opportunity, while competent, to express their own wishes on how they want to be treated, what is in their best interests and what level of quality of life they are prepared to accept should they become unable to decide for themselves. In practice, advance directives have a number of disadvantages. The 'living will' can be ambiguous and therefore open to interpretation. If vaguely worded it will not reassure the patient and will furthermore lead to debate about its actual meaning. On the other hand, if it is too specific it may be too restrictive. It is thus very difficult to find the appropriate form of words adequately to describe what the patient actually requests. It can lack flexibility and thus not only be unable to change as a situation develops but also be unable to respond to unforeseen events.

The alternative of proxy consent can have similar problems. Although it is more flexible it leaves many questions unanswered. Can the proxy fully reflect the patient's wishes or is the decision likely to be based on a form of substituted judgement? Will there be a great deal of discussion between the proxy and the patient to ensure that the proxy fully understands the patient's preferences in a wide selection of medical situations? Can the proxies actually carry out those wishes, if known, or will they suffer from guilty feelings if they feel they have let the patient die? Of course, some decisions are clearly going to be based upon future quality of life but, because an acceptable quality of life means different things to different people, it needs to be interpreted according to what the patient would have wanted.

The first question that must be asked is whether advance directives are actually needed in the UK. Is there any evidence that medical staff inappropriately use medical technology to the detriment of their patients? Unlike in the USA where the propensity towards litigation may lead to the inappropriate use of technology because doctors and hospitals fear lawsuits if they fail to do everything technologically possible to prolong a patient's life, there seems to be no evidence of the same happening in the UK. Furthermore, the system in the USA whereby doctors and hospitals are paid per item of service subconsciously encourages the prolonged use of expensive advanced medical technology, irrespective of future quality of life. The same situation does not apply to the UK as yet, although it remains to be seen what effect the recent Government reforms regarding hospital trust status and the purchaser/provider split will have.

It has been claimed that a poorly drafted natural death act can lead to the erosion of patient rights rather than fulfilment of patient wishes.[6] For example, the California Natural Death Act was passed in 1976 following the Karen Quinlan Case.[7] In this act a legally enforceable declaration can only be executed 14 or more days after a person is diagnosed as being terminally ill – terminal illness being defined as an illness that will imminently cause the patient's death. Thus, Quinlan herself would have been excluded. Further problems in the USA legislation are that the types of treatment that can be refused are limited to extraordinary treatment, there is no provision for proxy consent and there is no penalty to health-care workers who fail to honour the advance directive.

A significant problem with many of the statutes in the various US states is the requirement for the patient to be certified as qualified (in many cases by two physicians) in order to have their living wills followed. As argued by Heintz,[8] based on the principle of autonomy, a patient needs to be neither certified nor qualified but only mentally competent at the time of making the will.

Furthermore many statutes define a 'terminal condition' as one which, regardless of the use of life-sustaining procedures, would produce death and where the use of these procedures only serves to postpone the moment of death. Thus, these statutes exclude conditions such as Alzheimer's disease and the persistent vegetative state. Indeed, in the terminal cases envisaged, a living will is not needed because the patient is about to die. One US state actually has legislation stating that a living will can only be executed after a diagnosis of a terminal illness. Thus, US law actually appears to restrict patient freedom since a living will is only allowed when death is imminent, whether or not life-sustaining treatment is administered. One may further argue that this is precisely what many people would describe as futile treatment. Hence, it should not be administered, irrespective of whether or not there is a living will.

It may be claimed that the enactment of an advance directive law will improve communication between patient and doctor. In the USA, the Patient Self Determination Act ensures that, on admission to hospital, patients are advised of their right to refuse treatment and to write an advance directive.[9] All that actually happens is that the patient is handed a multi-page information sheet. This probably worsens communication between the doctor and the patient.

Thus, arguments that these laws enrich patient autonomy are not entirely accurate. Indeed, the law at times merely appears to be obstructive. Heintz, commenting on the Hawaii Natural Death Act, claims that he would not be surprised if the new act generated litigation where previously there had been none.[10] Annas, in turn, states that the use of complex forms and obstructive strategies makes it likely that treatment decisions will actually be made by the hospital's lawyers and the (proxy's) lawyers and not by the (proxy) and the physician.[11]

It must also be remembered that advance directives, whether in the form of living wills, proxy consent, or indeed a combination of the two, if introduced, are going to have different impacts on different specialities. Rheumatologists and dermatologists work to a completely different timescale to anaesthetists, the treatment they offer being carried out over months, years or even a lifetime. Anaesthetists, on the other hand, mainly act in emergency situations, with only seconds or a few minutes in which to take decisions and act accordingly. In the emergency situation, such as a major overdose or road traffic accident, questions of consent do not immediately spring to mind. Sometimes patients have to be admitted unexpectedly to the ICU following a complication of surgery. Thus, in the anaesthetic workplace, apart from the possible administration of blood, few situations can be predicted and hence patient consent (or dissent) to a specific situation may be difficult to obtain in advance.

Furthermore, to be of any use the existence of an advance directive has to be known to the health-care staff treating the patient. A sudden catastrophic event may preclude the passing on of this information. Should, then, a centralized system be set up that has to be referred to in each emergency? The possibilities of mistakes occurring with this form of data collection and retrieval are immense. The introduction of advance directives will therefore create more problems than may be solved.

Quality of Life

The preservation of life is a fundamental principle of both law and medicine. This does not mean, however, that doctors are compelled to offer a patient all available means at their disposal in order to prolong his or her life. Technological advances have resulted in gradually shifting the problem from the means of reversing the dying process to questions regarding the quality of life sustained and preserved.[12] Thus, in a US court case, it was stated that:

> Prolongation of life ... does not mean a mere suspension of the act of dying, but contemplates at the very least, a remission of symptoms enabling return towards a normal, functioning, integrated existence.[13]

In this respect, the patient in the case history, despite what would have been heroic measures to prolong his life, had no chance of returning to a normal life. Questions, however, still arise. How ill was the man prior to his accident? He was obviously well enough to drive a car. There are clearly many people, such as those who are bed-bound, who are in a much worse state than he was. People, therefore, are prepared to accept different levels of quality of life, which in turn makes the concept difficult to define and evaluate.

Ordinary/Extraordinary Treatment

In the above case history, it was decided not to operate and to withdraw inotropes and supplemental oxygen and decrease ventilation. How did the health-care staff come to decide this?

One of the fundamental principles aiding the decision-making process is the distinction between ordinary and extraordinary treatment. This appears to offer doctors and patients a reasonable and straightforward basis of assessing what is obligatory treatment, or what Gillon[14] describes as 'how much to strive to keep alive'.

Ordinary means have been defined as all medicines, treatments and operations which offer a reasonable hope of benefit for the patient and which can be obtained and used without excessive expense, pain or other inconvenience. Extraordinary means are all medicines, treatments and operations which cannot be obtained or used without excessive expense, pain, or other inconvenience, hence causing an intolerable burden, or which, if used, would not offer a reasonable hope of benefit.[15]

However, one of the main problems with this distinction is that the terms 'benefit' and 'burden' are open to interpretation. For example, it has been claimed that doctors should distinguish between an effect and a benefit. An effect is limited to a part of the patient's body whereas a benefit improves the patient as a whole.[16]

On the other hand, in judging how burdensome a particular treatment is, consideration has to be given to the degree of risk, cost and physical and psychological hardship involved relative both to a particular patient, his or her overall condition, potential for improvement, resources and sensibilities, and to a particular doctor (or medical team), his or her time, effort and other obligations.[17] The criteria for assessing whether a proposed treatment is burdensome are therefore not precise and will differ according to the patient's circumstances. Similarly, individual doctors and, more importantly, individual patients will have different priorities.

Nevertheless, it must be recognized that doctors are not treatment technicians: they are not required to administer futile treatment nor can the patient or family request it.[18] A treatment that fails to improve the patient's prognosis, comfort, well-being, or general state of health is futile.[19] Because it is not medically indicated it is not ethically obligatory. Schneiderman and his colleagues[20] have proposed that treatment should be regarded as futile if in the last 100 cases it has been useless. Furthermore, they claim that if a treatment merely preserves permanent unconsciousness or cannot end dependence on intensive care, that treatment should be regarded as futile. Others are not so prepared to accept such a wide interpretation of futility and believe that the concept of futility should only be applied to the medical assessment of physiological futility.[21]

I personally believe that not only is futility a medical judgement but also that futility varies according to the resources available. Hence, if resources were unlimited, many cases presently described as futile would cease to be so. For example, if there were unlimited ICU beds, no patient would be refused admission, irrespective of how remote the chances of survival were. Hence, the concept of futility may very well have significant economic ramifications.

The problem with decision making is that the science of outcome prediction in the ICU is not exact. Various decision-making aids, such as the APACHE program, Therapeutic and Injury Severity Score, the Mortality Prediction Model, The Riyadh Intensive Care Program and the Glasgow Coma Scale, have all been used in the ICU to try to help doctors correctly predict a patient's prospects of survival. All are derived from a large data bank of previous patients and therefore do not take any account of individual patients, new drugs or technological advances.

Nonetheless, if it is agreed that a certain treatment is physiologically futile, then ethically it is imperative that such a treatment is not offered because resources are finite. It is interesting, therefore, to point out that, in the recent case of *Airedale NHS Trust* v. *Bland*,[22] it was argued and accepted by the law lords that treatment was futile. If that is the case, then it must also be futile for every other patient in a persistent vegetative state. Consequently, it could be argued that it is unethical to keep them all alive because it would clearly be a misuse of resources. This would be a logical extension of the Bland decision.

Double Effect

In the example used in this chapter, the patient was given analgesic drugs, following the withdrawal of treatment, to ensure that he remained pain-free and comfortable. However, these drugs, due to their effect on the body, may possibly have led to an earlier death. Their administration appears acceptable due to the application of the principle of double effect.

This principle is mainly used to allow doctors to treat patients despite the knowledge that undesirable side-effects may arise out of that treatment. For example, the administration of pain-relieving drugs is allowed even in doses that may coincidentally speed up death. It is claimed that:

> In this case, of course, death is in no way intended or sought, even if the risk of it is reasonably taken; the intention is simply to relieve pain effectively, using for this purpose painkillers available in medicine.[23]

The principle therefore emphasizes the central moral importance of intentions, and elicits a sharp distinction between intended and foreseen (but unintended) consequences.[24] There can be consequences foreseen to be inevitable which do not count as intended.[25]

The Appleton Consensus states that pain and suffering should be vigorously treated, even if this leads to an earlier death.[26] The principle of double effect, although usually used in this context of terminal pain relief, may also be used to justify the use of opiates in the relief of coughing and breathlessness.[27] Thus, the principle appears to allow an agent to bring about indirectly a bad effect that it is not permissible to bring about directly.[28]

The Roman Catholic Church also accepts the principle of double effect.

> There is a distinction between intending death and foreseeing that there is a serious risk of death as a result of one's act. The distinction is well understood and significant.[29]

However, the Roman Catholic Church does not accept all cases of double effect. When the dose of morphine is increased automatically at every administration or at daily intervals despite the patient neither being in pain nor distressed, this is clearly a case of active euthanasia, albeit by instalments.[30]

There are a number of arguments against the principle. For instance, one of the conditions for the principle to be valid is that the intention of any act must be solely to produce the good effect. The problem with this is that when one knows that a bad effect will result from one's action then it seems to be simply self-deceiving to say that one does not intend it.[31] In this way, the principle clearly encourages moral dishonesty.

The principle further claims that a person does not intend all the consequences of an intentional action.[32] What counts as an intended effect is not, however, very clear. Intentions are difficult to define. How does one draw the line between intended means and foreseen inevitable consequences? The term 'double effect' relates to side effects which may be brought about in addition to the effect that is aimed at. A side effect is claimed to be one not intended by the agent. This cannot be correct, as the following example will show.[33]

Consider an anaesthetic agent, the main effect of which is to put the patient to sleep. A side effect is the production of hypotension. In a particular operation hypotension may be very desirable. Both drug A and drug B will anaesthetize the patient, but drug A causes more hypotension (a side effect) than drug B. Therefore in a particular operation requiring hypotension drug A is chosen. The side effect here is surely intended. Similarly, consider an anaesthetic for an operation in which no hypotension is required. If drug A is again used, instead of B, and the patient develops hypotension how can the anaesthetist deny responsibility by claiming it was only a foreseen consequence? What else did the anaesthetist expect?

Therefore, by far the greatest difficulty with the principle lies with explaining how one does not necessarily intend a consequence that is foreseen. Almost anything can be foreseen as a side effect rather than intended as a means. It would also be easy to say after an action that there was no intention to cause harm. If the agent was fully aware of the consequence before deciding to carry out the action, responsibility for that action must be accepted. The consequence of the action cannot be described as unintended, accidental or indirect.

The double effect argument would therefore appear useful only to those holding absolutist principles and reflects the moral absolutism of standard Roman Catholic morality. The following example clearly illustrates this. A good Roman Catholic may not directly kill himself. However, if he is engaged in a just war he may throw himself on a grenade that lands in his foxhole to save his comrades. This is permissible as long as he does not intend to kill himself but only to absorb the shrapnel with his body, although he can surely foresee that this will lead to death. One effect, it is claimed, is intended (the absorbing of the shrapnel); the second effect (his death) is foreseen but not intended.[34] Many readers, I believe, would find it hard to accept there is a difference.

Does this mean that the principle of double effect is never acceptable? It appears that one of the few acceptable uses of the principle is in the context of terminal pain relief because one aspect that has not yet been mentioned is choice. No-one would doubt that it is a moral imperative to prescribe painkillers for the relief of terminal pain. Not to do so would be one of the most immoral omissions in medicine. Therefore there is no choice but to prescribe them; the doctor has no other option and does not need to justify their prescription. The side effects of the drugs are therefore irrelevant. By analogy, in the anaesthetic drug example given above, if there was no other drug available apart from the one which will also cause hypotension, then there is no other choice available apart from the administration of that drug. The possibility of side effects is again irrelevant.

Acts/Omissions

Although it is arguable whether the administration of sedating drugs could be proved to lead to the earlier death of a patient, the withdrawal of life-supporting treatment certainly does, and this is of great concern to doctors. Does the withdrawal of life-supporting treatment from the patient, which directly leads to the patient's death within a very short space of time, amount to the act of killing?

The British Medical Association[35] rejects killing but is prepared to allow the withholding of life-saving treatment, even though that omission will lead to an earlier death than if treatment were given. In these cases, it is claimed, it is not the 'omitter' who is killing, but the disease or condition from which the patient suffers. This argument is based on the acts and omissions doctrine in which actions that result in some undesirable consequence are, in general, morally worse than inactions, or failures to act, that have the same consequence. Most people would accept this because they do not feel as morally responsible for their omissions as they do for their actions. There is thus a widespread and deeply held intuition that there is an important distinction between killing and letting die. To many, an action carries the presumption that the person carrying out the act incurs the responsibility of intention; an omission does not.[36]

The distinction between acts and omissions is however subject to a number of significant criticisms:

1 New technology makes the distinction difficult and sometimes impossible to put into practice.
2 It has been argued that there is no necessary valid moral distinction.
3 Some writers have further maintained that directly and painlessly killing a patient may be a morally superior decision to leaving him to a slow undignified death.

If considered in terms of the intentions or of the consequences of the action or omission, there seems to be no necessary ethical difference at all between killing and letting die (at least in some cases). For example, one can commit murder by omission. If during a routine operation the anaesthetist notices a ventilatory disconnection and deliberately fails to reconnect so that the patient dies, then he has deliberately killed the patient, albeit by an omission. Making a patient die by an omission is therefore not analogous to no action at all and is open to the same degree of moral appraisal as the act of killing the patient. If one has a duty to act, and fails to do so, one is morally (and legally) responsible for the consequences arising out of that omission. An omission is therefore not merely not doing. Something not done is omitted if it ought to have been done, or was needed or was expected.

Hence, there is no necessary moral difference between an act and an omission.[37] If the motives, intentions and other background factors are held constant and equal in both cases, there can be no moral difference. Furthermore, the main criticism of the doctrine must be that there can be no moral or legal justification for giving a doctor the right to withhold treatment such as connecting a patient to a respirator and yet to refuse him the right to withdraw treatment by disconnecting a patient already so connected. It would be absurd to suggest that if respirators required periodic recharging a doctor would have the right in certain circumstances not to recharge the respirator – an omission – but would not have the right in the same circumstances to unplug a continuously operating respirator – an action.

Despite the element of action in treatment withdrawal, it should be classified as a refusal to continue treatment rather than an act of killing. This has very recently been confirmed by the House of Lords decision in the *Bland* case in which it was held that it would be appropriate to withdraw feeding from a patient in a persistent vegetative state.[38]

The American Medical Association[39] have also accepted that there is no distinction between withholding and withdrawing life-sustaining treatment, and this applies to all medical treatment which prolongs life, including nutrition and hydration.

In summary, what is morally true about acts causing deaths is equally true of omissions causing death, other things being equal. There is no necessary moral difference between the two. It is simplistic to assume that a death which results from not connecting a patient to a respirator is morally preferable to a death that results from disconnecting a patient from a respirator.[40] Thus there is no moral or legal difference between withholding and withdrawing treatment. Despite this, it is not universally accepted by doctors who, psychologically, find it much more difficult to stop treatment than to withhold it. Once a particular treatment is started, it is difficult to stop it. It is relatively easy not to offer a patient artificial ventilation but much more difficult to withdraw it especially as, in the eyes of all health-care staff concerned, the act of removing a patient from the ventilator leads to the patient's death.

Resource Allocation

It is now well recognized that every public health-care system cannot fully meet the demands placed upon it. Demand has outstripped supply. ICUs have a potential for limitless expense. However, because resources are finite, treatment offered to one patient or group of patients necessarily results in another patient being denied treatment, or at least having treatment delayed.

The general public must realize that, over the next few years, some very awkward questions regarding the allocation of resources to the health-care industry will be asked. Politicians, as always, will not answer them. They will make the rules but will certainly not take responsibility for the treatment or non-treatment of individual patients. That is the responsibility of doctors who, in turn, have the duty to inform the public if resources have fallen way below demand.

Scarcity will lead to society (or others chosen by society) having to establish priorities of resource allocation. Although, at present, members of society believe they have a right to all forms of treatment, they must be prepared to reassess what can and cannot be achieved and impose limits on these achievements. There is, however, great disagreement on which criteria should be used in resource allocation.[41] What appears clear, however, is that it will be the supply side that will be regulated since it is very difficult to regulate demand directly. Indeed, by regulating the supply side, demand can, in turn, be diminished to a certain extent. For example, in the ICU situation, decreasing the number of available beds by one will tighten the criteria for admission, and doctors will therefore not bother to refer certain patients. As stated earlier, the definition of futility varies according to the resources available. It must be recognized, however, that this situation cannot go too far. The number of beds cannot, for example, be suddenly cut by five (out of, say, a previous total of seven) because of the public outcry that will ensue. Already, some health authorities have decided that certain treatments, such as in-vitro fertilization and tattoo removal, are not essential, will not be provided in hospitals under their control. The demand for these treatments is therefore shifted on to the private health service.

It is also very important to recognize the implications of supply-induced demand, which means that, for each new scientific and skill

development – whether of electronic technology, complex drug struc-
tures or surgical techniques and body tissue replacements – the availability of a new service will create a demand in excess of the ability
to meet that demand, thereby adding to the overall burden of rationing.[42] For example, the increasing availability of organ transplanta-
tion will increase demands on the ICU. In turn, the improved successful treatment of certain illnesses in the ICU, as for example
pneumocystis infection in AIDS patients, will increase demand.

At the individual ICU level, many questions remain unanswered.
In the case history detailed at the beginning of this chapter, what
would have happened if there were no available beds in the ICU?
What should the staff have done if the patient had taken the last
available bed and another patient required admission with a potentially recoverable illness? Should there be rigid criteria which
patients must satisfy before being admitted? Should one of these be
the probability of survival, since it is recognized that patients with a
less than 50 per cent chance of survival incur costs that are twice as
high as those with a chance of survival of over 50 per cent?[43] Unfortunately, attempts to predict survival have not been particularly successful. However, it is clearly the responsibility of the ICU staff to
resolve these various dilemmas. Otherwise, the hospital administration, by means of the financial control given to it with the recent
introduction of purchaser/provider contracting, will do it instead.

Legal Inconsistencies

The law is inconsistent and fudges many of the issues. One major
problem with the legal arguments is that despite the fact that doctors
are allowed to stop all life-supporting treatment and administer large
doses of narcotics to keep the patient comfortable, the law does not
accept the administration of a large dose of potassium which achieves
the same end result, only more quickly. For example, in the recent
Bland case,[44] the administration of a lethal dose of a drug would have
spared the family and staff two extremely distressing weeks waiting
for the patient to die. It would also have made economic sense.

The law recognizes the test of best interests of the patient unless
the interest of state supersedes. Thus, active euthanasia is illegal.

The issue of consent when dealing with incompetent patients also
requires clarification, with guidance issued to health-care staff.

Conclusion

It is accepted that, in many ways, this discussion has raised more questions than have been answered. I make no apology for this. Many of the issues are highly complex, and philosophical debate continues. However, arguably no one group, be it of doctors, lawyers, philosophers or accountants, has a right to decide what is right or wrong for the rest of society. Open debate amongst all members of the community is urgently required, especially on the issue of resource allocation. On the other hand, the law fudges many of these issues in the belief that it is serving the interests of society. From the practitioners' view, it is time for reassessement and clarification.

Notes

1   Pace, N, Plenderleith, J.L. and Dougall, J.R. (1991), 'Moral principles in withdrawing advanced life support', *British Journal of Hospital Medicine*, **45**, pp. 169–170.
2   Mason, J.K. (1996), 'Consent to treatment and research in the ICU', in Pace, N. and S.A.M. McLean (eds), *Ethics and the Law in Intensive Care*, Oxford: Oxford University Press.
3   Ibid.
4   Pace, N. (1993), 'Ethical problems in ITU', *Current Anaesthesia and Critical Care*, **4**, pp. 208–12.
5   See Chapter 3 of this volume.
6   Heintz, L.L. (1988), 'Legislative hazard: keeping patients living, against their wills', *Journal of Medical Ethics*, **14**, pp. 82–6.
7   In re Quinlay (1976), 70 NJ, 10 355 A. 2d 647 Cert denied 429 US 922.
8   Heintz, op. cit., note 6 supra.
9   For discussion, see Capson, A. (1986), 'Legal and Ethical problems in decisions for death', *Law, Medicine and Health Care*, **14**.
10 Heintz, op. cit., note 6 supra.
11 Annas, G.J. (1991), 'The health care proxy and the living will, *New England Journal of Medicine*, **324**, pp. 1210–13.
12 McCormick, R.A. (1974), 'To save or let die; the dilemma of modern medicine', *Journal of the American Medical Association*, **229**, pp. 172–6.
13 In re Dinnerstein (1978), Mass App. 380 NE2d 134.
14 Gillon, R. (1986), 'Ordinary and extraordinary means', *British Medical Journal*, **292**, pp. 259–61.
15 Kelly, G. (1951), 'The duly to preserve life'. *Theological Studies*, **12**, p. 550.
16 Schneiderman, L.J., Jecker, N.S. and Jonsen, A.R. (1990), 'Medical futility: its meaning and ethical implications', *Annals of Internal Medicine*, **112**, pp. 949–54.
17 Linacre Centre (1982), *Euthanasia and Clinical Practice: Trends, Principles and Alternatives*, Working party, London: Linacre Centre.
18 Tomlinson, T. and Brody, H. (1990), 'Futility and the ethics of resuscitation', *Journal of the American Medical Association*, **264**, pp. 1276–80.
19 cf. Schneiderman *et al.*, *op. cit.*, note 16 supra.
20 Ibid.
21 Hastings Center (1987), *Guidelines on the Termination of Life Sustaining Treatment*

and the Care of the Dying, Bloomington, Ind.: Indiana University Press and the Hastings Center.

22 *Airedale NHS Trust* v. *Bland* [1993] 2 WLR 316.

23 Sacred Congregation for the Doctrine of the Faith (1980), 'Declaration on Euthanasia', Vatican City, *Acta Apostolicae Sedis*, **72**, pp. 542–52.

24 Beauchamp, T.L. and Childress, J.F. (1989), *Principles of Biomedical Ethics* (3rd edn), New York: Oxford University Press. Downie, R.S. and Calman, K.C. (1987), *Healthy Respect: Ethics in Health Care*, London: Faber and Faber.

25 Kennedy, I. (1981), *The Unmasking of Medicine*, London: Allen & Unwin.

26 Stanley, J. (1989), 'The Appleton Consensus: suggested international guidelines for decisions to forego medical treatment', *Journal of Medical Ethics*, **15**, pp. 129–36.

27 Dunstan, E.J. (1989), 'First know the patient: resolving multiple problems in old age', in G.R. Dunstan and E.A. Shinebourne (eds), *Doctors' Decisions: Ethical Conflicts in Medical Practice*, Oxford: Oxford University Press, pp. 187–96.

28 Cf. note 24 supra.

29 See note 17, supra.

30 Ibid.

31 Gillon, R. (1986), 'The principle of double effect and medical ethics', *British Medical Journal*, **292**, pp. 193–4.

32 Cf. move 24 supra.

33 Pace, N., 'Withholding and withdrawing medical treatment', in Pace and McLean, *op. cit.*, note 2 supra.

34 Engelhardt, H.T. (1986), *The Foundations of Bioethics*, New York: Oxford University Press.

35 British Medical Association (1984), *Handbook of Medical Ethics*, London: British Medical Association.

36 Cf. note 17 supra.

37 Tooley, M. (1976), 'The termination of life: some issues', Manuscript, Research School of Social Sciences, Australian National University.

38 *Op. cit.*, note 22 supra.

39 American Medical Association (1990): AMA Council on Scientific Affairs (1990), 'Persistent vegetative state and the decision to withdraw or withhold life support', *Journal of the American Medical Association*, **263**, pp. 426–30.

40 Gillon, R. (1988), 'Euthanasia, withholding life-prolonging treatment and moral differences between killing and letting die', *Journal of Medical Ethics*, **14**, pp. 115–17.

41 Gillon, R. (1985), 'Justice and allocation of medical resources', *British Medical Journal*, **291**, pp. 266–8.

42 Dyson, R. (1996), 'Rational allocation of resources: management perspectives', Pace, N. and McLean, S.A.M. *op. cit.*, note 2 supra.

43 Ridley, S., Biggam, M. and Stone P. (1993), 'A cost benefit analysis of intensive therapy', *Anaesthesia*, **48**, pp. 14–19.

44 *Op. cit.*, note 22 supra.

2 Managing Patients in a Persistent Vegetative State since *Airedale NHS Trust* v. *Bland*

BRYAN JENNETT CBE, MD, FRCS
Professor Emeritus of Neurosurgery, Institute of Neurological Sciences, University of Glasgow

To understand why the management of vegetative patients presents medical, ethical and legal problems it is first necessary to be clear about the medical facts of this condition. It is also necessary to be aware of the emergence in the USA over the past decade of a consensus about this issue, since this has influenced recent events in the UK.

Vegetative patients have suffered severe brain damage that puts the cerebral cortex – the thinking, feeling part of the brain – out of action. The patient is awake at times, with eyes open, but shows no evidence of awareness – no psychologically meaningful responses to external stimuli, no commands obeyed and no words uttered. But many reflex responses remain, such as withdrawal of the spastic paralysed limbs from a painful stimulus, which may provoke grimacing and groaning. It is widely accepted that vegetative patients are unconscious and incapable of suffering mental distress or physical pain. The evidence for this comes not only from clinical observation but from research studies on the level of metabolic functioning of the cerebral cortex and basal ganglia which, in vegetative patients, is at the level associated with deep surgical anaesthesia. In addition, the pathological dissection of the brains of vegetative patients who have died shows extensive destruction of the cerebral cortex or widespread disconnection of the cerebral cortex from the rest of the brain, or a combination of both. There is not therefore a single lesion, similar in all vegetative patients, but a range of pathologies depending on causation. The common factor is that there is no longer sufficient cerebral cortex, either surviving or connected, for the continuation of consciousness. It is known that wakefulness (eye opening) and reflex activity depend on mechanisms in the lower, more primitive, parts of the brain and are independent of the cortex which is, however, needed for awareness.

Vegetative survival affects a small proportion of patients rescued by resuscitation and intensive care from devastating acute brain insults that would previously have proved fatal. Head injury accounts for about half of these acute cases; the next most common cause is an anoxic episode (acute oxygen deprivation in the brain) due to cardiac arrest, near drowning or strangulation; other causes are hypoglycaemia in diabetics and a variety of intracranial conditions, such as haemorrhage, infection or tumour. Children with severe developmental diseases and adults with degenerative conditions can gradually become vegetative as their condition progresses (as with, for example, Alzheimer's disease and Huntington's chorea). The debate about the appropriate management of vegetative patients has, however, focused on those who have suffered acute insults.

After acute insults patients may recover to varying degrees after being vegetative for some weeks, and occasionally after several months. Children more frequently recover than adults, and traumatic cases recover more often than non-traumatic. Many medical authorities have declared that the vegetative state can be considered permanent (as distinct from persistent) after one year, and several consider that an earlier decision can be made in non-traumatic cases. A recent authoritative US report based this view on a review of over 750 cases reported in the medical literature.[1]

In reviewing claims for recovery from the vegetative state it is important to distinguish between recovery to some degree of independence, which is obviously a desirable outcome, and the restoration only of very limited responsiveness, without speech. The latter is the usual outcome when recovery begins after many months and it is a matter of debate whether such limited recovery, associated with some awareness of their plight, can be regarded as a better outcome for patients than the insentient vegetative state. Nonetheless the possibility of a reasonable recovery in some patients has led the British Medical Association (BMA) to recommend that vegetative patients in the early months should be treated by vigorous rehabilitation.[2] Certainly it is important to maintain adequate nutrition and to avoid complications such as contractures and bedsores whilst awaiting spontaneous recovery. There is, however, no good evidence that sensory stimulation programmes, drug regimes or electrical stimulation of the brain can promote recovery from the vegetative state. In practice few active rehabilitation units are prepared to admit such patients because of the poor prognosis.

Continued survival in the vegetative state requires only basic nursing care and tube feeding. In the early months a number of patients die, normally from chest infections, but those who survive the first year are relatively stable and can live for many years. Several survivals of 18 and 20 years are recorded, one of 37 and one of 40 years. Such prolonged survivals are not usually associated with exceptional care, and some have occurred despite a decision to withhold antibiotics in the event of infections and not to resuscitate should cardiopulmonary arrest take place.

Estimates of the numbers of vegetative patients at any one time depend crucially on how long patients have to be in this state to qualify. US estimates are based on an interval of one month after the acute insult, giving much larger numbers than if only those still vegetative after three or six months are counted, because many patients have died and some have recovered by this time. The best estimates for the UK are about 1000 cases at least six months after an acute insult; based on the US figures there might be as many again derived from chronic conditions.

Once the vegetative state is declared permanent (as distinct from persistent) there is therefore the prospect of prolonged survival in this state. The question then arises as to whether continuing life-sustaining treatment is appropriate and/or obligatory. This has medical, ethical and legal perspectives which focus on whether such treatment can be considered to confer any benefit on the patient and therefore to be in his or her best interests. Considering that it was not, some US families in the late 1970s requested that food and water be withdrawn from their vegetative relatives, in order to allow them to die with dignity. Although doctors often agreed, hospital authorities were sometimes reluctant to do this without a court order, and at least 50 such cases have now reached the US courts – where the families' requests have almost always been granted. The courts in the USA have, however, come to be regarded as an inappropriate forum for making such sensitive decisions, since they tend to polarize opinions, attract unwanted publicity, delay decision-making and involve unnecessary expense. Moreover several US judges have stated that it is now appropriate for the decision to withdraw tube feeding to be made by doctors in consultation with the family, without seeking court approval, unless there is a dispute between the involved parties or the patient has no family to speak for him or her.

No-one knows how many cases have been dealt with informally without court approval in the USA, because it has never been declared necessary to seek a court order before stopping treatment. Indeed, such decisions have been seen as in accord with the recommendations of the 1983 President's Commission on Decisions to Forego Life Sustaining Treatment.[3] This Commission, which included doctors, nurses, lawyers, theologians and philosophers, considered a wide range of circumstances in which treatment could be withdrawn either because it was refused or was considered not in the patient's best interest; moreover it made specific reference to withdrawing tube feeding from vegetative patients. More recently the US medical establishment has made several authoritative statements about the diagnosis, prognosis and management of vegetative patients. These include the American Academy of Neurology (1989),[4] the American Medical Association (1990),[5] the American Neurological Association (1993),[6] and the Multi-society Task Force (1994).[7] These all state that, once the vegetative state has been declared permanent, the withdrawal of tube feeding is appropriate as this can be considered to be treatment that is not in the patient's best interest.

Courts in the USA have placed considerable emphasis on trying to discover how a particular patient would have wanted to be treated (substituted judgement), and one case (Nancy Cruzan)[8] was referred to the Supreme Court because the Missouri Attorney General demanded clear and convincing evidence of the patient's own wishes before agreeing to treatment withdrawal on the grounds of the family's assertion that this was what she would have wished. By a majority decision the Supreme Court considered it constitutional for a state to demand such direct evidence of a patient's wishes, but that no state need require it.[9] It also reasserted the legality of discontinuing life-sustaining treatment and declared that tube feeding was such a treatment. In the event, the case went back to the original Missouri court where new witnesses were produced to attest to Nancy's previous views, and treatment was withdrawn. Commentators mostly agreed with the dissenting judges on the Supreme Court that it was unrealistic to expect young patients who were the victims of sudden, unexpected brain damage to have made a formal advance directive, and that not to allow the family's views to prevail seriously limited the autonomy of the vegetative patient. This and other cases have led to widespread discussion in the public domain in the USA of the management of patients who are permanently vegetative.

By contrast, this condition was almost unknown to the British public until the *Bland* case came to court in November 1992, and there had been little discussion in the medical literature. Bland was a 21-year-old, left vegetative after anoxic brain damage in a football stadium disaster three years previously, whose doctors and parents wished to allow to die by discontinuing tube feeding. However, in 1991 a Working Party of the Institute of Medical Ethics[10] had declared that withdrawal of tube feeding was ethically acceptable, but pointed out that the legal position was unclear. It recommended fuller discussion in medical and public circles. This point was raised a few months later in the *British Medical Journal* in a paper by a neurosurgeon and a lawyer who contrasted the USA and UK situations.[11] They also referred to a Scottish case where informal legal advice was that a decision could be made by the doctors and the family, and treatment was withdrawn. The paper also made anonymous reference to the emerging case of *Airedale NHS Trust* v. *Bland*,[12] in which the coroner had advised the doctor who was considering treatment withdrawal that a criminal investigation would be likely to follow. To emphasize his point the coroner had sent a copy of his letter to the doctor to the Chief Constable.

The following year the BMA Ethics Committee produced a discussion document recommending that treatment withdrawal could be considered after one year provided that two doctors independent of the treating doctor confirmed the diagnosis and prognosis.[13] That paper was published a few weeks before the *Bland* case came to the Family Division of the High Court.[14] In this case, the Health Authority in Airedale sought a declaration that it would not be unlawful to withdraw tube feeding, as recommended by the treating doctor after consulting the family. The Official Solicitor opposed the declaration and, when it was granted, took the case to the Court of Appeal[15] and then to the House of Lords.[16] In the event, all nine judges involved in the three hearings unanimously supported the declaration on the grounds that this was non-beneficial treatment which a doctor therefore had no duty to provide. The courts recommended that future cases should come for judicial review, although several of the judges indicated that they hoped that a less formal decision-making process might be developed in time. They also recommended that Parliament should consider the issue, and a House of Lords Select Committee was set up, which reported in January 1994.[17] By this time the BMA, after considering responses to its discussion document, had published guidelines approved by its Council.[18]

The Lord's Committee report confused the issue by failing to reach agreement as to whether to regard artificially provided nutrition and hydration as medical treatment and also by declaring that, if antibiotics were withheld at an earlier stage, the need for a decision about withdrawing tube feeding need never arise. This is simply not in accord with medical experience of vegetative patients who commonly survive for years without antibiotics. The Committee recommended that professional bodies should draw up a Code of Practice, as had happened with the definition of brain death, thereby hinting that judicial review of every case might not then be necessary.

However, in March 1994 all NHS Trusts and Health Authorities in England and Wales received from the Official Solicitor a practice note on the persistent vegetative state, indicating that each case required referral to the Family Division of the High Court, together with reports from at least two neurological experts, one of which should have been requested by the Official Solicitor. In fact, a few weeks before this practice note was issued, a second case had been brought to the High Court, as an emergency, because a feeding tube had fallen out and the doctors wished not to replace it. In the event, both the High Court and the Appeal Court heard the case within 48 hours and agreed to declare this lawful.[19] Moreover they dispensed with the need for an independent neurological report, although the Official Solicitor had requested this. Since then only two other cases have been referred to the English High Court, and there has been one case in the Republic of Ireland[20] that was appealed to the Supreme Court.[21] In all cases treatment withdrawal was declared not to be unlawful.

The position is, therefore, that doctors in England and Wales now no longer have the freedom to withdraw tube feeding without a court hearing, unlike their colleagues in the USA. Moreover recent declarations by the Health Council of the Netherlands (1994)[22] and by the New Zealand Medical Association (1994)[23] have each recommended treatment withdrawal once the vegetative state is declared permanent, without reference to a court. It is to be hoped that the recommendations currently being completed by the Law Commissions in both Scotland and England will include a statutory provision that doctors who discontinue tube feeding in accordance with agreed guidelines will be exempt from criminal and civil liability or disciplinary action, without the need for a prior court declaration for each case.

Although it seems that a consensus has been reached on this issue, it is only fair to note the objections and reservations that some have expressed. It has been argued that stopping tube feeding is doing no more than withdrawing futile treatment once a trial of treatment has failed, and is therefore in line with the many decisions now commonly made to withhold or withdraw life-saving or life-sustaining treatment in acute hospitals every day.[24] However, apart from discontinuing renal dialysis, such decisions usually apply to situations where death is imminent – when patients need intensive care, emergency surgery or cardiopulmonary resuscitation. Moreover an added reason for withdrawing treatment in such instances is often the wish to relieve dying patients of the burdens of these interventions. Critics of withdrawing tube feeding from vegetative patients point out that, with the possibility of many years' survival, these patients can neither be considered to be dying nor can their treatment be causing them any suffering because they have no awareness. However, both ethicists and lawyers have frequently stated that there is no difference between withholding and withdrawing treatment that is considered futile.[25] The principal difference with vegetative patients is that their trial of treatment has lasted a year rather than a few hours or days. Perhaps the nearest parallel is the discontinuation of dialysis, which is quite commonly now done at a patient's request. There is also now an emerging consensus that competent patients with serious paralysing conditions can legitimately request discontinuation of life-sustaining treatments, and that doctors should comply with such requests.[26]

Of course, vegetative patients cannot refuse treatment, and the question is how to respect their autonomy. Most commentators agree that the existence of a living will or advance directive identifying tube feeding in a vegetative state as an unwanted treatment can greatly facilitate decision-making.[27] However, this is seldom available, and the next best guide must be the opinion of families with their knowledge of the patient's values.

The law is also clear that the cause of death after withdrawal of tube feeding is considered to be the original brain damage, not the dehydration that results from stopping tube feeding. Nonetheless some have argued that, as death is an inevitable consequence of stopping tube feeding, this omission should be considered as murder. However, a distinction is drawn between the intended and foreseen consequences of this decision. The intention is to discontinue futile treatment, not to bring about death. It is argued that, as the treatment does not benefit the patient, there is no moral or legal obligation on the doctors to provide such treatment.

However, some moralists, particularly Roman Catholics and orthodox Jews, have questioned whether treatment that prolongs life can be considered of no benefit. They uphold the sanctity of life against the views of many other moralists and theologians who consider that a biological life without the possibility of awareness or exercising free will or any enjoyment of life is not one which it would be obligatory to support. Other objectors are concerned that allowing withdrawal of treatment from vegetative patients seems to sanction euthanasia and thus poses a threat for other severely disabled patients. Again, the courts have explicitly stated that this is not an example of euthanasia, and many moralists have also taken this position. However, it is a matter of opinion whether the vegetative state is sufficiently discrete and extreme to allow its management to be defined clearly, without the fear of embarking on a slippery slope.

Another argument is that providing food and fluid is an aspect of normal basic care and should not be considered to be medical treatment. A counter-argument is that tube feeding of an unconscious patient who cannot swallow is substituting a lost physiological function in the same way that mechanical ventilation or dialysis does. The Institute of Medical Ethics[28] emphasized that the symbolic significance of feeding the disabled or helpless patient no longer applies when there is no interaction with the patient, no question of assuaging hunger or thirst, and no prospect of recovery by so prolonging life.

Yet another issue is whether death following the stopping of tube feeding might cause distress to the patient or to his watching family. All the evidence is that this does not happen, if there is good nursing care to maintain hygiene in the mouth. There may be some accentuation of reflex activity initially, but soon the patient becomes comatose and dies peacefully in 10–14 days. Sedatives to reduce the early reflex activity may be advised, to avoid family concern.

The matter of resources has not so far been mentioned, but has been confronted by Gillon[29] who maintains that the ethical principle of fairness in the allocation of health care resources raises questions about deploying large sums on maintaining vegetative patients. Indeed, he suggests that those wishing for this to be done should seek funding outside the NHS. In fact this occasionally happens when multi-million pound personal damages are awarded to allow a vegetative patient to be nursed at home with paid professional carers. A proposal under discussion in the USA is for some health insurances to exclude futile treatment unless a vitalist premium surcharge has been paid.[30]

It was considered that the *Bland* case might precipitate a rush of cases seeking similar relief from the courts. In fact there have been few. It needs to be made clear that discontinuing tube feeding is offered only as one option for management, and that it would normally be considered only if the family wished it. Even in the USA only a minority of families with a vegetative member requests this course. However, a recent editorial in the *New England Journal of Medicine*, accompanying the report from the Task Force, suggested three possible approaches to the dilemma of the vegetative state.[31] One would be to redefine death to include the vegetative state as was done 20 years ago for brain death – but it was acknowledged that practical issues and public opinion would make this unacceptable. The second would be to declare that treatment should routinely be discontinued after a certain length of time in vegetative patients, thereby easing the burden of families who have to make this decision and argue their case. The third, and favoured, approach would be to shift the burden from those who want to discontinue treatment to those who wish it to be continued. The presumption should be that a vegetative patient would not want to be kept alive, and that treatment would normally be discontinued. Families holding what this editorial writer calls 'the idiosyncratic view that treatment should be continued'[32] would have to justify their stance by documenting the wishes of the patient for continued treatment as expressed earlier. This certainly addresses an issue that concerns many health professionals caring for vegetative patients and their families – namely, that continued treatment often seems to be more for the benefit of the families and their consciences rather than it is for the benefit of the patient or to fulfil his or her own wishes.

Notes

1   Multi-Society Task Force on PVS (1994), 'Medical aspects of the persistent vegetative state', *New England Journal of Medicine*, **330**, pp. 1499–1508 and 1572–79.
2   British Medical Association (1993), 'Guidelines on treatment decisions for patients in the persistent vegetative state', *Annual Report*, Appendix 7, London: British Medical Association.
3   President's Commission for the Study of Ethical Problems in Medicine (1983), *Deciding to Forgo Life Sustaining Treatment*, Washington, DC: US Government Printing Office.
4   American Academy of Neurology (1989), 'Position of the American Academy of Neurology on certain aspects of the care and management of the persistent vegetative state patient', *Neurology*, **39**, p. 125.
5   American Medical Association Council on Ethical and Judicial Affairs (1990), 'Persistent vegetative state and the decision to withdraw or withhold life support', *Journal of the American Medical Association*, **263**, p. 426.
6   American Neurological Association Committee on Ethical Affairs (1993), 'Persistent vegetative state', *Annals Neurology*, **33**, p. 386.
7   *Op. cit.*, note 1 above.
8   *Cruzan* v. *Director, Missouri Dept. of Health*, 110 Sct. 2841 (1990).
9   Annas, G.J. (1990), 'Nancy Cruzan and the right to die', *New England Journal of Medicine*, **323**, p. 670.
10 Institute of Medical Ethics Working Party Report (1991), 'Withdrawing life supporting treatment from patients in a persistent vegetative state after acute brain damage', *Lancet*, **337**, p. 96.
11 Jennett, B. and Dyer, C. (1991), 'Persistent vegetative state and the right to die: the US and Britain', *British Medical Journal*, **302**, p. 1256.
12 *Airedale NHS Trust* v. *Bland*, Family Division of High Court (1993), 821.
13 British Medical Association (1992), Discussion paper on treatment of a patient's persistent vegetative state.
14 See note 12.
15 Ibid., 833 (Appeal Court).
16 *Op. cit.*, 858 (House of Lords) note 12 supra.
17 *Report of the Select Committee on Medical Ethics*, HL21–1, London: HMSO, 1994.
18 See note 2.
19 *Frenchay Healthcare NHS Trust* v. *S.* [1994] 2 All ER 403.
20 Wall, M. (1995), Appeal in Irish 'right-to-die' case, *Lancet*, **345**, p. 1296.
21 Wall, M. (1995), Irish Supreme Court approves 'right-to-die' case, *Lancet*, **346**, p. 368.
22 Health Council of the Netherlands (1994), *Patients in a Persistent Vegetative State*, Publication no. 1994/12, The Hague.
23 New Zealand Medical Association Public Issues Advisory Committee (1994), *Policy Paper: Persistent Vegetative State*, Wellington, New Zealand Medical Association.
24 Jennett, B. (1992), 'Letting vegetative patients die: ethical and lawful and brings Britain into line', *British Medical Journal*, **305**, p. 1305.

25   For further discussion, see Chapters 4, 5 and 9 in this volume.
26   American Academy of Neurology, *op. cit.*, note 4 supra.
27   For further discussion, see Chapter 3 in this volume. See also McLean, S.A.M. (1995), 'Advance Directives' in N. Pace and S.A.M. McLean (eds), *Law and Ethics in Intensive Care*, Oxford: Oxford University Press.
28   *Op. cit.*, note 10.
29   Gillon, R. (1993), 'Patients in the persistent vegetative state: a response to Dr. Andrews', *British Medical Journal*, **306**, p. 1602.
30   Rie, M.A., Murphy, D. and Fox-Buchanan, S. (1994), *Model Legislation for Benefit Limited Health Plan ICUs in Colorado: Implementing the Output of the GUIDe Project*, American Society of Law, Medicine and Ethics.
31   Angell, M. (1994), 'After Quinlan: the dilemma of the PVS', *New England Journal of Medicine*, **330**, p. 1524.
32   Ibid.

3 Are Advance Directives Really the Answer? And What was the Question?

ANN SOMMERVILLE
Adviser to the BMA on Medical Ethics

The extensive legal and moral debate triggered in 1991 and 1992 by the case of Anthony Bland[1] fuelled an existing clamour for the re-examination of some of society's basic preconceptions. Those preconceptions included the notion that life is always preferable to death and that life-prolonging medical treatment is necessarily a benefit to the person who receives it. The case even raised questions about what it means to be 'alive' and how to define a 'person'.

It excited disquiet and the questioning of boundaries not only on such high-flown philosophical matters as being and non-being but also on public policy issues such as the role of declaratory statements in the criminal justice system and the difference between allowing death to occur slowly by doing nothing and actively intervening to cause a quick end. There was debate about how an individual's interest in preventing the indignity of a non-consensual invasion of his or her body could be weighed against the state's interest in preserving life. Questions were raised about whether a severely mentally incapacitated person could have such interests or, indeed, any interests at all. The perceived integrity of the medical profession was seen to be potentially in doubt, and many predicted that the *Bland* case would ultimately lead to a devaluation of life and an acceptance of euthanasia. None of this debate was new, however. Courts in the USA had already thrashed out all the same arguments through a series of similar cases.[2]

In the UK, the case led some people who had never previously heard the term 'persistent vegetative state' to consider how they would want to be treated were they to lose the ability to think or communicate. Advance directives – a concept borrowed from the

USA – seemed to provide one answer, but there was widespread confusion about their status and scope. Eventually, the *Bland* case went to the ultimate appeal court, the House of Lords, whose judgement reflected much heart-searching and included a recommendation for the parliamentary review of the whole gamut of issues raised, including advance directives. Accordingly, a Select Committee of the House of Lords was set up to examine the evidence. Part of its remit was 'to consider the ethical, legal and clinical implications of a person's right to withhold consent to life-prolonging treatment, and the position of persons who are no longer able to give or withhold consent.[3] This involved clarifying the status of anticipatory decision-making and deciding whether there should be a statute on the subject. In early 1994 the Select Committee concluded that such a statute would be superfluous.

A central premise of this chapter, however, is that factors other than the House of Lords' report will ultimately decide how advance directives develop and whether or not they work well. An important factor is the common law, which by the end of 1994 had upheld the advance refusal of the first English litigant.[4] Other factors include the degree to which the public and consumer groups are really committed to advance directives, the attitudes of health care purchasers, health professionals and such bodies as the British Medical Association and Royal College of Nursing, and the extent to which all of these are prepared to take steps to make patient choice a reality. Although included in the list of factors considered, the BMA's views are not synonymous with the opinions and conclusions given in this chapter.

Why Advance Directives?

As society has attempted to protect itself from the realities of mental degeneration and death, responsibility for care of the mentally incapacitated, the elderly and the dying has been increasingly confined to institutions, hospitals and health professionals. This is what Illich in the mid-1970s called the 'medicalization' of death.[5] Although many other aspects of life – conception, childbirth, the process of ageing, manifestations of unhappiness or stress – can also be said to have been medicalized, these other facets of ordinary human experience have not been marginalized in our society as have the processes of degeneration and death. Even though, as Benjamin Franklin said, the only certainties in life are death and taxes, it seems that we put thought into avoiding the latter but not considering the former.

Advance directives or 'living wills' attempt to deal with medicalization and marginalization. They aim to permit individuals to have a voice in situations where they are otherwise unable to control what is done to them. Their purpose is to empower the individual to make future choices using present mental capacity and knowledge. The degree to which they achieve this aim depends on factors which need further examination, and this chapter attempts to place some of the rhetoric about autonomy into a practical context. The effectiveness of the advance directive depends ultimately upon wide recognition that individual views, rather than clinical opinion alone, must dictate treatment.

Part of the stimulus for advance directives derives from an increasingly misplaced fear of overtreatment at the end of life, mistrust in medical technology or lack of confidence that health professionals recognize when 'enough is enough'. But although bad practice in the form of futile prolongation of life or inappropriate resuscitation exists and should not be underemphasized, there is a growing consensus among health professionals and the courts about its unacceptability. *Patients* are being transformed into *clients* or *health-care consumers* with bargaining powers. Advance directives are both a symptom and an effect of changing practice. At the same time, lessons are being learned from the hospice movement about communication and caring for the whole person rather than responding to a set of symptoms. In practical terms, however, it must also be said that such lessons cannot be fully integrated into settings where staff–patient ratios are severely dissonant with those in the hospice context, and advance directives can do nothing to address this.

What is the Scope of an Advance Directive?

There have been many suggestions concerning the potential scope of advance directives. One useful starting-point may be the English Law Commission's description in its 1991 discussion document:

> The purpose of an advance directive is to enable a competent person to give instructions about what he wishes to be done, or who he wishes to make decisions for him, if he should subsequently lose the capacity to decide for himself. Advance directives are usually discussed in the context of medical treatment and relate mainly to the patient's right to refuse or change treatment in a disabling chronic or terminal illness.[6]

Although this definition fits into an evolving pattern of thinking about the legitimate scope of advance directives, close examination also shows it to be unsatisfactory for the current stage of debate in the UK.

The first part of the definition, for example, combines what many people see as two functions: making an anticipatory choice for oneself about specific matters and appointing another person to make proxy choices as appropriate when the need arises. Deciding in advance for oneself demands a degree of certainty about the decisions to be made and a certain clairvoyance about future options. Choosing a proxy decision-maker simply requires the individual to have confidence that the person appointed will remain alive and sane longer than himself and will indeed carry out what the appointer would like to happen. Various potential problems arise in connection with appointing a proxy, some of which are touched on later.

The second part of the definition firmly places advance directives in the category of 'end of life' medical decisions (which is the only role envisaged for them by the House of Lords too), although the Law Commission encompasses directives which change treatment rather than just refuse it. This might be seen as a variation on the common view of advance directives as only being appropriate to refuse procedures. From a legal viewpoint, however, patients can only *direct* non-treatment. If they aim to request a procedure or choose between options, then their document has to be called something other than a directive since it will not have the legal power to direct anyone. The scope of the English common law until now has only covered refusal and courts are unlikely to see health professionals as bound by statements which limit the exercise of clinical judgement by selecting between treatment options, although they might require doctors to take them into account.[7]

Comparison can be made between the manner in which the scope of advance directives has been defined in the UK and how advance directives originally developed in the USA. They were invented by Luis Kutner, a Chicago lawyer, as a means by which competent individuals could provide, in advance, evidence to rebut the legal presumption that life-prolonging treatment could be given to them when they were unable to decide for themselves.[8] The same presumption holds in the UK. Erin and Harris[9] argue that the assumption that people always want their lives sustained is frankly erroneous since evidence suggests 'that the vast majority of people would wish life-sustaining treatment withdrawn in certain situations.[10] They overturn the notion of presumed consent and propose 'as the default position that, under circumstances of irreversible loss of competence, life-sustaining treatment be withheld from all patients in the absence of an advance directive to the contrary'.[11] That is, only statements positively requesting life-prolonging treatment would have any value and health professionals should automatically allow all incompetent patients without one to die. Although Erin and Harris go on to identify some important practical disadvantages to such a system, their proposal may unfortunately have more current relevance than they suppose, as will be discussed later.

Table 3.1 The three stages in the evolution of advance directives in the USA

	Date	Legislation	Scope
Stage 1	1976	California National Death Act	• Allows withdrawal of treatment • Directive must be in a particular format • Patient must be terminally ill and death imminent
Stage 2	mid-1980s	Launch of Uniform Rights of the Terminally Ill Act	• Allows withdrawal of treatment and tube feeding • No mandatory form. Beginning of individualized form • 'Terminal' illness covers coma, PVS, dementia
Stage 3	1985	Indiana Living Wills and Life-prolonging Procedures, Declaration	• Allows for requests for, as well as refusal of, treatment

It is possible to trace the evolution of advance directives both in the USA and the UK through three principal stages of development.[12] Table 3.1 summarizes the development of advance directives in the USA. The first generation of US laws established a model directive which could only be triggered if the patient was dying and the directive conformed to the established format. A decade later, the second generation dispensed with the mandatory form and allowed a much broader definition of terminal illness as the triggering factor. The third generation, whose prototype is seen in the Indiana legislation, incorporates the looser definition of the second generation model and permits requests for, as well as refusal of, treatment.

Discussion in the UK follows some aspects of the same pattern even though we have no statute to match US law. Initially, in the UK, advance directive forms were only available from organizations supporting voluntary euthanasia and were generally viewed as being applicable to terminal illness. A second phase witnessed arguments for the application of advance directives to non-terminal conditions, such as persistent vegetative state. The House of Lords in the *Bland* decision[13] endorsed this development. Bodies, such as the BMA, also maintained that advance statements of treatment preferences should be able to cover any condition the patient wants to provide for, but that positive requests could only be honoured if they were clinically appropriate and not detrimental to other patients.

The King's College and Terrence Higgins Trust model directive can be seen as fitting into the third generation of formats. It provides not only for refusal of treatment but for the option of asking 'to be kept alive for as long as reasonably possible using whatever forms of treatment are available'. It also permits personal requests such as the preservation of life until a particular nominated person can be called to the bedside to say goodbye. One of the important points about this type of directive is that it shows that the discussion concerns a *right to choose* rather than a *right to die*. Given the anxiety about access to medical services of some patient groups, such as smokers or the elderly, this third generation of advance directive requesting treatment may well deserve attention. For the patient, the obvious drawbacks are that it leaves open the definition of 'reasonable' and 'available'. Also some variations of this type of directive are discouragingly complex both for their drafters and interpreters: a document which is not easily understood risks being ignored or misinterpreted.

Since every modern textbook and declaration of health-care ethics calls for partnership with patients and listening skills, there seems no compelling reason for limiting the potential application of anticipatory statements or directives to chronic illness or, indeed, any illness at all. They could be accommodated as a regular part of the dialogue and continuous negotiation which is supposed to exist between patients and health professionals. Pregnant women with birth plans for the management of labour exercise a form of anticipatory decision-making, although, in most cases, women in labour do not lack capacity and can review their options according to circumstances. The point to be made here is, if advance statements really can be useful, why not adapt them to suit the myriad requirements of people facing any form of reduced capacity, whether temporary or permanent? People with Alzheimer's disease, for example, know with certainty that if they live long enough they will experience dementia. There may be a wide range of matters they would want to decide for themselves in advance rather than simply appointing an attorney with enduring powers to act for them. Arguably also, an anticipatory decision that an individual wanted her money used to maintain herself in a specific nursing home rather than other alternatives could be the basis of an advance directive. Fears are sometimes raised by doctors that relatives, anxious to get their hands on a demented patient's savings, may attempt to override the patient's strongly expressed wish to remain in the nursing home she had chosen. A witnessed statement of her intentions when competent could provide protection.

The BMA has argued that an authorizing statement would be useful – perhaps even more useful than a refusing directive – but this is partly based on the premise that the most clear and explicit refusing directives will probably apply to futile treatments which good professional practice would disallow. Authorizing statements accommodate decisions which are so personal that only the individual undertaking them could decide. For example, a person facing incapacity might wish to agree in advance to genetic testing which she does not need herself but which would benefit her children or grandchildren. She might agree to elective ventilation for organ donation if she already intends to offer to be an organ donor. At present a schizophrenic can only be sectioned for treatment under the Mental Health Act when he or she becomes dangerous but, without prior agreement, might miss out on help at a much earlier stage of illness. In lucid intervals, such a person could make provision for treatments during those intermittent periods when capacity fails. Prior agreement of this sort can be seen as more respectful of patient autonomy than a compulsory treatment order.

While it is acknowledged in common law that a patient cannot *require* a doctor to take specific positive actions, there is arguably scope for an anticipatory statement to authorize medical or other treatment. New ideas take time to permeate society. If society is serious about acknowledging patient rights and choices, including those expressed in advance, people need to become accustomed to anticipatory decision-making as a means of dealing with recurrent or familiar problems, rather than solely as a method for dealing with the frightening and the unusual.

The Last Resort of the Unheard?

Advance directives have been made in the UK for over 20 years but have only received attention comparatively recently. The way in which they are drafted and the degree to which they are implemented varies, there being no standard format and no statute to enforce them. Many health professionals are confused about the implications of advance directives or erroneously equate them with requests for euthanasia – probably because the earliest guidance and examples of advance directives were drawn up by the Voluntary Euthanasia Societies. In the late 1980s agencies, such as Age Concern,[14] published advice on advance directives, fuelling the assumption that they were likely to be useful only or mainly to the elderly. This is ironic since, both in the UK and the USA, the high-profile legal cases – namely, the US cases of Karen Quinlan and Nancy Cruzan and the UK cases of Tony Bland and 'T' –[15] which discuss the importance of advance directives, but where in fact directives were conspicuous by their absence, involved people under 25 years old.

Recognition of the relevance of advance directives to people of all ages owes much to the *Bland* case and patient advocacy groups. The Terrence Higgins Trust and the Alzheimer's Disease Society have drawn attention to the particular application of directives to the onset of progressive mental impairment. Although these organizations have undoubtedly influenced the public perception of advance directives, the advance directive still retains a residual image as the last resort of marginalized groups.

US surveys[16] showed that advance directives, like organ donor cards, are seen by the public as a 'good thing', but that spontaneous take-up has fallen far short of the number who express theoretical support. A recent UK survey[17] indicated that, while 84 per cent of the 2000 respondents (average age 69.1 years) supported the idea of *everyone* making advance directives, exactly the same percentage said that they did not have one. Only 13 per cent of the respondents had made an advance directive and, in younger age groups, the percentage is likely to be even lower. Another survey demonstrated that the function of an advance directive in relation to incapacity was broadly misunderstood by people who thought that having a legally witnessed document would simply increase their chances of being heard when they (competently) express their views in hospital. Many writers have drawn attention to the fact that advance directives can only really become effective in communities willing to confront their own mortality. One of the perceived advantages of advance directives and other anticipatory statements is that they encourage open discussion of death and mental incapacity. But in practice this only works where individuals are already receptive to the opportunity, and, as stated earlier, death has become marginalized in present day society. Thus, unless they have had specific training or long experience, health professionals are just as likely as other people to distance themselves from potentially disturbing discussions.

Common law recognition of advance directives is recent. If the basic conditions outlined by Lord Donaldson in the 'T' case are fulfilled,[18] the binding force of advance directives at common law in England and Wales seems secure. This means that if a competent, informed and unpressured adult makes a clear anticipatory refusal of treatment and the circumstances envisaged by the patient subsequently arise, health professionals would be bound by that refusal. In Scotland, there has been no case law, although the House of Lords' comments in the *Bland* case about advance directives would be relevant. One of the leading speeches in *Bland* came from a Scottish Law Lord, Lord Keith of Kinkel who stressed that any mentally competent person is at liberty to decline treatment and can also do this in anticipation of later loss of competence. In Lord Keith's view, to administer medical treatment contrary to such a refusal is unlawful and constitutes both a tort and the crime of battery.

The English and Scottish Law Commissions are both working on legislation which will change some aspects of the way decisions are made for people who cannot make decisions for themselves. Advance directives, however, barely gain a mention in the Scottish Law Commission consultation paper of 1991.[19] The Commission reassures us that these directives are used in the USA because of

> ... unnecessary treatment being given to terminally ill patients and expensive private health care which can impoverish patients and deprive their families of their anticipated succession rights. These difficulties do not arise to the same extent in Scotland.[20]

In England, the Law Commission published draft legislation in March 1995,[21] which, if enacted, would legally oblige health professionals to take account of the ascertainable past and present wishes of a mentally incapacitated person in every case. The Commission draws distinction, however, between the legal effect of an advance expression of views or preferences and advance decisions. Its proposed legislation only gives specific statutory recognition to clear decisions to refuse particular forms of treatment. Even if this Bill becomes law, doctors will need to assess the scope of the patient's decision and its applicability to the circumstances. Clause 9(3) of the Bill negates any advance refusal if the patient has not specifically recognized the possibility of death as a result of nontreatment. Effectively, therefore, health professionals will retain a degree of discretion except in cases where the directive unambiguously refuses specific treatment in all circumstances, such as the Jehovah's Witness type of directive.

Eventually, enduring powers of attorney may be extended to cover health care. Both the Scottish and English Law Commissions suggest this as a possible extension of the law and both recommend limits on what such an attorney could agree to or refuse on behalf of an incapacitated person. Feeding, nursing, pain relief or other palliative care could not be refused by the attorney. The Scottish Law Commission has more faith in the medical profession and says that proxy 'power to consent is less important since doctors will generally not propose treatment that is not in the patient's best interests.'[22] The English Law Commission is less sure about this and would not allow attorneys to consent to a range of treatments which doctors might suggest but which require the additional permission of a judicial forum. These would include some sterilizations, donation of non-regenerative tissue or bone marrow and some kinds of medical research.

The House of Lords

In effect, the House of Lords has had two bites at the issue of advance directives. As already mentioned, in the *Bland* case there was agreement that medical treatment could not be given contrary to clear anticipatory instructions refusing it. Lords Browne-Wilkinson and Mustill also stressed that they considered it imperative for Parliament, rather than the courts, to rule on the wider issues raised by the case.

A contradictory view came from the Lords Select Committee on Medical Ethics.[23] After a year of taking evidence on end-of-life issues, the 14 members of Committee astonished some observers by reaching agreement on some contentious issues. They published 21 conclusions, all of which indicate a cautious, conservative handling of the issues and general confirmation of the status quo. Finally, while commending the development of advance directives, they found it unnecessary for Parliament to introduce legislation, although they did recommend that a professional code of practice on advance directives should be developed.

How Important are the Recommendations?

An essential question is: what will become of these recommendations and how much force do they have? The answer is not much,
unless other interested bodies choose to take them up. One might
expect the Department of Health to act on them but its response[24] to
the Lords, published in May 1994, is non-committal on many points
and passes the buck on others.

Where Did the Recommendations Come From?

The Lords' recommendations closely reflect the evidence put to them
by organizations of health professionals, including the BMA and
Royal College of Nursing. In particular, the recommendations on
advance directives briefly encapsulate the long flirtation that the
BMA has had with the notion of advance directives – except that the
BMA changed its traditional view and supported the English Law
Commission's proposals for legislation on advance directives during
the period in which the House of Lords' Committee was sitting, and
this was not mirrored by the Lords' final statement.

Prior to that, the BMA's views had gone through several stages.
Initially lukewarm to the notion of advance directives, the BMA saw
them as only potentially helpful in a few cases. In the 1990s the
relationship developed more spark as the BMA sought opportunities
for improved doctor–patient dialogue. Nevertheless, while the Association was happy to live with the concept of advance directives, like
a reluctant bridegroom it had cold feet about formalizing the relationship by means of statute. It argued that respect for patient choice
could be achieved through improved medical education, clear professional guidance (such as a code of practice) and the changing
emphasis on willingness to listen to patients. Statute, the BMA argued, was superfluous - partly (but not only) because long experience had shown that whatever goes into Parliament tends to emerge
in quite another form.

Although the BMA no longer objects to statute, its original prediction that legislation would be superfluous now seems closer to becoming reality. Much depends on the reaction to the code of practice
published by the BMA in April 1995[25] in response to the House of
Lords' report. In time this should set the standard for 'good professional practice' and help ensure consistency in the way advance
directives are handled. Although the code of practice has been
endorsed by medical and nursing royal colleges, considerable further effort will be required before the guidance is widely known in
the mainstream of medical practice.

Do Advance Directives Offer Genuine Advantages?

The House of Lords' report lists advantages and disadvantages which witnesses raised in regard to advance directives. The perceived advantages include giving patients control of their destiny and therefore peace of mind, providing opportunity for dialogue, guiding health professionals in difficult cases and removing responsibility for difficult decisions from relatives.

The primary perceived advantage of advance directives lies in protecting patient autonomy beyond the onset of incapacity but this may arguably be a 'symbolic' rather than a practical expression of autonomy. Many forms of advance directives offer the drafter a choice of specifying personal instructions and/or nominating a proxy to decide. US surveys indicate that people are most likely to select proxy decision-making by their family or their doctor. A US study[26] published in 1992 indicated that, of 104 patients with a life-threatening illness who were offered advance directives, 69 took up the offer and most asked for non-aggressive treatment if 'the burdens of treatment outweigh the expected benefits', although none gave any other personal instructions and all of them designated a proxy. However, other evidence[27] suggests that proxies are more likely than patients themselves to opt for life-prolonging treatment. While choosing to transfer the decision is just as much an expression of autonomy as deciding oneself, it does not require an advance directive to do so.

In any case, people are not entirely autonomous in their decision-making, but are influenced to some degree by the advice and information they receive and how the options are portrayed to them. It is increasingly recognized that the concept of non-directive counselling on complex issues is often no more than a sham.[28] Dialogue with health professionals is an important facet of making an informed advance directive, but health professionals, although exhorted to make their advice non-directive, find this hard to achieve. Nor is it easy to find specialized counselling about the likely future options for patients with specific diseases. Autonomy is only protected if the instructions are available at the right moment and the directive is clear. An ambiguous statement will complicate, rather than simplify, the situation.

Discussions of 'autonomy' sometimes appear to juggle theories but offer little by way of practical guidance. In Dworkin's view, when an individual is conscious but mentally incapacitated, 'two autonomies are in play: the autonomy of the demented patient and the autonomy of the person who became demented. These two autonomies can conflict, and the resulting problems are complex and difficult.[29] Of course, some philosophers resolve this dilemma by attributing no autonomy to the demented person and recognizing the 'residual interests' of the previously competent individual as paramount. A cluster of fascinating psychological and philosophical questions arise here about an individual's ability to make decisions, in advance, on matters of life and death on behalf of the person he or she will be in the future when some part of the individual 'self' – mental faculties, memories and awareness of continuity – has been lost. As Dworkin implies, the competent person who makes the anticipatory decision can be seen as fundamentally different and 'other' to the incapacitated individual who lives out (or does not) the consequences of the decision. While individuals can only make advance directives for 'themselves', a person who becomes severely mentally disordered or brain-damaged is, in some sense, no longer 'herself'.

Much of Western philosophy has been preoccupied with the importance of 'personhood', personal identity and the relationship between mind and body. Harris, for example, sees the individual's capacity to assess and value his life as fundamental[30] to personhood. There is a tradition of trying to resolve problems of identity by citing continuity of mind and mental state as the important criterion. Yet, continuity of the body is irrelevant. If the mind ceases to function as a mind, then that 'person' ceases to exist although the bodily shell may continue. A competent individual therefore is arguably not making advance decisions for him or herself but for the relics of that individual which he or she once was.

Although it is philosophically complex, on a practical level this issue is not necessarily intractable. If we allow 'persons' to make testamentary disposition for their material possessions, why not permit the same for their bodily shell after the cessation of the rational faculties? 'Ownership' of the body was the notion that sparked off the original idea of a living will: Luis Kutner's proposal was that a competent adult should be able to execute a document 'analogous to a revocable or conditional trust, with the patient's body as the *res* (the property or asset), the patient as the beneficiary and grantor, and the doctor and the hospital as trustees'.[31] The concept of property is based on the idea that there is a system of rules governing access to, and control of, some resources, whether material or incorporeal. In this case the property would be very much corporeal, and the owner, when competent, might be assigned legal rights about how it is treated in future. The owner of the body would retain an enduring interest in the body until it decays and would continue to inhabit it or be allowed to vacate it in accordance with his prior direction.

Some modern philosophers, such as Parfit,[32] argue that survival of identity need not be viewed as an 'all or nothing' issue but as a matter of degree, and this has some intuitive plausibility. One of his arguments is that, in the natural course of life, we experience a series of 'successive selves' and he quotes Proust's notion that:

> ... we are incapable, while we are in love, of acting as fit predecessors of the next persons who, when we are in love no longer, we shall presently have become.[33]

It is trite to observe that people's views change with their circumstances. Parfit imagines the possibility of the diffusion of 'self' along several different potential branches of development. He talks, for example, of 'my most recent self', 'one of my earlier selves' and 'one of my distant selves' – each of these showing a different degree of psychological connectedness with the past self. From a practical perspective, would this mean that a greater weight should be attached to an advance directive made comparatively recently by an individual who is still more or less the same self? If we recognize varying degrees of psychological continuity with former and future selves, it leaves unresolved the same question of whether it is morally correct for subsequent selves to be locked in by the provisions of an advance directive which fails to reflect their current interests. In life, of course, we do recognize that individuals make bad or risky choices in the development of their 'successive selves' but that these should generally be respected.

Theorizing aside, concern for the welfare of people with severe and permanent incapacity or dementia is often used as an argument for imposing limits on the scope of advance directives. The incapacitated individual may show all signs of wanting to be nourished, to receive treatment and to live, oblivious to the views of the former self. Despite such difficulties, it is not my intention to diminish the importance of respect for autonomy, imperfect though the exercise of it may be in practice.

Some disadvantages of advance directives were noted by the House of Lords. They include the difficulties patients experience in making their views known unambiguously, the risks of pressure or other forms of abuse being brought to bear upon the drafter and the danger of misdiagnosis. Unfortunately, however, none of these are restricted to anticipatory decision-making, but may apply to any treatment situation. Admittedly, the matter of ensuring unambiguous expression may be more complex in the case of anticipatory refusals. An example from the *Lancet*[34] drew attention to a dilemma facing doctors treating an elderly woman with advanced cancer of the colon and intestinal obstruction. Her acute pain was unamenable to narcotics but could have been relieved by a colostomy under local anaesthetic. Her advance directive refused any 'heroic' intervention in the case of incurable illness and did not distinguish between life-prolonging and pain-relieving measures. On the brief evidence given, however, such a directive might have been justifiably challenged under the criteria specified by Lord Donaldson in the 'T' case[35], as arguably, the patient had insufficient information when she drafted the directive. It might also be argued that the circumstances which arose were not precisely those envisaged in advance.

A potentially more damaging disadvantage would arise if advance directives were seen as a covert measure for reducing treatment costs or limiting the amount of care given to the elderly and terminally ill. Any encouragement by health professionals for the drafting of directives would then create suspicion and mistrust. A comparison of costs and benefits was offered in the Schneiderman study[36] which, although it admittedly involved relatively small patient numbers, showed that while most patients with advance directives wanted to limit expensive high-technology treatments, in the actual implementation of their directive there was no significant difference in overall provision of terminal care or costs between these patients and others who made no anticipatory choice. This conclusion obviously leads to the question of whether advance directives are likely to work or have any genuine value outside the realm of theoretical debate.

Do Advance Directives Work in the Real World?

The study mentioned above indicated that, in 1992, advance directives made little or no difference to treatment of the seriously ill in the state of California. No significant differences were found between those with and without advance directives in terms of patient satisfaction, general well-being, length of survival and amount of narcotics given. Patients with directives spent more days in hospital than those in the control group without directives, and similar treatment costs were incurred by all patients in the last month of life. The authors identify several reasons for this lack of divergence. They suggest, for example that doctors may simply have ignored the directive or limited 'heroic' treatment in equal measure to those with and without directives or that the document was not applicable to the circumstances. One of the most significant findings is that, contrary to expectation, most of the patients in the study retained decision-making capacity in the terminal stages. For those facing mental incapacity through diseases such as AIDS, 'discussion before death was so extensive it precluded dependence on the advance directive'.[37] Clearly, it is inadvisable to generalize from such limited data, but one inevitable conclusion is that even where advance directives are potentially most useful, they are superfluous in practical terms if good opportunities for dialogue already exist.

It is appropriate to ask how meaningful anticipatory decision-making is likely to be in the context of the prevalent social and medical realities in the UK. Not least, it must be questioned whether good opportunities for negotiation and dialogue exist in the context of terminal care. Arguably, if it is difficult to negotiate aspects of terminal care when one is competent to do so then anticipatory attempts stand very little chance. One recently published Scottish study[38] seems to indicate some of the practical problems. The study monitored care given to 50 hospitalized dying patients, of which only two received aggressive interventions before death. More than half the patients retained competence and consciousness until shortly before death, but were unable to obtain basic minimal interventions to maintain their comfort, such as a drink of water on demand. The authors concluded that 'contact between nurses and the dying patients was minimal; distancing and isolation of patients by most medical and nursing staff were evident; this isolation increased as death approached'.[39]

The UK is five years into a managed market of health care. A culture of public expectation about treatment choices has been raised by such measures as the Patient's Charter. But, as yet, the promised patient rights in the market are illusory in practice. Patients do not have control of their health care, and sometimes individual care is fragmented by health authorities changing the hospitals with whom they have block contracts if a better bid is made by another facility. Often, it is not health professionals who make choices but the purchasing authorities. Patient audit, patient satisfaction surveys and new complaints mechanisms have a potential to change the picture. If advance directives are to become commonplace and implemented, this will be achieved from the bottom up by the accelerated 'consumerization' of health care and the need for health facilities increasingly to adapt to client demand within a highly competitive market.

There have been anecdotal reports of a few NHS Trusts saying 'we do not accept advance directives here', in the same way as they decline to offer some loss-making clinical services. But health-care purchasers, including fund-holding GPs, can pick and choose among the hospitals competing for patients. Ultimately those who pay the piper will call the tune on making provisions for advance directives *if* people feel strongly enough about the issue. Sufficient demand from the public could result in purchasers demanding the sort of care that respects advance directives for the proportion of patients who want this. But this brings attention back to the fact that, in the UK, anticipatory decision-making is a minority activity.

Another factor influencing the usefulness of directives concerns the venue where treatment is provided. Community-based services, short-stay hospital or hospice care, community nursing and better liaison between the NHS, social services and voluntary sector can promote patient choice. Even when complicated technical interventions are required, people who die in their own homes supported by carers, specialized nurses or hospice outreach programmes are likely to have greater control over the final stages of life. There are persistent fears, however, that hard-pressed health authority budgets will increasingly be used to purchase acute services rather than provide palliative care for people at home. Funding for hospice and palliative care is no longer ring-fenced as it was in the past. Palliative care services have to win contracts from purchasers who no longer have specific palliative care budgets.

Advance directives refuse life-prolonging measures. Advance statements may also be needed to address issues other than the mere refusal of medical interventions. The current reality is that the NHS is ceasing to fund long-term care of the elderly, and local hospitals are being closed as preference is given to establishing centres of excellence for acute care. There is a danger that the mentally incapacitated and dying will become the object of 'benign neglect' rather than of technological interventions to keep them alive. This might be seen as a practical reflection of the proposal by Erin and Harris[40] of a presumption of non-treatment unless advance effort has been made to rebut that notion.

Fears undoubtedly abound that life-prolonging measures are likely to be increasingly unavailable for patients with poor long-term prognoses, even if they want them. In its position paper to the House of Lords Select Committee, the Alzheimer's Disease Society implies that a concentration on autonomy may distract from broader needs. It suggests that people might be willing to sacrifice the right to consent to treatment if they could use a living will to will themselves appropriate medical care when they need it. The Society goes on to say that the good terminal care for people with dementia is decreasing and 'it is likely that many people in the last stages of Alzheimer's disease will have very little prospect of high quality and appropriate health care in the early part of the next century'.[41] This is not to say that advance directives will become superfluous but rather that they may need to change to allow those who want treatment to register a claim.

In real life the practicalities of combining directives with proxy decision-makers may also raise difficulties. The pattern of population trends is such that the proportion of older people in the UK who may want to appoint proxies will exceed the number of those they know and can be confident will survive them. Women, in particular, live longer than men, are more likely to experience widowhood and are less likely to remarry. At present half of the women of 65 years and over and a fifth of older men live alone. Dementia occurs in about 5 per cent of the population over 65 and in up to 20 per cent of those over 80. The very old (85 years and over) often live in institutional settings and carry the highest risk of dementia. Will there be trusted proxies available for them in future?

Conclusion

All the signs are that advance directives – at least in their present form – may not be the best or only answer for people with deteriorating mental faculties. Despite the rhetoric, only a small minority of people presently have sufficient confidence to commit themselves about future choices, and they may be aiming wrongly to ward off treatments which are increasingly never even on offer. In a climate of genuine patient choice, advance statements could usefully broaden in scope and offer a way forward to better communication and negotiation. In practice this can only be achieved if opportunities for unhurried or repeated discussion are built into the provision of health care. These are rarely available at present. The attitudes of health professionals are also vital. Hopefully the Code of Practice published by the BMA will establish a baseline and give patients a voice and consistency in the manner they are cared for at the end of life.

Notes

1   *Airedale NHS Trust* v. *Bland* [1993] 1 All ER 821.
2   See, for example, Chapter 16 of Kennedy, I. and Grubb, A. (1994), *Medical Law: Text with materials*, London: Butterworths; or, more briefly, Chapter 15 of Mason, J.K. and McCall Smith, A. (1991), *Law and Medical Ethics*, London: Butterworths.
3   Report of the Select Committee on Medical Ethics, HL Paper 21-1, HMSO 1994, p. 7.
4   *Re C (Adult: Refusal of Medical Treatment)* [1994] 1 WLR 290.
5   Illich, Ivan (1976), *Limits to Medicine: Medical Nemesis: the Expropriation of Health*, New York: Boyars Marion.
6   Law Commission (1991), *Mentally Incapacitated Adults and Decision-Making: An Overview*, Consultation Paper no. 119, London: HMSO, at para. 6.2, p. 137.
7   See, for example, Re J (a minor) (wardship: medical treatment) [1990] 3 All ER 930 where Lord Donaldson stated and reiterated in subsequent cases that 'No one can dictate the treatment to be given', at para. g–h, p. 934.
8   Lush, Denzil (1993), 'The history of living wills', *Eagle Magazine*, August–September.
9   Erin, C.A. and Harris, J. (1994), 'Living Wills: Anticipatory Decisions and Advance Directives', *Reviews in Clinical Gerontology*, **4**, pp. 269–275.

10 Ibid., at p. 270.

11 Ibid.

12 See the discussion by D. Lush in *op. cit.*, note 8 supra.

13 See note 1 above.

14 Age Concern (1988), *The Living Will: Consent to Treatment at the End of Life*, Working Party Report, London: Age Concern Institute of Gerontology and King's College Centre of Medical Law and Ethics.

15 Re Quinlan, 70 NJ, 10, 355, A.2d, 647 (1976); *Cruzan* v. *Director, Missouri Dept of Health*, 111, L.Ed 2d, 224, 110 S Ct 2841 (1990); *Airedale Trust* v *Bland*, *op. cit.* note 1 supra; Re T (adult: refusal of treatment) [1992] 4 All ER 649.

16 Dworkin, for example, mentions an American poll of 1991 in which 87 per cent of interviewees claimed to support withdrawal of treatment in accordance with an advance directive but only 17 per cent of interviewees in another poll had signed one. Dworkin, R. (1993), *Life's Dominion*, London: HarperCollins, p. 180.

17 Survey published in *Yours* magazine, December 1994.

18 *Op. cit.*, note 15 supra.

19 Scottish Law Commission (1991), *Mentally Disabled Adults: Legal Arrangements for Managing their Welfare and Finances*, Discussion Paper no. 94, Edinburgh: HMSO.

20 Ibid., as para. 5.108, p. 312.

21 Law Commission Document 231 (1995), London: HMSO.

22 Ibid. *Op. cit*, at para 5.108, p. 312, note 19 above.

23 *Op. cit.*, note 3 above.

24 Government response to the Report of the Select Committee on Medical Ethics, HMSO, 1994.

25 Advance statements about Medical Treatment (1995), London: BMJ Publishing Group.

26 Schneiderman, L. *et al.* (1992), 'Effects of offering advance directives on medical treatments and costs', *Annals of Internal Medicine*, **117**, pp. 599–606.

27 Seckler, A.B. *et al.* (1991), 'Substituted judgement: how accurate are proxy predictions?', *Annals of Internal Medicine*, **115**, pp. 92–8.

28 See, for example, in the genetic field, Clarke, Angus (1991), 'Is non-directive genetic counselling possible?' *Lancet*, **338**, 19 October, p. 998.

29 Dworkin, R. *op. cit.*, note 16 above, p. 192.

30 Harris, J. (1985), *The Value of Life*, London: Routledge, p. 16.

31 *Indiana Law Journal*, **44**, 1969, pp. 539–554 at p. 552.

32 Parfit, Derek, 'Personal Identity', reprinted in Ted Honderich and Myles Burnyeat (eds) (1979), *Philosophy As It Is*, Harmondsworth: Pelican.

33 Proust, Marcel (1949), *Within a Budding Grove*, London, quoted and translated by Parfit, *op. cit.*, note 32 above, p. 205.

34 Rosner, F. (1994), 'Living Wills', *Lancet*, **343**, 23 April, p. 1041.

35 *Op. cit.*, note 15 above.

36 Schneiderman *et al.*, *op. cit.*, note 26 above.

37 Ibid., p. 605.

38 Mills, M., Davies, H. and Macrae, W. (1994), 'Care of dying patients in hospital', *British Medical Journal*, **309**, pp. 583–6.

39 Ibid., p. 605.

40 *Op. cit.*, note 9 above.

41 Position paper based on written evidence submitted to the House of Lords Committee on Medical Ethics by the Alzheimer's Disease Society, June 1993.

4 Law at the End of Life: What Next?

SHEILA A.M. McLEAN

When the House of Lords established a Select Committee[1] in the aftermath of the case of Anthony Bland,[2] it was surely a widespread hope that their conclusions would provide a radical revision of the UK laws concerning the end of life. That the question 'what next?' can still be posed is evidence of the fact that, for many, this hope was ultimately ill-founded. Certainly, it seems unlikely that the Report of the Select Committee will have satisfied all of the judges who heard the *Bland* case, perhaps most notably Lord Mustill who concluded his judgement by saying '... I must admit to having felt profound misgivings about almost every aspect of this case.'[3]

It is no longer the case that issues at the end of life can be seen solely as matters for the criminal law which continues to maintain its prohibition on killing. Survival is a matter which also has ramifications for the civil law in the light of increasingly ageing populations and the preservation of existence by rapid medical advance. As Giesen has said:

> Death and dying are issues which in recent years have increasingly become matters of concerned public discussion worldwide ... . It is submitted two factors are mainly responsible for this development. First, the process of dying has been shifted from a private setting to the more public setting of health care institutions, or from the home to the hospital. ... Secondly, advances in medical technology and pharmacology have made it possible to prolong the lives of terminally or otherwise hopelessly ill patients who have little (or no) hope of a cure.[4]

Yet, as the Hastings Center point out: '... the new powers of medicine have proved to be a mixed blessing. Our capacity to prolong life in many cases exceeds our capacity to restore health.'[5]

Not only, however, has public discussion been generated and engaged in on this area, but our civil courts have increasingly been involved in the process of decision-making. The involvement of the law is a relatively new feature in this area, with much of practice having been previously left unreported and unscrutinized. It is taken here as being unexceptional that the law should be involved as the ultimate mechanism for the protection of individuals and the creation and monitoring of standards and practices.

However, the *fact* of legal involvement is in itself insufficient to meet the concern that decision-making should not merely be conducted within a framework, but that this structure should be both transparent and consistent. The thrust of this chapter will relate to these latter points. The – not uncontroversial – propositions to be considered will be as follows:

1   The law has developed in a piecemeal way, resulting in inconsistencies in dealing with situations which are in fact of the same genus. Yet we are entitled to expect consistency or formal justice from our law with like cases being treated in a like manner.
2   We are still in need of a radical revision of our law, both to achieve consistency and also to reflect adequately social and other mores.

The law is not, nor should it be, a static instrument, maintaining, without thought, the status quo. Rather, and perhaps in the tradition of American Realism, the law should be a flexible and sensitive tool, whether it is proactive or reactive. The forum in which such sensitivity arises may differ from jurisdiction to jurisdiction, but whether judge-made or statutory, the problems must be tackled. Unlike the tradition in the USA, judges in the UK are often reluctant to make new law on a case-by-case basis. Thus, to return to the case of Anthony Bland,[6] the majority of the judgements sought to declare the decision taken as being readily encapsulated by current law (a debatable proposition, and one which led some of Their Lordships into deep intellectual waters), whilst others, most notably Lords Browne-Wilkinson and Mustill, were unprepared to swim with their colleagues. In puzzling over this question, Lord Browne-Wilkinson, for example, had this to say:

> ... behind the questions of law lie moral, ethical, medical and practical issues of fundamental importance to society. ... Existing law may not provide an acceptable answer to the new legal questions which it [the ability to sustain life artificially] raises. Should judges seek to develop new law to meet a wholly new situation? Or is this a matter which lies outside the area of legitimate development of the law by judges and requires society, through the democratic expression of its views in Parliament, to reach its own distinctions on the underlying moral and practical problems and then reflect those decisions in legislation?

His conclusion was that he was in 'no doubt that it is for Parliament, not the courts, to decide the broader issues'... .[7]

However, to return to the question of formal justice, that consistency in law is one of its fundamental values is difficult to dispute. In the common law systems, such as those of England and the USA, consistency is sought by dependence on precedent (although it must be said that rigid adherence to precedent is sometimes criticized as rendering the law relatively inflexible). In the civilian legal tradition, certainty is achieved substantially by codification – a method of establishing and promulgating standards and rules to which adherence is mandatory. In jurisdictions such as Scotland, which owe much to the civilian tradition but are perhaps best described as mixed jurisdictions, precedent plays a part, but novel situations are resolved by reference to principle.

Thus, whatever the legal approach adopted, it is clear that an inherent characteristic of a developed legal system remains its commitment to formal justice. Logically, therefore, an important issue for the law – if it is to achieve this – is the categorization of problems into discrete classes. Thus, if all cases of fraud are dealt with under the same set of rules, routinely applied without fear or favour, then the law is successful on this level at least. Equally, it would not be expected that cases of arson would be subject to the same set of rules, since this represents a different class or category of offence. Formal justice is not offended by this categorization.

It is first, therefore, important to explain why it is argued here that the law in respect of death and dying is currently inconsistent, and to do this it is necessary to establish that the range of decisions required to be taken are indeed of the same kind. Before seeking to do this, however, it is imperative to confront directly the essence of the issue. At present it can be argued that the UK approach to decisions at the end of life breaks the problems down by using a number of devices which are, broadly speaking, situational. Thus, as will be shown, the approach to the handicapped neonate may differ substantially from the attitude taken to the patient in persistent vegetative state, to the enforceability of an advance directive or to the request of a patient for active termination of life.

Yet, in each of these cases we are talking of one thing only – the attainment of a 'good' or 'easy' death. In other words, no matter who the individual might be, and no matter his or her condition, the actual decision, however reached, is a decision for or against death. We are, in its purest form, considering euthanasia. If it is possible to strip away the fear and hostility frequently aroused by the use of that word and remind ourselves of its etymology rather than the horrific pictures conjured up by the experience in the not-too-distant past of involuntary euthanasia (which, arguably, is in fact only murder under a different name), a rational approach may be taken.

Jonathan Glover[8] describes euthanasia as falling into three principal categories, which will be adopted here:

1   *voluntary euthanasia*: that is the ending of someone's life with their consent and in their interests;
2   *non-voluntary euthanasia*: the ending of someone's life without reference to their wishes, in a situation where they can express no such choices, again in their best interests;
3   *involuntary euthanasia*: the ending of someone's life either without regard to their wishes when they are competent to give them, or against their expressed wishes, supposedly in their best interests.

As has already been said, the third category is arguably indistinguishable from murder (since motive is irrelevant to that crime) and need not concern us further here, so it is with the first two categories that this chapter, and our law, are vitally concerned. There are two principal aspects to their definition which lead to the claim that they are of the same genus. The first is that the result is the ending of life and the second is the intrusion of the concept of best interests. In other words, these cases are distinguishable *only* on the basis that in one case the consent of the individual is available and given and in the other that consent is not available from the particular person. Thus, arguably, and leaving aside for the moment the ways in which decisions in respect of the *incapax* might be taken, these cases are, for all significant purposes, on all fours, and we can legitimately anticipate that they will be dealt with in a similar manner by our law. This is not to denigrate the importance of consent, which normally renders intervention lawful, but rather to indicate that there is a paradox in accepting non-consensual decisions whilst simultaneously rejecting those which demonstrate the autonomy which makes consent a central concept in both law and ethics.

If the above is accepted, then it is not sufficient to satisfy the requirement of formal justice that, for example, all patients in PVS are treated the same, whilst (under different rules) all handicapped neonates are accorded the same treatment. It must rather be that *all* decisions which result in death as an outcome are subject to the same considerations and raise the same concerns. In other words, it is vital that the similarities of the cases, rather than their differences, are focused on if we are to build and develop a coherent set of standards which will satisfy our legitimate demand for transparency and clarity, for equality of treatment and for certainty of outcome.

Of course, it might be argued that the situations are so different that a different approach is merited. Arguably, it would not detract from, but would rather strengthen, the argument presented here if this were conceded. What this chapter seeks to do is to consider the underlying, rather than the cosmetic, issues at stake. If one function of the law is to provide some form of certainty, based on principle, then we must both identify the principle and demand its consistent application. The value at stake, therefore – at least as far as current law is concerned – is not the right of the individual to make decisions about his/her life or death. Maybe it should be, but this is not the case at present, and since this chapter seeks to deal with legal reality, and to postulate reform, it is important that this caveat is borne in mind.

A brief review of the current UK laws will therefore suggest that it is matters other than consistency and formal justice which have informed decision-making. In fact, most jurisdictions have probably wittingly or unwittingly, reached a similar situation. The source of this is two-fold. First, law often and perhaps inevitably does develop in a piecemeal fashion, at least where it is judge-made. An example of this can be seen in English law in respect of prenatal damage. Put simply, a woman who causes her foetus harm prenatally cannot (except in one circumstance) be sued as a result of that damage by that child after birth.[9] The reason for this is that it would disrupt the family unit. Yet that same behaviour may result in the child being removed from the home after birth.[10] Which disrupts the family unit more?

The point here is that these cases are decided by different legal processes, or in different courts. They are categorized as different issues, because – as in the case of decisions at the end of life – no overview is taken, and the differences between them are concentrated on to the detriment of consideration of their similarities. In particular, the underlying values which were intended to be served by the laws are addressed in an inconsistent manner – where they are addressed at all.

To return to the cases of concern here, it is obvious after only brief consideration that the same – perhaps even wider – inconsistencies are evident. Broadly, the situations encapsulated by Glover's first two categories can be described thus:

- the handicapped neonate;
- the patient in persistent vegetative state;
- the patient who rejects life-saving treatment;
- the patient who executes an advance directive;
- the patient who seeks euthanasia.

In a series of cases generally heard by our civil courts (with the exception of the trial of Dr Leonard Arthur,[11] the attitude of the judiciary has been consistent in dealing with the handicapped neonate. Taking them with a broad brush, a decision not to treat, or not to continue treating, where the parents do not wish treatment to continue and where doctors are satisfied that it is not 'in the best interests' of the child for it to survive, will not be unlawful, so long as the doctor's (in)actions conform to a 'responsible body of medical opinion'.[12] In other words, non-voluntary euthanasia is endorsed by UK law.

Equally, and however else it may be described, the judgement in the case of Anthony Bland provides further endorsement of non-voluntary euthanasia. As with the case of the handicapped neonate, the presumption – whichever route was selected to reach it – was that although '... there is a legitimate moral and legal presumption in favor of preserving life and providing beneficial medical care with the patient's informed consent',[13] nonetheless '... avoiding death should not always be the preeminent goal; not all technologically possible means of prolonging life need or should be used in every case.'[14]

As to the individual who refuses life-saving treatment, where that decision is not provoked by apparent third-party intervention or duress, and providing the individual is legally capable of making it, an assault would technically be committed if treatment were continued. This position is very clear and stems from the notion that the autonomy of the individual should not be overridden (a point which will be referred to again below). In the Canadian case of *Mallette* v. *Shulman*,[15] Mr Justice Robins put the position clearly:

> At issue here is the freedom of the patient as an individual to exercise her right to refuse treatment and accept the consequences of her own decision. Competent adults ... are generally at liberty to refuse medical treatment even at the risk of death. The right to determine what shall be done with one's own body is a fundamental right in our society... .[16]

This statement is echoed in UK decisions, with Lord Butler-Sloss adding that 'A decision to refuse medical treatment by a patient capable of making the decision does not have to be sensible, rational or well-considered.'[17]

In other words, the patient may – for whatever reason – prefer death to life. It may, of course, seem that this category of patient sits uneasily with the others, since what is happening here could be argued to be merely an extension of the act of suicide. However, it is suggested that this group of patients *is* properly considered under the heading of euthanasia, for the reason that their decision, in their best interests, is sufficient to override the pre-existing duty of care owed by their medical advisers. Thus, this is not simply a private act of suicide, but is rather an example of the principle of autonomy coming into competition with, and defeating, other values which would prevail in other circumstances. It is a public and not a solely private act, and might even be described as a kind of passive euthanasia. Importantly also, even if this latter proposition is not accepted, it demonstrates yet again that – whatever the rhetoric of a preference for life – our law is not prepared to damage other important values, such as autonomy, in order to enforce that postulated preference. Rather, the law acknowledges that some deaths may be better than some lives.

The next category concerns patients who have made a clear and unequivocal statement of intent in respect of their treatment choices and in advance of the circumstances arising. It is not necessary to go into this in detail here, but it is interesting to note that – although there appears to be considerable enthusiasm for the advance directive, and although the outcome is the same as in the above cases – there is nonetheless an apparent reluctance to accord them definitive status. The major exception to this is the recent case of Re C,[18] where the court took what, in the light of history, was a remarkable stand. In not only endorsing the choice of someone diagnosed as mentally ill, but also in validating an anticipated decision, the court recognized, in the clearest possible terms, the right of an individual to make life-threatening decisions on the basis *solely* of his or her preferences for a certain type or quality of life, and irrespective of the therapeutic interest in treatment.

But this case was unusual, not least because the treatment concerned was extremely specific, and its status is not yet clear. Although at least one judge in the *Bland* case began the process towards the recognition of advance directives, their development is still viewed with some suspicion. Paradoxically, the reasons most frequently given are that they might not reflect the currently held views of the individual (were they capable of currently holding views);[19] in what way, one wonders, does this differ from the neonate whose views are never known, or Anthony Bland whose views were never expressed? A further argument relates to the fact that the situation may have changed,[20] presumably thus rendering the previously expressed choices less than rational (at least in clinical terms). In reality, this is arguably no different from the position of the person who rejects life-saving treatment on an apparently 'irrational' basis. In other words, the similarities are greater than the differences, and consistency might be thought to demand that advance directives are given the force of law.

Finally, there is what has proved to be the most troublesome case – that of the individual who seeks active euthanasia. The question of the difference, if any, between acts and omissions has generated volumes of academic and other comment, and is inevitably the subject of consideration in many of the chapters in this book. Whatever one's moral conclusion as to the validity of the distinction, it is worth pointing out that, legally speaking, there is no qualitative difference between the two where there is a pre-existing legal duty of care. As Schreiber, J. said in the US case of *Matter of Conroy* (1985)[21], ... the line between active and passive conduct in the context of medical decisions is far too nebulous to constitute a principled basis for decisionmaking'.[22] In addition, it must be clear that omitting to save life and actively taking it arise from the same intention and have the same consequences. As Lord Mustill succinctly said in the *Bland* case, 'It is intent to kill or cause grievous bodily harm which constitutes the mens rea of murder, and the reason why the intent was formed makes no difference at all'.[23] Arguably, therefore, we might expect the law to treat the act in the same way as the omission. This, however, it does not do.

To summarize, therefore, current law in the UK can be said to endorse a number of things: first, autonomy is an important principle and, second, life is not always preferable to death. However, the brief examination of the situations in which there is a perceived need to utilize these principles has shown that they are not applied in a manner which can escape the criticism of being uncertain and uneven. Paradoxically, the decision that life is not always preferable to death seems to be more readily endorsed where the individual has no autonomy (non-voluntary euthanasia) and, with the exception of treatment refusal (which, it has been argued, might be categorized as a form of passive euthanasia), the clear and autonomous decision that death is preferable is one which the law will either half-heartedly recognize (as in the case of the advance directive) or will reject outright (as in the case of active euthanasia).

One further matter must be disposed of before considering the second strand of my argument. Leaving aside those individuals who are not autonomous, but for whom tests (however satisfactory) have been devised which permit them to attain a 'good' death, it is clear that the most problematic group for our law-makers has been those who are expressing an autonomous preference for death. In Canada, a recent attempt to claim the right to make such decisions was defeated,[24] and in most jurisdictions the doctor acceding to such a request would be guilty of a criminal act. However bizarre this conclusion might seem, however paradoxical given the law's failure to condemn non-voluntary euthanasia, it could be said that, no matter how important autonomy is, there are good reasons for limiting it in these situations.

These reasons might most forcefully relate to the individual as a member of a community. Certainly, we already limit the rights of individuals simply to do or say exactly what they please. Laws concerning assault, rape, defamation and nuisance are examples of autonomy-limiting laws. Their rationale goes beyond the individual and encroaches into the good order of society. The individual's autonomy is not permitted to atomize the community in which he or she lives, and rightly so. Therefore, if it were clear that permitting an individual to make an autonomous choice for death would have significant deleterious effects on the rest of the community, the legal tradition is there to defeat the primacy of the claim from autonomy. But does this evidence exist?

It is rather trite, but nonetheless necessary, to start from the question of suicide in attempting to answer this question. Suicide is no longer a criminal offence. The individual is free to choose death no matter what are the consequences for family and friends. The moral tone of the community may be dented, but is not permanently damaged, by this exercise of autonomy. However, active euthanasia can be seen as a very different phenomenon. Here, the individual asks another, third party, to carry out a kind of surrogate suicide – to shoulder the burden of committing the act. Whatever the reason for this (and it may simply be the lack of the opportunity to kill oneself), for some, the involvement of a third party renders the act qualitatively different. It is therefore not the death but the manner of the death which is said to distinguish the two situations.

Of course, were third parties *obliged* to accede to such requests, there would be a legitimate and incontrovertible source of concern, since their own autonomy could be said to be overridden by that of another. But assuming that this is not seriously suggested, what is the balance to be achieved between the interests of the community and the principle of autonomy or self-determination? Interestingly, it seems that the answer to this is held clearly by UK law. In a case concerning treatment refusal, Lord Donaldson made wide-reaching comments on this very issue. He said:

> This situation gives rise to a conflict between two interests, that of the patient and that of the society in which he lives. The patient's interest consists of his right to self-determination – his right to live his own life as he wishes, even if it will damage his health or lead to his premature death. Society's interest is in upholding the concept that all human life is sacred and that it should be preserved if at all possible. *It is well established that in the ultimate the right of the individual is paramount.* (emphasis added)[25]

Or as Lord Mustill put it in the *Bland* case:

The interest of the state in preserving the lives of its citizens is very strong, but it is not absolute.[26]

In any event, might it not additionally be argued that the interests of society are best discovered by reference to what that society believes its interests to be? Although opinion poll evidence must be regarded as, in some ways, suspect there is a growing body of information from such surveys which suggests that many communities do not in fact see the legalisation of euthanasia as being inimical to their interests as a whole. The *Lancet*, for example, reported in 1993 that opinion poll evidence from the Netherlands suggested that 70 per cent of adults do not wish euthanasia to be a criminal offence.[27]

To conclude this part of the discussion, therefore, a number of strands have emerged. First, given that the issues at stake in each of the groups described above can be said to be the same – that is, the value of life over death – it could be argued, indeed it *is* argued, that their treatment should proceed on the same basis. It is therefore obligatory to criticize a legal regimen which permits death where the individual has made no choice for it yet criminalizes it where a competent decision has been made. This criticism could, of course, be overcome either by outlawing all of these situations or by permitting all of them. It is not the purpose of this chapter to opt for either solution – merely to point to the disparity between the conclusions.

Second, our law recognizes that the concept of the sanctity of all life is not an absolute principle. Again, whether or not one agrees with this position, that this is accepted should mean that the situations in which death is a legitimate or preferable option should be approached with this in mind. Principles, rather than sophistry, should guide the law here. Better a law which offends some members of the community than one which does harm to the very principles on which that society is run.

The House of Lords Select Committee and Beyond

As was said at the beginning of this chapter, the establishing of the House of Lords Select Committee was widely seen as an opportunity to clarify the lawfulness of decisions at the end of life. For my part, at least, it was also devoutly hoped that the Committee would take account of the two conclusions reached above and would react by reinforcing the need for consistency in the law.

The remit of the Committee was as follows:

... to consider the ethical, legal and clinical implications of a person's right to withhold consent to life-prolonging treatment, and the position of persons who are no longer able to give or withhold consent;
and to consider whether and in what circumstances actions that have as their intention or a likely consequence the shortening of another person's life may be justified on the grounds that they accord with that person's wishes or with that person's best interests;
and in all the foregoing considerations to pay regard to the likely effects of changes in law or medical practice on society as a whole.[28]

However, any hope that the whole spectrum of cases would be dealt with by the Committee is dashed by the statement that 'medical practice in respect of neonates'[29] was not specifically raised by the terms of reference (surely a debatable interpretation). However, it was conceded that they 'cannot be excluded from any consideration of decision-making about the withholding or withdrawing of medical treatment.'[30] Although this last statement might raise hopes again, their consideration of this issue is effectively confined to three paragraphs in which they report the views of the British Paediatric Association, their opposition to routine scrutiny of these cases by the courts and their suggestion that a code of practice be drafted to cover such cases – a code which the Association itself was currently involved in seeking to draft.[31]

Nowhere in the Select Committee Report is the position of the neonate viewed from the perspective which has been outlined above. The question of amalgamating all decisions for death in an effort to identify and clarify common principles is not seriously addressed. Thus, the members of the Committee were not informed in their conclusions by concern for the kind of consistency which is argued for here. Rather, they chose to continue the debate in terms of situation rather than values. It is scarcely surprising, then, that – in my view at least – their Report is ultimately unsatisfactory.

In fact, this dissatisfaction extends even to the areas which the Committee did feel able to consider. Even if the lessons to be learned from the law concerning the handicapped neonate were not available for their consideration, consistency and principle might still have emerged from consideration of those groups whose situations they *did* feel themselves able to address. Sadly, however, this too was not to be.

Perhaps unsurprisingly, their starting-point was the sanctity of life:

Belief in the special worth of human life is at the heart of civilised society. It is the fundamental value on which all others are based, and is the foundation of both law and medical practice. The intentional taking of human life is therefore the offence which society condemns most strongly.[32]

However, it was also acknowledged that:

> Alongside the principle that human life is of special value, the princi-
> ple is widely held that an individual should have some measure of
> autonomy to make choices about his or her life.[33]

Equally unsurprisingly, those who submitted evidence to the Select
Committee were not in agreement either about what each of these
principles encapsulated or the weight to be given to them should
they appear to conflict. The task of marrying the major differences of
opinion was almost certainly impossible. To that extent, calls for
public consultation as an exercise in democracy are doomed to collect information about the range of opinions but to fail to satisfy all
of them. This is not to suggest that the process is of no value, but
rather to recognize its limitations. Ultimately, responsibility for concluding on these complex matters rests with the law – either judge-
made or statutory. Either way, it is arguably naive to assume that it
is, in any real sense, democratic.

Leaving this aside, however, let us turn to a critique of the Select
Committee Report. Although the search for consistency was
abandoned at the first hurdle, many of the Select Committee's conclusions reflect and endorse other values. The cautious enthusiasm
for the advance directive,[34] for example, reinforces the primacy of
autonomy, as does the fact that no recommendation was made which
would eat into the competent patient's right to refuse life-preserving
treatment. Both of these conclusions will be welcomed by many, but
criticized by others. However, what is lacking in them is substantially that they sit uncomfortably with other conclusions reached.

If the underlying reason for endorsement in these cases is the
autonomy of the individual, and that autonomy is given pre-emi-
nence over the abstract concept of the sanctity of life, how is it
possible to distinguish between the exercise of autonomy in these
cases and in those which amount to voluntary active euthanasia?
The Select Committee circumvented this whole ethical quagmire by
merely stating that 'The right to refuse medical treatment is far removed from the right to request assistance in dying',[35] concluding
that the arguments in favour of legalizing euthanasia were not 'sufficient reason to weaken society's prohibition of intentional killing'.[36]
Few reasons are given for this conclusion.

One point, however, which is well made is that the fact that, in
individual cases, euthanasia might be thought by some to be appropriate is insufficient to require legal change. As the Report says:
'... individual cases cannot reasonably establish the foundation of a
policy which would have such serious and widespread repercus-

sions.'[37] Equally, it echoes a point raised above concerning the ramifications of choices for death, saying:

> ... death is not only a personal or individual affair. The death of a
> person affects the lives of others, often in ways and to an extent which
> cannot be foreseen. We believe that the issue of euthanasia is one in
> which the interest of the individual cannot be separated from the
> interest of society as a whole.[38]

If scrutinized for sense, this is manifestly true; if scrutinized for
consistency with the other conclusions reached, this cannot stand as
an argument against legalizing euthanasia. Death is a matter which
affects others, but this is true of *all* deaths, not merely those which
would result from euthanasia. Nor can the distinction be based on
the involvement of others in the death. Where neonates are allowed
to die, where advance directives are followed, where artificial nutrition and hydration are lawfully removed and where laws respect the
wishes of a person to end their life by refusing treatment, third
parties already *are* involved. As has already been argued, even if
there were some validity in the distinction between acts and omissions, it vanishes in the context of pre-existing duties. Thus, the
doctor who withdraws or withholds treatment is legally an active
participant in the death – in other words he or she *is* already a third
party for these purposes.

Moving from euthanasia *per se*, the extent to which the Report
clarifies the law in a transparent and principled manner can be observed by the Lords' attitude to specific situations. What is to be
done with, or for, the person in PVS, maintained by artificial nutrition and hydration? What of the person in intractable pain? The
response of the Select Committee to these questions represents, it is
submitted, a fudging of the issue – a pragmatic and doubtless compassionate fudge, but a fudge nonetheless. In essence, the Select
Committee, in the first example, neatly side-stepped the question by
suggesting that changes in clinical management should mean that
the question of whether or not to remove artificial nutrition and
hydration should seldom arise.[39] All very well, but what of the cases
when they *do* arise? The answer would seem to be that this should be
a matter for a new judicial forum,[40] although on what basis, and
subject to what constraints of practice or principle, this forum should
operate is not clear.

As to the patient in intractable pain (and therefore presumably a
likely candidate to request euthanasia), their case is met in two ways:
first, by an endorsement of the principle of double effect, an established part of certain theologies and already accepted by the law in
the UK;[41] and, second, by stating that the doctor should be acting in

accordance with a responsible body of medical opinion, will be returned to later in the chapter.

In cases where pain has become intractable the Report says:

> ... we are satisfied that the professional judgement of the health-care team can be exercised to enable increasing doses of medication (whether of analgesics or sedatives) to be given in order to provide relief, even if this shortens life. ... In some cases patients may in consequence die sooner than they would otherwise have done but this is not in our view a reason for withholding treatment that would give relief, as long as the doctor acts in accordance with responsible medical practice with the objective of relieving pain or distress, and with no intention to kill.[42]

This is not the place to discuss the long-standing debate about the application of this principle, nor the plausibility of distinguishing foresight from intention in reality. These issues are flagged, however, because they demonstrate that this principle is by no means uncontentious.

The application of double effect does, however, also endorse the view that quality of life may be every bit as important as quantity and serves by implication to reinforce the claim made earlier that not all life is preferable to death.

It might be argued, however, that the application of this principle also obfuscates the issue. What is the value being served? Dr Cox, for example, might well have argued that, although of no therapeutic value, his injection of potassium chloride certainly ended the pain (and the life) of his patient.[43] He might have reasoned that his act, whilst foreseeably resulting in death was not intended to do this, yet he was convicted of attempted murder.

Further avoidance of the issue is seen by the Select Committee's wholehearted endorsement of improvements in palliative care.[44] Certainly, no-one would quibble with this as a goal to be striven for, but the Committee itself accepted that palliation was not universally possible. What of those for whom none is available or effective? The encouragement of developments in palliative care is arguably a complement to, and not a substitute for, the need to address the fundamentals of the issue.

Ultimately, therefore, whilst initially welcome, the pleas of Lords Browne-Wilkinson and Mustill for Parliamentary consideration and resolution of these complex legal, ethical and social issues have taken us little forward. The government's response to the Select Committee Report[45] may be described at best as insipid, and certainly is in no way classifiable as radical.

Conclusions

In summary, it will be seen that the goals identified in this argument as being of primary value have not been met. A variety of different tests were applied to reach a variety of conclusions, with no apparent search for logic or consistency. It has been argued here that this is largely a result of the failure to perceive that, in essence, decisions about the end of life (one's own or someone else's) are more similar than they are dissonant and, as such, deserve consideration from a common set of values. The Select Committee and the government have merely perpetuated the categorization which, it has been submitted, is inappropriate and unhelpful. As a result, the outcome of the exercise is no more satisfying than was the pre-existing situation.

One further item must, however, be addressed before concluding. It has already been noted that, in commenting on the principle of double effect, the Select Committee introduced a modification to it which does not appear in the theology from which it is derivative: namely, that the doctor is acting in accordance with a responsible body of medical opinion. It should, of course, come as no surprise that the House of Lords paid significant attention to medical practice, given that the Committee was entitled the Select Committee on Medical Ethics. That matters of life and death should be seen contextually rather than broadly was probably predictable from the moment this title was settled upon.

Yet, why should context have such relevance? The UK Central Council for Nursing, Midwifery and Health Visiting was quick to object to this title,[46] although it appears that they may have taken a lone stance on this. But their objection merits consideration. Surely much more than medical ethics is involved in these decisions? The fact that they most often arise in a hospital setting does not make them solely or even predominantly medical. This classification does, however, shed important light on the final constraint which shaped this Report, and which smoothed the path for the decision in the *Bland* case.

For some of the judges in the *Bland* case, the fact that doctors regard these decisions as being medical was sufficient so to render them.[47] For others, the fact that nasogastric feeding was initiated by medical staff and pursued under their supervision, was sufficient to make this medical.[48] The logic of this, then, was that decisions about whether or not the feeding should be continued were questions not of ethics but of medical practice. Thus, the test used in other cases involving doctors could be applied, namely that drawn from the case of *Bolam* v. *Friern Hospital Management Committee* (the Bolam Test).[49] That is, if a doctor acts in accordance with a practice accepted as reasonable by a responsible body of medical opinion, then he or she is not negligent.

It must be said that the application of this test in cases of operational negligence is not uncontentious,[50] but by what stretch of the imagination can it be said to be satisfactory in situations where what is at stake is not whether or not the doctor acted with due skill and care, but rather whether or not an individual should live or die? Lord Mustill, at least, commented on this anomaly, although he did not feel that the *Bland* judgement critically hinged on the application of this test.[51] Nonetheless, he was sufficiently concerned to comment, obiter, that although 'I accept without difficulty that this principle applies to the ascertainment of the medical raw material such as diagnosis, prognosis and appraisal of the patient's cognitive functions …'[52] nonetheless '[B]eyond this point, however, it may be said that the decision is ethical, not medical, and that there is no reason in logic why on such a decision the opinions of doctors should be decisive.'[53] This view echoes the concerns of the Law Commission, which stressed that 'A test developed to deal with matters of clinical judgement is not necessarily the most appropriate one to use in circumstances where the balancing of other interests may be required.'[54]

It has been argued here that there are non-medical questions which must be addressed from a principled perspective. The principles endorsed have included autonomy, but the need for legal consistency has formed the central plank of this chapter. The only remaining question, then, is how would a principled perspective best be achieved? Manifestly, it will only be attainable if the values identified here are adverted to by whichever manifestation of the law is given ultimate responsibility, that is whether law continues to be judge-made or becomes codified or legislative. Opinion as to the best way forward is divided.

In some traditions – for example, in the American Realist model – the judiciary have the power to shape the law and are seen as the best forum for so doing. In terms of this theoretical approach, judges – usually acting within the framework of a written constitution or bill of rights – interpret the intentions of those who drafted the written statement, enlightened by prevailing social and other mores. However, even in this tradition, the role of the judiciary in so doing is not uncontroversial. As Schreiber, J. said in *Matter of Conroy*, 'As an elected body, the Legislature is better able than any other single institution to reflect the social values at stake.'[55]

Perhaps not surprisingly, the weight of opinion in the UK, at least in recent years, seems to fall on the side of parliamentary rather than judicial determination. Apart from the pleas of Lords Browne-Wilkinson and Mustill already referred to, other voices have been raised in support of a parliamentary resolution. Perhaps most notably, the Law Commission highlighted its concerns on this point, saying:

The desirability of piecemeal decision-making through caselaw is questionable. Decisions of the courts, particularly in sensitive areas, tend to be confined to the particular facts, and there is a reluctance to give pronouncements on principles of general application. This can mean that there is no real consistency between different decisions, and make it difficult to elicit guidelines with any real reliability.[56]

The failure to seek such consistency, to identify these ethical guidelines, coupled with the hijacking of broad ethical matters by medicine (and with full backing of the law), does little to meet the concerns expressed earlier concerning accountability and transparency of decision-making. These failures merely continue the unhelpful process of false and contrived categorization and obscure the way forward. It cannot be said that the radical revision of the law which, at the outset of this chapter, was said to be needed has in fact taken place. Rather, existing flaws have been further entrenched in the legal approach. That this could have been predicted is clear; yet it is equally clear that it is unfortunate.

Notes

1 House of Lords Select Committee (1994), *Report of the Select Committee on Medical Ethics*, HL Paper 21, London: HMSO.
2 *Airedale NHS Trust v. Bland* [1993] 1 All ER 821.
3 Ibid., at p. 896.
4 Giesen, D. (1990), 'Law and ethical dilemmas at life's end', *Law and Moral Dilemmas Affecting Life and Death*, Council of Europe, Proceedings of the XXth. Annual Colloquy on European Law, Glasgow, pp. 82–3.
5 Hastings Center (1987), *Guidelines on the Termination of Life-sustaining Treatment and the Care of the Dying*, Report, p. viii, Bloomington: Indiana University Press.
6 *Op. cit.*, note 2 above.
7 Ibid., at pp. 877–8.
8 Glover, J. (1977), *Causing Death and Saving Lives*, Harmondsworth: Penguin, (reprinted 1984).
9 Congenital Disabilities (Civil Liability) Act 1976 s. 1.
10 Cf. *D. v. Berkshire C.C.* [1987] 1 All ER 20. For a discussion of this and other cases, see Fortin, J.E.S. (1988), 'Legal protection for the unborn child', *Modern Law Review*, **51**, (1), p. 54.
11 *R v. Arthur, The Times* 5 November 1981, pp. 1, 12.
12 This is the so-called 'Bolam Test', taken from the case of *Bolam v. Friern Hospital Management Committee* [1957] 2 All ER 118.
13 Hastings Center Report, *op. cit.*, note 5 above, Preface p. viii
14 Ibid.
15 [1991] 2, *Medical Law Review*, 306, at p. 314.
16 Ibid., at p. 167.
17 *Re T* [1992] 3 *Medical Law Review*, 306, at p. 314.
18 *Re C (Adult: Refusal of Treatment)* [1994] 1 WLR 290.
19 Cf. Robertson, J. (1991), 'Second thoughts on living wills', *Hastings Center Report*, **21**, (6),p. 6.

20   Cf. ibid.
21   486 A 2d 1209 (NJ 1985).
22   Ibid., at p. 1234.
23   Ibid., at p. 890.
24. *Rodriguez* v. *British Columbia* [1993] SCJ No. 94, 30 September 1993.
25   *Re T, op. cit.,* note 17 above, at p. 312.
26   Ibid., at p. 891.
27   *Lancet* 1993, **341**, p. 426.
28   Ibid., at p. 7.
29   House of Lords Select Committee, *op. cit.,* p. 47, para. 229.
30   Ibid.
31   Ibid.
32   Ibid., p. 13, para. 34.
33   Ibid., p. 13, para. 40.
34   Ibid., p. 54, paras 263 and 264.
35   Ibid., p. 48, para. 236.
36   Ibid., p. 48, para. 237.
37   Ibid.
38   Ibid.
39   Ibid., p. 52, para. 257.
40   Ibid., p. 50, paras 245 and 246.
41   Ibid., p. 49, para 242.
42   Ibid.
43   Dr Cox was tried and convicted of attempted murder at Winchester Crown
     Court, 18 September 1992. At a subsequent disciplinary hearing of the General
     Medical Council he was not struck off the register.
44   Ibid., p. 49, para. 241.
45   *Government Response to the Report of the Select Committee on Medical Ethics,* Lon-
     don, HMSO, 1994.
46   House of Lords Select Committee *op. cit.,* note 1 above, Paper 21–11, at p. 139.
47   Cf., for example, the judgement of Lord Goff.
48   This is an argument which must surely be regarded with some scepticism.
49   *Op. cit.,* note 12 above.
50   See, for example, Mason, J.K. and McCall Smith, R.A. (1994), *Law and Medical
     Ethics,* (4th edn), London: Butterworths; Brazier, M. (1992), *Medicine, Patients
     and the Law,* (2nd edn), Hardmondsworth: Penguin; McLean, S.A.M. (1989), *A
     Patient's Right to Know: Information Disclosure, the Doctor and the Law,* Aldershot:
     Dartmouth.
51   *Airedale NHS Trust* v. *Bland, op. cit.,* note 2 above, at p. 895.
52   Ibid.
53   Ibid.
54   The Law Commission (1991), *Mentally Incapacitated Adults and Decision-Making:
     An Overview,* Consultation Paper no. 119, London: HMSO, p. 33, para. 2.24.
55   *Op. cit.,* note 21 above, at p. 1220.
56   *Op. cit.,* note 54 above, p. 90, para. 3.37.

PART II

5 Safeguards for Physician-assisted Suicide: The Oregon Death with Dignity Act

CHERYL K. SMITH
Attorney and writer

Introduction

Attempted suicide and suicide are no longer crimes in the USA, although many jurisdictions specifically prohibit, by statute, assisting in a suicide.[1] None of these statutes makes an exception for assisting in the suicide at the request of a person who is terminally ill. It is not clear, in most cases however, whether such statutes were passed with these individuals in mind.[2]

In attempts to give dying persons the legal right to control the time and manner of their own death, with the aid of a physician, a variety of tactics were employed in the first half of the 1990s, including legislative proposals, initiatives and legal challenges to state-assisted suicide laws.[3] Bills that would legalize physician-assisted suicide or active euthanasia were introduced in eight states between 1990 and 1993, although none were passed.[4] In the majority of cases they failed even to move out of the committees where they were initially proposed.[5] The two most successful proposals, unsurprisingly, were brought through the initiative process rather than through the legislature.[6]

The Oregon Death with Dignity Act, now known as Oregon Measure 16 of 1994, is the third such 'right to die' initiative to be placed on the ballot in the USA.

In November 1994 the Oregon Death with Dignity Act passed by 51–49 per cent of the vote and was to go into effect the next month.

Although the Oregon Death with Dignity Act was to be effective 30 days after its passage, it was temporarily stopped by a federal

69

judge after a group of physicians and patients, represented by an Indiana attorney, filed a complaint asking that it be enjoined.

In that complaint, the plaintiffs argued that the law, which would allow competent adults with a terminal disease to obtain a prescription for the purpose of ending their life, is unconstitutional and unlawful. They argued, first, that the law deprives terminally ill Oregonians from protection of certain laws, i.e., the law that provides a criminal prohibition against assisted suicide and the law that provides for commitment of mentally ill persons. The complaint also stated that the law violates the Americans with Disabilities Act, the Religious Freedom Restoration Act, the First Amendment right to freedom of association, and the Equal Protection and Due Process clauses of the 14th amendment to the US Constitution.

A hearing on the complaint was held on December 19, 1994 and an opinion was handed down on December 27, 1994. That opinion further postponed the implementation of Measure 16.

After further hearings in May 1995, US District Judge Michael Hogan ordered a permanent injunction against Measure 16.[7] He dismissed a number of plaintiffs and defendants, and found that the law violates the equal protection clause of the 14th amendment to the US Constitution.[8] I will not discuss the constitutional arguments in depth as that is beyond the scope of this chapter.

Initiatives and Referenda

Initiatives and referenda are alternatives to direct legislation. The two processes are not well understood and are frequently confused with each other. Twenty-one US states have provisions for law-making by initiative; 25 allow law-making through the referendum process.[9]

Initiative Process

The initiative process is a method for true grass-roots law-making. It may be used to propose constitutional amendments or create legislation. Initiative legislation is *initiated* by citizens, supported by voters through signing of petitions and placed on the general election ballot for a vote by the citizens of the state. It may be direct or indirect.

Direct initiatives allow direct placement on the ballot of a proposed measure (either statute or constitutional amendment) after the acquisition of a specific number of signatures on a citizen petition. This was the method used in both the California and Washington Death with Dignity Act campaigns.

Indirect initiatives must be submitted to the legislature for approval after the acquisition of a specific number of signatures on a citizen petition and prior to placement on the ballot.

Referendum

Referendum is a process whereby a state law or constitutional amendment that was already approved by legislature is *referred* to voters for approval prior to becoming effective. Three variants to this process exist: citizen petition, legislative referendum and constitutional referendum.

Under the citizen form of referendum, citizens of a state petition the legislature for a referendum on legislation that is, or was, being considered. Legislative referendum, alternatively, allows the legislature to voluntarily submit laws to voters for their approval. Constitutional referendum is used when a state's constitution requires that certain questions be submitted to voters.

Oregon Initiative Requirements

In Oregon, placement on the ballot of an initiative measure to make statute law requires that a detailed process be followed. First, an original and two copies of the prospective petition must be filed with the Elections Division of the Secretary of State's Office.[10] This prospective petition must designate no more than three chief petitioners and must be signed by 25 registered voters.[11] As soon as the petition is filed, the Secretary of State must immediately send the full text to the Attorney General.[12] The Secretary of State must also seek public input on whether the text of the proposed law contains only one subject.[13]

The Attorney General is required to prepare a draft ballot title for the initiative measure and file it with the Elections Division no later than the fifth business day after receipt of the proposed initiative measure.[14] The draft ballot title must contain a caption that does not exceed ten words; a question that does not exceed 20 words; and a summary that does not exceed 85 words.[15] The Attorney General must also ensure that the ballot title meets a minimum readability standard and is impartial, concise and accurate.[16]

Once received, the Secretary of State must publish the notice and solicit comments on the draft ballot title through various sources.[17] Registered voters are then given ten working days to comment on the draft ballot title; these comments must be considered by the Attorney General when writing a certified or revised ballot title.[18] (Individuals who have given written comment then have the further right to appeal the certified ballot title to the Supreme Court of Oregon.)

If the ballot title is appealed within ten days of certification, it must then be expeditiously reviewed by the Supreme Court and a final determination made.[19]

After preparing cover and signature sheets as required by law,[20] petitioners file them with the Secretary of State for review and approval.

The next step in the process is the collection of voter signatures. In order to qualify an initiative for the ballot, registered voters' signatures equalling 6 per cent of the 'total votes cast for all candidates for governor at the last election in which a candidate for governor was elected to a full term'[21] must be collected no less than four months prior to election. (That equated to 66 771 signatures required to qualify the Oregon Death with Dignity Act – a number that was far surpassed with more than 95 000 signatures ultimately collected.)

The signatures are then verified as soon as possible upon their receipt by the Secretary of State and, if that requirement is met, the initiative measure is certified for placement on the official election ballot and printed in the voters' pamphlet and on the ballot.[22]

Oregon Law on Assisted Suicide

Oregon is one of more than half of the US states that have a statute making assistance in suicide a criminal offence.[23] It also has a statute that makes assisted suicide a defence to murder when the conduct at issue 'consisted of ... aiding ... without duress or deception, another person to commit suicide'.[24] That statute codified *State* v. *Bouse*,[25] brought in 1953, in which the court interpreted the prior assisted suicide statute[26] to cover participation such as 'furnishing the means for bringing about death'.[27] Although the case leaves some ambiguity regarding the definition of 'furnishing', it puts Oregon physicians who write a prescription for drugs to end the life of a dying person at risk of prosecution.

The advance directive statute[28] also addresses assisted suicide. It differentiates withholding or withdrawing 'a life-sustaining procedure or ... artificially administered nutrition and hydration' in accordance with the provisions of the statute from affirmative or deliberate acts or omissions to end life, including assisted suicide, suicide, mercy killing and assisted homicide.[29]

In order to protect physicians who are currently writing prescriptions for lethal medication at the request of their terminally ill patients and to provide an opportunity for physicians who would like to provide such help but are currently not so doing, a new law was required.

Drafting the Initiative

The principal message in television advertisements opposing the Death with Dignity initiatives in California and Washington was that they contained no safeguards for vulnerable individuals. (Although the real objections may have been different – for example, that only God gives life and only God should take life – I will deal here with the issue of safeguards because it was pivotal in swaying the electorate, whereas religious or other arguments may not have been.) Some of the fears voiced by opponents were that patients would be coerced, doctors would make an incorrect diagnosis, the patient might be acting out of depression, there might be a conspiracy to bring about a patient's death, or that the state would become a 'suicide capital'.[30]

The Oregon Death with Dignity Act was written very narrowly, with safeguards specifically enumerated in the bill. It addressed not only those concerns voiced during the previous campaigns, but drew on recommendations from both the writings and advice of various medical and legal professionals.[31]

In order to make the initiative consistent with current Oregon law, much of the language, particularly as regards definitions, was taken from the current law on advance directives,[32] which was passed in 1993 by the legislature, with the cooperation and support of a number of health-care organizations.[33]

Safeguards

Only adults who are capable, terminally ill residents of Oregon and who are voluntarily expressing a wish to die are eligible to make a written request to a physician for a prescription to end their life in a humane and dignified manner, under section 2.01 of the Measure.

The principal difference between Measure 16 and previous proposals is that it is purely a prescribing bill. The law does not expressly allow a physician to administer an overdose of a lethal drug; the patient is required to take the final act that brings about death. This general limitation addresses the concern that physicians should not deliberately cause death, thereby violating their Hippocratic tradition as healers.[34] While previous initiatives were opposed by state medical associations, the Oregon Medical Association decided to remain neutral on Measure 16.

Other safeguards in Measure 16 include the following:

- The attending physician must determine that the patient is terminally ill, capable and is making a voluntary and informed request; and must request notification of next of kin.

- The consulting physician must confirm the patient's diagnosis, voluntariness, capability and informed decision-making.
- If either physician believes that the patient has a psychiatric or psychological disorder, or is suffering from depression which causes impaired judgement, the patient must be referred for counselling.
- The patient must make an informed decision based on knowledge of the diagnosis, prognosis, potential risks, results and alternatives, including comfort care, hospice care and pain control.
- The physician must ask the patient to notify his or her next of kin.
- The patient must make one written and two oral requests.
- The patient may rescind the request at any time and in any manner, and the physician must give a final opportunity for the patient to make a rescission.
- Waiting periods of 15 days between the initial oral request and the writing of the prescription, and 48 hours between the written request and the writing of the prescription must elapse.
- All information must be documented in the medical record.
- Only Oregon residents are covered by the law.
- The Health Division is required to review records annually, in order to collect information regarding compliance and to provide an annual statistical report.
- Wills and contracts may not be conditioned on requests under the Act.
- Insurance or annuity policies may not be conditioned on requests under the Act.
- Mercy killing, lethal injection and active euthanasia are not authorized.

Duties of the Attending Physician

Section 3.01 requires the attending physician to make an initial determination that the patient has a terminal disease, is capable and has made a voluntary request. He or she is also required to obtain an informed decision, to refer the patient to a consulting physician and to a counsellor if appropriate, to ask the patient to notify his or her next of kin, to offer an opportunity to rescind the request, to document all the steps in the medical record and to ensure that all the steps are carried out in accordance with the Act before writing a prescription.

All conversations between patient and physician in this regard are to be documented in the medical record, potentially to be reviewed by the state, thereby improving current physician practice and further protecting patients. These conversations may also be more open and honest. Under currently accepted medical practice, physicians may prescribe large doses of medication for patients under the guise of pain control and the 'double effect'. Double effect allows the prescription and administration of large doses of medication purportedly intended only to control the pain, with the patient's death being only an unintended effect. Under this new law rather than maintain the pretence that death is unintended, patients and physicians may make rational decisions and discuss what is really taking place.

Duties of the Consulting Physician

The consulting physician, under section 3.02, must examine the patient and his or her medical records in order to confirm the diagnosis and prognosis, to determine that the patient is capable and to verify that the request to end his or her life is voluntary and informed.

This requirement of a confirming opinion has been included in virtually all proposals for physician-assisted death.[35] Such a confirming opinion not only protects the patients from misdiagnosis, erroneous decision-making or coercion, but also helps to assure the public that no unilateral decisions are being made.

Referral for Counselling

Section 3.03 mandates a referral for counselling if either the attending or consulting physician believes the patient to have a psychiatric or psychological disorder, or to be suffering from a depression that causes impaired judgement. The purpose of counselling, as defined in section 1.01 (4), is to ensure that patients are not suffering from a disorder that may be impairing their judgement. It also provides an opportunity for another opinion regarding the patient's mental state and helps to ensure that he or she is not requesting the assistance of a physician for reasons that are unacceptable under this law.

One of the principal concerns voiced in television advertisements opposing the Death with Dignity Initiatives is that patients who want a physician-assisted death are depressed. The requirement to refer a patient to a counsellor under Measure 16 will encourage, if not mandate, physicians to consider the possibility of depression before acceding to the request. However, because many dying people become depressed, yet have previously stated their beliefs regarding assisted death, depression *in itself* does not rule out the physician's assistance under Measure 16. It does encourage him or her, however, to make referrals to deal with problems that may not yet have been considered, such as isolation, finance or pain control.[36]

Informed Decision

The patient must make an informed decision, as defined in section 1.01 (7), based on knowledge of the diagnosis, prognosis, potential risks, results and alternatives, including comfort care, hospice care and pain control. This requirement was included in section 3.04 because of the importance and finality of a decision to die.

Informed decision, as defined by Measure 16, is similar to informed consent. Informed consent can be seen as an 'affirmative duty of disclosure' by a physician,[37] to a competent and rational patient. The requirement that physicians obtain informed consent prior to performing surgery or other treatments is well established in American law. In *Schloendorf* v. *The Society of New York Hospital*, Justice Cardozo stated that '[e]very human being of adult years and sound mind has a right to determine what shall be done with his own body. …'[38]

Oregon law requires that physicians explain to patients the treatment or procedure they will perform, alternatives to that procedure, and any related risks.[39] Because the decision to end one's life is even more important than procedures that *may* bring about death or other complications, the drafters of Measure 16 made the informed decision requirement even more rigorous than that of informed consent. In addition, because the patient him or herself will undertake the 'procedure' that ultimately brings abut death, the requirement of informed consent is not appropriate.

Besides potentially failing to find the appropriate solution to the problem – for example, better pain control, respite care or hospice care, a physician who fails to meet that affirmative duty of disclosure has not only failed ethically but risks litigation – in this case by the survivors.[40] Capability, while also expressly required by the Measure, is implicit in informed consent. In addition, because deciding to die should be a last resort, in informing of alternatives, physicians are expressly required to discuss other options, including palliative care, hospice care and pain control.

Informing Next of Kin

Section 3.05 requires that the attending physician ask patients to inform their next of kin of their decision. However although this action is strongly encouraged it is not a requirement. While family communication and support in the dying process has a significant value, in some cases patients may be estranged from their family or have antithetical views, and therefore may choose not to inform family members.[41] This provision acknowledges the ideal of involving the family, but balances that ideal against patient autonomy and confidentiality.

Physicians may not notify the family against patient's wishes due to the confidential nature of information disclosed during the physician-patient relationship. In addition to an ethical prohibition against revealing confidential disclosures without consent of a patient,[42] ORS 677.90 states that '[t]he Board of Medical Examiners for the State of Oregon may ... suspend or revoke a license to practice [medicine] ... for willfully or negligently divulging a professional secret'.

Written and Oral Requests

In order to receive a prescription for medication to end life in a humane and dignified manner, the patient is required, by section 3.06, to make one written and two oral requests. This provision, in conjunction with the waiting periods, more clearly delineates the concept of enduring or persistent request, which is the standard in the Netherlands, as well as in various other proposals.[43] It helps to ensure that the request is well considered and is not, for instance, a response to a bad day. The requirement that one of the requests be written also ensures that the event is properly documented, not only to make a record but for reporting requirements.

Right to Rescind Request

The right to rescind a request at any time and in any manner, regardless of mental state, is an important provision mandated by section 3.07. The requirement that the physician must offer the patient an opportunity to rescind his or her request several times during the process assures the patient that he or she is not under any coercion and that having a change of mind is acceptable.

The physician is also required to discuss the request with the patient and provide another opportunity for rescission prior to writing a prescription. Going ahead with obtaining a prescription should be a wholehearted decision; in fact, patients who receive a prescription still have the right to change their mind at any time.

Waiting Periods

Section 3.08 governs waiting periods under the Measure. A period of not less than 15 days must elapse between the initial oral request and the writing of a prescription. No less than 48 hours must elapse between the written request and the writing of a prescription. This provision further elucidates the requirement of a persistent request and addresses the concern expressed by opponents of previous Death with Dignity initiatives that a patient may request assistance in dying on one day and be dead by the next. It helps to ensure that the request is well considered and allows time for a change of heart. It also provides the patient and physician an opportunity to resolve the problem that may have led to the request.

Although this provision could arguably cause greater patient suffering if the initial request comes towards the end of the dying process, it encourages deliberate choice while simultaneously protecting vulnerable individuals.

Medical Record Documentation Requirements

Section 3.09 enumerates detailed requirements for the documentation or filing of specific information in the patient's medical record. This helps to ensure compliance with the law by providing a method for verifying that all the required steps were taken by the involved parties. These records are open to review by the Health Division, according to rules developed after passage of the law.

Because this medical record documentation provision, along with the Health Division review requirement, provides mechanisms for the verification of discussions between patient and physician, medical practice for terminally ill patients wishing to die will, arguably, be improved. In addition, problems that may arise from this new practice will be identified more easily.

Residency Requirement

The requirement in section 3.10 that only requests made by Oregon residents may be granted under this Measure addresses the concern that the state might become a 'suicide mecca'. The weakness in this provision is that is does not define 'resident'. Current Oregon law is not helpful on this count either; no general definition of 'resident' exists, and most statutes that have residential requirements do not define the term.[45]

Reporting Requirements

Section 3.11 (2) grants rule-making authority to the Oregon Health Division for the collection of data relating to requests for prescriptions to end life in a humane and dignified manner.[45] The drafters felt that rather than requiring that certain data elements be collected by statute, the Oregon Health Department would be in a better position to make this determination. Although they may mandate reporting of all cases where requests are made, this information is not open to the public.

The public will be informed, however, of statistics generated by the Division on an annual basis, under section 3.11 (3). In addition, under the statute governing rule-making, the public will have an opportunity to comment on the proposed rules developed by the Health Division regarding data collection and record review.[46]

Effect on Wills, Contracts, Insurance and Annuity Policies

Section 3.12 (1) states that no provision in a will, contract or other agreement that would affect whether a person makes or rescinds a request under Measure 16 shall be valid. Subsection (2) also prohibits the conditioning of an obligation under a current contract upon the making or rescinding of a request by a person under Measure 16. Both of these provisions relate to the requirement under, and philosophy behind, Measure 16 that a person who decides to make, or not to make, such a request must be acting out of free choice and without undue influence by others.

Likewise, section 3.13 prohibits the sale, procurement, or issuance of an insurance or annuity policy that is conditioned on the making or rescinding of a request for medication to end life in a humane or dignified manner. It also states that ingestion of such medication shall not have 'an effect upon a life, health, or accident insurance or annuity policy'. This section acts to ensure that such actions are based on autonomous choice rather than on duress or external economic factors.

Construction of Act

Section 3.14 clarifies that nothing in Measure 16 authorizes lethal injection, mercy killing or active euthanasia. It also provides that action taken under the Measure shall not constitute suicide, assisted suicide, mercy killing or homicide under the law. This provision would affect current laws regarding reporting of cause of death, construction of wills, and criminal prosecutions.

Under ORS 146.090, the current statute governing death investigations, deaths that are 'apparently homicidal, suicidal or occurring under suspicious or unknown circumstances' or 'resulting from ... the use ... of toxic agents' must be investigated by the medical examiner. Measure 16 would exempt deaths that would otherwise require investigation, assuming that prescription drugs are not usually considered 'toxic agents'.

ORS 146.003 defines cause of death as 'the primary or basic disease process or injury ending life', while manner of death is defined as 'the probable mode of production of the cause of death, including natural, accidental, suicidal, homicidal or undertermined.' Section

3.14 creates a potential problem in relation to these definitions, in that ending of life under its provisions does not constitute suicide and obfuscates cause of death to be reported under current statutes.

Measure 16 could also affect probate law and inheritance under wills, in that by exempting actions under its provisions from classification as homicide or suicide, the statute prohibiting a 'slayer' from inheriting (by considering them to predecease the decedent) would be inapplicable. ORS 112.455(2) defines a slayer as 'a person who, with felonious intent, takes or procures the taking of the life of another'.

Although no Oregon cases are on point, in a Pennsylvania case, a woman who supplied pills and assisted her mother in taking them, causing her death, was precluded from inheriting from her sister's estate.[47] Without Measure 16, a court could arguably construe assistance in a suicide to be procurement of the taking of life of another.

Obviously, criminal prosecutions of physicians who prescribe medication to patients who ultimately use it to end their lives would be preempted by Measure 16, if its provisions were adhered to. In addition, commitment to mental facilities of dying patients who wanted to end their lives may presumably be more difficult than at present.[48]

Another law that could potentially be affected is ORS 161.205(4), which allows persons 'acting under a reasonable belief that another person is about to commit suicide' to use physical force upon the individual to the extent reasonably believed necessary to thwart that result. Since actions under Measure 16 are not to be considered suicide, they would not fall under these laws.

Other Provisions

Measure 16 contains a number of other provisions including immunities and liabilities, a severability provision and a recommended request form.

Immunities and Liabilities

Section 4 deals with immunities and liabilities. Its provisions protect those individuals who participate in good faith, and penalizes anyone who attempts to subvert the law or coerce a patient. Rather than name specific groups of health care providers, the drafters intended for this provision to cover any participant who has a role in the process, even those who are simply present at the time the patient takes the medication.

The first part of section 4.01 – subsection (1) – protects persons participating in good faith in compliance with the Measure from civil or criminal liability or professional disciplinary action. It expressly extends that protection to individuals who are present at the time a patient takes the prescribed medication to end his or her life. This provision was included because the drafters strongly believed that since no-one should have to die alone, the family, physician or other supportive individuals should be allowed to be present when the person takes the prescription.

Judge Hogan relied heavily on these two sections in his final opinion determining that Measure 16 is unconstitutional, in particular on the standard of 'good faith compliance'. He determined that this standard preempts the general statutory standard of care which requires that 'A physician ... has the duty to use the degree of care, skill and diligence which is used by ordinarily careful physicians ... in the same or similar circumstances in the community of the physician ... or a similar community.'[49]

Although one could argue that because the statute is silent on this issue, the intent was to preempt the statute, as the drafter of these provisions I can safely state the purpose was to grant broad immunity to any persons lawfully participating in any aspect of the process, rather than to immunize persons from charges resulting from deliberate, reckless or negligent conduct. The absence of a provision such as that contained in the advance directive statute, stating that the standard is not exclusive of other standards of care,[50] does not imply an intent to preempt. Exclusivity is only guaranteed by an explicit clause to that effect.

Section 4.01 (2) protects individuals participating in good faith in compliance with the Measure from being penalized by professional organizations, associations or health-care providers. Examples include loss of hospital privileges at a religious hospital or loss of licence or discipline by a medical board that ethically opposes such participation.

Section 4.01 (3) prohibits using actions taken under Measure 16 as grounds for neglect or the appointment of a guardian or conservator. This provision is intended to prevent individuals from claiming that asking for, or receiving, a prescription under the Measure constitutes either incapacity or other grounds to justify the protection of person or property.[51]

Health-care providers and facilities would not be required to participate in the provision, to a qualified patient, of medication to end his or her life in a humane and dignified manner. This reflects the focus on choice and autonomy of the individual – both patient and physician – and is consistent with current advance directive law in Oregon.[52]

A health-care provider who is unwilling or unable to participate, however, would be required to transfer medical records to a new health-care provider, on request.

Severability

The purpose of section 5.01 is to sever various provisions of the Measure in the event that any part of it is found to be invalid. This ensures that the whole law is not invalidated if one part of it is found to be invalid, for constitutional or other reasons.

Form of Request

Section 6.01, along with section 2.02, sets out requirements for the form of a written request for medication as authorized under Measure 16. In addition to containing statements that the requirements of the Measure have been met, the form must also be witnessed by two individuals.

   The witnessing requirement is taken from the current advance directive statute.[53] Witnesses must confirm that the person signing the request is personally known to them or has provided proof of identity; the request was signed in their presence; the signer appears to be of sound mind and is not under duress, fraud or undue influence; and the signer is not a patient for whom they are acting as the attending physician. In addition, one of the witnesses may not be a relative, entitled to a portion of the person's estate, or own, operate or be employed at a health-care facility where the person is a patient or resident. If the patient is an in-patient at a long-term care facility,[54] one of the witnesses must be an ombudsman.[55] The ombudsman provision is similar to a provision found in Oregon's advance directive law,[55] and is intended to protect more vulnerable individuals who reside in nursing homes.

Conclusion

Measure 16, the Oregon Death with Dignity Act, is the most tightly drafted piece of physician-assisted death legislation to come before the people in the USA. The safeguards, written in response to concerns voiced in previous campaigns for right to die legislation, while helping to protect vulnerable patients from perceived or real abuses, encourage doctors and patients to freely discuss issues surrounding the dying process.

   A study in the Netherlands, where assisted suicide and euthanasia are tolerated but are not legal, showed that two-thirds of patients who asked their physicians for assurance that they would be assisted in dying when in the final stage of their disease did not need the assistance because other suitable alternatives were given.[56]

When Measure 16 is found to be constitutional and enforced, which is inevitable given Judge Hogan's convoluted analysis on the equal protection clause, patients will no longer need to fear involuntary commitment for raising the issue of assisted suicide, and physicians will no longer need to hide behind the double effect or fear prosecution or lawsuits for helping their patients to end their lives on their own terms.

The Oregon Death with Dignity Act is a narrow aid-in-dying bill that both reflects the lessons learned from previous efforts to pass similar laws and attempts to expand the legal boundaries for helping dying Oregonians to exercise control over end-of-life decisions.

Notes

1 According to the Choice in Dying, of New York, 32 states have statutes that explicitly criminalize assisted suicide: 11 criminalize assisted suicide by common law, and in six states the law is unclear. In 1994, courts in two of these states, Washington and Michigan, declared their statutes unconstitutional. Both of those decisions were later reversed by higher courts.

2 One known exception is Connecticut's statute, CONN. GEN. STAT ANN. § 53a–56(a).

3 Compassion in Dying, a Washington state organization formed to offer direct assistance with the rational suicides of terminally ill persons, has filed lawsuits in several states challenging their criminal statutes on assisted suicide on constitutional grounds. In *Compassion in Dying, et al. v. State of Washington*, 1994 WL 174250, Judge Barbara Rothstein found the Washington law unconstitutional on the grounds that it 'places an undue burden on the exercise of a protected Fourteenth Amendment liberty interest by terminally ill, mentally competent adults acting knowingly and voluntarily, without undue influence from third parties, who wish to commit physician-assisted suicide' and that it violates equal protection of the law 'by prohibiting physician-assisted suicide while permitting the refusal or withdrawal of life support systems for terminally ill individuals.'

4 Smith, C. and Trepkowski, M. (eds) (1993), *AID-IN-DYING; Legislative Proposals 1990–1993*, Eugene: The Hemlock Society USA, p. 1. All but two of these were brought by legislators in response to requests from constituents.

5 Ibid., p.1.

6 Washington state citizens, in 1990, voted down an active euthanasia bill, Initiative 119, by 54 to 46 per cent. California's Initiative 161 was defeated by the same percentage in 1992. These initiatives would have legalized both physician-assisted suicide and voluntary active euthanasia.

7 Eugene Register Cunard (1995), August 4, at A1.

8 *Lee v. State of Oregon* (1995), Civil No. 94–6467–HO. D. Ore. August 3.

9 *The Book of States*, 1992–93 edn, vol. 29 (1992), Lexington, KY: Council of State Governments.

10 ORS 250.045.

11 ORS 250.045(1),(3).

12 ORS 250.065.

13 The Oregon Constitution, Article IV, para. 1 requires that an initiative petition deal with only one subject.

14   ORS 250.065(3).
15   ORS 250.035(1).
16   ORS 250.039.
17   ORS 250.067(1).
18   ORS 250.067(2).
19   ORS 250.085.
20   ORS 250.045.
21   Oregon Constitution, Article IV, para. 1,(2)(b).
22   ORS 250.067(3).
23   ORS 163.125(b) states: 'Criminal homicide constitutes manslaughter in the second degree when ... [a] person intentionally causes or aids another person to commit suicide.'
24   ORS 163.117.
25   199 Or.676, 264 P2d 800 (1953).
26   The statute at that time, ORS 163.050, stated: '... any person who purposely and deliberately procures another to commit self-murder or assists in the commission thereof, is guilty of manslaughter.
27   Ibid. at 703
28   ORS 127.505 – 127.660.
29   ORS 127.570.
30   For an overview of arguments both for and against assisted suicide, see Smith C. (1993), 'What about legalized assisted suicide?', *Issues in Law and Medicine*, **8**, (4), Spring.
31   Drafts of the Initiative were circulated to various professionals in the Right to Die field, as well as physicians, law professors, counsellors and other professionals. For examples of writings regarding safeguards, see, for example, Quill, T., Cassel, C. and Meier, D. (1992), '*Care of the hopelessly ill: proposed clinical criteria for physician-assisted suicide*', *New England Journal of Medicine*, **327**, pp. 1380–4; and Smith, *op. cit.*, note 4 above, pp. 23–32.
32   ORS 127.505 – 660.
33   Interestingly, one aspect of the measure being attacked by opponents who favoured ORS 127.505–127.660 is the definition of 'incapable', despite the fact that the definition was taken directly from that statute.
34   I refer here to the Hippocratic tradition because, although the Hippocratic oath undoubtedly reflects some of the underlying values in medicine, it is rarely studied in medical schools and is sworn to by only 6 per cent of medical students (*New York Times*, 15 May 1990, at B6.) In addition, while the oath requires physician to relieve pain, it also prohibits the giving of deadly drugs. In cases of unrelenting terminal pain, both courses may not be possible.
35   *Op. cit.*, note 4 above, pp. 18–19.
36   In one study of suicides by persons over the age of fifty, common stressors such as financial problems, stress of illness, substance abuse, and loss of a valued role, among others, were identified. Physicians receiving requests for assisted suicide from dying patients would be well advised to consider dealing with or referring patients to resources to assist with these stressors.
37   Appelbaum, P.S., Lidz, C. and Meisel, A. (1987), *Informed Consent*, New York: Oxford University Press.
38   211 NY 125, 129.130, 105 NE 92, 93 (1914).
39   ORS 677.097.
40   One of the earliest cases of informed consent litigation was *Salgo v. Leland Stanford Jr., University Board of Trustees*, 154 Cal. App. 2d 560, 317 P2d 170 (Dist. Ct. App. 1957). The court stated in that case that '[a] physician violates his duty to his patients and subjects himself to liability if he withholds any facts which

are necessary to form the basis of an intelligent consent by the patient to the proposed treatment'.

41 An example is gay patients with AIDS, who not only have to cope with dying an often terrible death, but with estrangement from unaccepting families.

42 Section IV of the American Medical Association's Principles of Medical Ethics states that '[a] physician shall respect the rights of patients, of colleagues, and of other health professionals, and shall safeguard patient confidences within the constraints of the law'.

43 See, for example, Smith, C. (1991), Euthanasia in the Netherlands: Medical record documentation requirements. *Topics in Health Record Management*, **12**, (1), August; Risley, R. (1989), *Death with Dignity: A New Law Permitting Physician Aid-in-Dying*, Eugene OR: Hemlock Society.

44 See, for example, ORS 412.520, requiring residency as an eligibility criterion for aid to the disabled.

45 ORS 183.025–.725 governs administrative rule-making.

46 ORS 183.335 contains requirements pertaining to notice, content, public comment and adoption of administrative rules.

47 In re Estate of Leslie N. Jamison, Deceased, No. 91–2420, Court of Common Pleas of Montgomery County, Penn., Orphans Division, Memorandum of Opinion by Taxis, Sr. J., October 1, 1993.

48 ORS 426.070 provides a procedure for civil commitment of persons who are considered dangerous to themselves because of a mental disorder. Under this law, a physician can have patients held for up to 12 hours against their will to evaluate their mental state.

49 *Lee* v. *State of Oregon* at p. 15.

50 ORS 127. (1)(b).

51 ORS 127.625 allows health care providers to opt out of participation in withdrawal or withholding of life support. It is more restrictive than Measure 16 in that it does not require the physician to transfer care of the patient to another physician; the patient's representative must do this, or, if none exists, the physician must discharge the patient or find another physician, 'without abandoning' him or her.

51 ORS 126.003–.403 governs guardianship and conservatorship.

52 ORS 127.515(4), which sets witnessing requirements, also contains a provision that the witnesses not be health-care representatives or alternative representatives (for purposes of carrying out advance directives). This provision is omitted from Measure 16's witness requirement.

53 Long-term care facility is also defined by law. ORS 442.015 (14)(b) defines long-term care facility to include residential facilities and homes, skilled nursing facilities and intermediate care facilities. Such facilities serve individuals who are elderly, have medical problems, or have mental illness, mental retardation or other developmental disabilities.

54 Ombudsmen are designated by the facility but have certain qualifications specified by the Department of Human Resources by rule. ORS 441.103 establishes the office of Long-Term Care Ombudsman and the duties of that position.

55 ORS 127.515 (4)(e).

56 Van Der Maas, P.J., *et al*, (1991), 'Euthanasia and other medical decisions concerning the end of life, *Lancet*, **338**.

Appendix A

THE OREGON DEATH WITH DIGNITY ACT

SECTION 1
GENERAL PROVISIONS

§ 1.01 DEFINITIONS

The following words and phrases, whenever used in this Act, shall have the following meanings:

(1)   "Adult" means an individual who is 18 years of age or older.

(2)   "Attending physician" means the physician who has primary responsibility for the care of the patient and treatment of the patient's terminal disease.

(3)   "Consulting physician" means a physician who is qualified by speciality or experience to make a professional diagnosis and prognosis regarding the patient's disease.

(4)   "Counseling" means a consultation between a state licensed psychiatrist or psychologist and a patient, for the purpose of determining whether the patient is suffering from a psychiatric or psychological disorder, or depression causing impaired judgement.

(5)   "Health care provider" means a person licensed, certified, or otherwise authorized or permitted by the law of this State to administer health care in the ordinary course of business or practice of a profession, and includes a health care facility.

(6)   "Incapable" means that in the opinion of a court or in the opinion of the patient's attending physician or consulting physician, a patient lacks the ability to make and communicate health care decisions to health care providers, including communication through persons familiar with the patient's manner of communicating if those persons are available. Capable means not incapable.

(7)   "Informed decision" means a decision by a qualified patient, to request and obtain a prescription to end his or her life in a humane and dignified manner, that is based on an appreciation of the relevant facts and after being fully informed by the attending physician of:
(i)   his or her medical diagnosis;
(ii)   his or her prognosis;
(iii)   the potential risks associated with taking the medication to be prescribed;
(iv)   the probable result of taking the medication to be prescribed;
(v)   the feasible alternatives, including, but not limited to, comfort care, hospice care and pain control.

(8)   "Medically confirmed" means the medical opinion of the attending physician has been confirmed by a consulting physician who has examined the patient.

(9)   "Patient" means a person who is under the care of a physician.

(10) "Physician" means a doctor of medicine or osteopathy licensed to practice medicine by the Board of Medical Examiners for the State of Oregon.

(11) "Qualified patient" means a capable adult who is a resident of Oregon and has been determined by an attending and consulting physician to have a terminal disease and who has expressed his or her wishes in a written and oral request to obtain a prescription for medication to end life in a humane and dignified manner in accordance with this Act.

(12) "Terminal disease" means an incurable and irreversible health condition that has been medically confirmed and will, within reasonable medical judgment, produce death within six (6) months.

SECTION 2
WRITTEN REQUEST FOR MEDICATION TO END ONE'S LIFE IN A HUMANE AND DIGNIFIED MANNER

§2.01 WHO MAY INITIATE A WRITTEN REQUEST FOR MEDICATION
An adult who is capable and has been determined by the attending physician and consulting physician to be suffering from a terminal disease, and who has voluntarily expressed his or her wish to die, may make a written request for medication for the purpose of ending his or her life in a humane and dignified manner, in accordance with this Act.

§2.02 FORM OF THE REQUEST
(1) A valid request for medication under this Act shall be in substantially the form described in Section 6 of this Act, signed and dated by the patient and witnessed by at least two individuals who, in the presence of the patient, attest that to the best of their knowledge and belief the patient is competent, acting voluntarily, and is not being coerced to sign the request.

(2) One of the witnesses shall be a person who is not:

(a) A relative of the patient by blood, marriage or adoption:

(b) A person who at the time the request is signed would be entitled to any portion of the estate of the qualified patient upon death under any will or by operation of law; or

(c) An owner, operator or employee of a health care facility where the qualified patient is receiving medical treatment or is a resident.

(3) The patient's attending physician at the time the request is signed shall not be a witness.

(4) If the patient is a patient in a long term care facility at the time the request is made, one of the witnesses must be an individual designated by the facility and having the qualifications specified by the Department of Human Resources by rule.

SECTION 3
SAFEGUARDS

§3.01 ATTENDING PHYSICIAN RESPONSIBILITIES
The attending physician shall:

(1)   Make the initial determination of whether a patient is capable, has a terminal disease and has made the request voluntarily;

(2)   Inform the patient of:

    (a)   his or her medical diagnosis;

    (b)   his or her prognosis;

    (c)   the potential risks associated with taking the medication to be prescribed;

    (d)   the probable result of taking the medication to be prescribed;

    (e)   the feasible alternatives, including, but not limited to, comfort care, hospice care and pain control.

(3)   Refer the patient to a consulting physician for medical confirmation of the diagnosis, and for a determination that the patient is capable and acting voluntarily;

(4)   Refer the patient for counseling if appropriate pursuant to Section 3.03;

(5)   Request that the patient notify next of kin;

(6)   Inform the patient that he or she has an opportunity to rescind the request at any time and in any manner, and offer the patient an opportunity to rescind at the end of the 15 day waiting period pursuant to Section 3.06;

(7)   Verify, immediately prior to writing the prescription for medication under this Act, that the patient is making an informed decision;

(8)   Fulfill the medical record documentation requirements of Section 3.09;

(9)   Ensure that all appropriate steps are carried out in accordance with this Act prior to writing a prescription for medication to enable a qualified patient to end his or her life in a humane and dignified manner.

§3.02 CONSULTING PHYSICIAN CONFIRMATION
Before a patient is qualified under this Act, a consulting physician shall examine the patient and his or her relevant medical records and confirm, in writing, the attending physician's diagnosis that the patient is suffering from a terminal disease, and verify that the patient is capable, is acting voluntarily and has made an informed decision.

§3.03 COUNSELING REFERRAL
If, in the opinion of the attending physician or the consulting physician a patient may be suffering from a psychiatric or psychological disorder, or depression causing impaired judgment, either physician shall refer the patient for counseling. No medication to end a patient's life in a humane and dignified manner may be prescribed until the person performing the counseling determines that the patient is not

suffering from a psychiatric or psychological disorder or depression causing impaired judgment.

§3.04 INFORMED DECISION

No person shall receive a prescription for medication to end his or her life in a humane and dignified manner unless he or she has made an informed decision as defined by Section 1.01(7). Immediately prior to writing a prescription for medication under this Act, the attending physician shall verify that the patient is making an informed decision.

§3.05 FAMILY NOTIFICATION

The attending physician shall ask the patient to notify next of kin of his or her request for medication pursuant of this Act. A patient who declines or is unable to notify next of kin shall not have his or her request denied for that reason.

§3.06 WRITTEN AND ORAL REQUESTS

In order to receive a prescription for medication to end his or her life in a humane and dignified manner, a patient shall have made an oral request and a written request, and reiterate the oral to his or her attending physician no less than fifteen (15) days after making the initial oral request. At the time the qualified patient makes his or her second oral request, the attending physician shall offer the patient an opportunity to rescind the request.

§3.07 RIGHT TO RESCIND REQUEST

A patient may rescind his or her request at any time and in any manner without regard to his or her mental state. No prescription for medication under this Act may be written without the attending physician offering the qualified patient an opportunity to rescind the request.

§3.08 WAITING PERIOD

No less than fifteen (15) days shall elapse between the patient's oral request and the writing of a prescription under this Act. No less than 48 hours shall elapse between a patient's written request and the writing of a prescription under this Act.

§3.09 MEDICAL RECORD DOCUMENTATION REQUIREMENTS

The following shall be documented or filed in the patient's medical record:

(1) All oral requests by a patient for medication to end his or her life in a humane and dignified manner;

(2) All written requests by a patient for medication to end his or her life in a humane and dignified manner;

(3) The attending physician's diagnosis and prognosis, determination that the patient is capable, acting voluntarily and has made an informed decision;

(4) The consulting physician's diagnosis and prognosis, and verification that the patient is capable, acting voluntarily and has made an informed decision;

(5)   A report of the outcome and determinations made during counseling, if performed;

(6)   The attending physician's offer to the patient to rescind his or her request at the time of the patient's second oral request pursuant to Section 3.06; and

(6)   A note by the attending physician indicating that all requirements under this Act have been met and indicating the steps taken to carry out the request, including a notation of the medication prescribed.

§3.10 RESIDENCY REQUIREMENT

Only requests made by Oregon residents, under this Act, shall be granted.

§3.11 REPORTING REQUIREMENTS

(1)   The Health Division shall annually review a sample of records maintained pursuant to this Act.

(2)   The Health Division shall make rules to facilitate the collection of information regarding compliance with this Act. The information collected shall not be a public record and may not be made available for inspection by the public.

(3)   The Health Division shall generate and make available to the public an annual statistical report of information collected under Section 3.11(2) of this Act.

§3.12 EFFECT ON CONSTRUCTION OF WILLS, CONTRACTS AND STATUTES

(1)   No provision in a contract, will or other agreement, whether written or oral, to the extent the provision would affect whether a person may make or rescind a request for medication to end his or her life in a humane and dignified manner, shall be valid.

(2)   No obligation owing under any currently existing contract shall be conditioned or affected by the making or rescinding of a request, by a person, for medication to end his or her life in a humane and dignified manner.

§3.13 INSURANCE OR ANNUITY POLICIES

The sale, procurement, or issuance of any life, health, or accident insurance or annuity policy or the rate charged for any policy shall not be conditioned upon or affected by the making or rescinding of a request, by a person, for medication to end his or her life in a humane and dignified manner. Neither shall a qualified patient's act of ingesting medication to end his or her life in a humane and dignified manner have an effect upon a life, health, or accident insurance or annuity policy.

§3.14 CONSTRUCTION OF ACT

Nothing in this Act shall be construed to authorize a physician or any other person to end a patient's life by lethal injection, mercy killing or active euthanasia. Actions taken in accordance with this Act shall not, for any purpose, constitute suicide, assisted suicide, mercy killing or homicide, under the law.

SECTION 4
IMMUNITIES AND LIABILITIES

§4.01 IMMUNITIES

Except as provided in Section 4.02:

(1)   No person shall be subject to civil or criminal liability or professional disciplinary action for participating in good faith compliance
with this Act. This includes being present when a qualified patient
takes the prescribed medication to end his or her life in a humane and
dignified manner.

(2)   No professional organization or association, or health care provider, may subject a person to censure, discipline, suspension, loss of
license, loss of privileges, loss of membership or other penalty for
participating or refusing to participate in good faith compliance with
this Act.

(3)   No request by a patient for or provision by an attending physician of medication in good faith compliance with the provisions of
this Act shall constitute neglect for any purpose of law or provide the
sole basis for the appointment of a guardian or conservator.

(4)   No health care provider shall be under any duty, whether by
contract, by statute or by any other legal requirement to participate in
the provision to a qualified patient of medication to end his or her life
in a humane and dignified manner. If a health care provider is unable
or unwilling to carry out a patient's request under this Act, and the
patient transfers his or her care to a new health care provider, the
prior health care provider shall transfer, upon request, a copy of the
patient's relevant medical records to the new health care provider.

§4.02 LIABILITIES

(1)   A person who, without authorization of the patient, willfully
alters or forges a request for medication or conceals or destroys a
rescission of that request, with the intent or effect of causing the
patient's death, shall be guilty of a Class A felony.

(2)   A person who coerces or exerts undue influence on a patient to
request medication for the purpose of ending the patient's life, or to
destroy a rescission of such a request, shall be guilty of a Class A
felony.

(b)   Nothing in this article precludes further liability for civil damages resulting from other negligent conduct or intentional misconduct
by any person.

(c)   The penalties in this Act do not preclude criminal penalties
applicable under other law for conduct which is inconsistent with the
provisions of this Act.

SECTION 5
SEVERABILITY

§5.01 SEVERABILITY

Any section of this Act being held invalid as to any person or circumstance shall not affect the application of any other section of this Act which can be given full effect without the invalid section or application.

SECTION 6
FORM OF THE REQUEST

§6.01 FORM OF THE REQUEST

A request for a medication as authorized by this act shall be in substantially the following form:

REQUEST FOR MEDICATION
TO END MY LIFE IN A HUMANE AND DIGNIFIED MANNER

I, _____, am an adult of sound mind.

I am suffering from _____, which my attending physician has determined is a terminal disease and which has been medically confirmed by a consulting physician.

I have been fully informed of my diagnosis, prognosis, the nature of medication to be prescribed and potential associated risks, the expected result, and the feasible alternatives, including comfort care, hospice care and pain control.

I request that my attending physician prescribe medication that will end my life in a humane and dignified manner.

INITIAL ONE:

____ I have informed my family of my decision and taken their opinions into consideration.

____ I have decided not to inform my family of my decision.

____ I have no family to inform of my decision.

I understand that I have the right to rescind this request at any time.

I understand the full import of this request and I expect to die when I take the medication to be prescribed.

I make this request voluntarily and without reservation, and I accept full moral responsibility for my actions.

Signed: _____

Dated: _____

DECLARATION OF WITNESSES

We declare that the person signing this request:

   (a) Is personally known to us or has provided proof of identity;

   (b) Signed this request in our presence;

   (c) Appears to be of sound mind and not under duress, fraud or undue influence;

   (d) Is not a patient for whom either of us is attending physician.

_____Witness 1/Date

_____Witness 2/Date

Note: One witness shall not be a relative (by blood, marriage or adoption) of the person signing this request and shall also not be entitled to any portion of the person's estate upon death. No witness shall own, operate or be employed at a health care facility where the person is a patient or resident. If the patient is an inpatient at a health care facility, one of the witnesses shall be an ombudsman.

6 Physician-assisted Suicide: A Social Science Perspective on International Trends

BARBARA J. LOGUE, Ph.D.
Mississippi Institutions of Higher Learning, Center for Policy Research and Planning

Introduction

The son, a prominent journalist, visits his 90-year-old mother every few days, knowing full well there is nothing he can do for her: she lies in a foetal position and blinks uncomprehendingly as he talks to her. Her only sound is a shriek of pain when attendants turn her body from side to side in an effort to heal her terrible bedsores. She is incontinent and must be hand-fed. On the other hand, 'heart and lungs are working, whatever is wrong with spine and limbs and mind. There is no respirator to be unplugged. No doctor can pronounce her a terminal case. The only sure prognosis is constant pain and misery as long as she lives' – and she may live indefinitely. Understandably, the man asks, 'Can't we put my mother to sleep?' [1]

'So sorry, we can't do it,' the law responds. 'We can only wait for a crisis, pneumonia perhaps, and then decline to treat her, allowing her to die, slowly, from the infection.' In short, because she cannot help herself, no-one else can help her either. The only options left open to relatives are to shoot her or smother her with a pillow, hoping the courts will be lenient, or to watch and wait and suffer too.

The dilemma is that, in the few countries where it has come under consideration at all, the availability of physician-assisted suicide is conditioned on a variety of criteria, ostensibly imposed to prevent abuses, that in fact serve to victimize people like the journalist's mother. Central among these is the requirement that the patient be mentally competent at the time the request is made. Guidelines for euthanasia impose the same requirement.[2] In the Netherlands, for example, applicants must satisfy the following criteria:

1   They must define their suffering as intolerable.
2   They must understand their medical situation and have weighed other options and alternatives.
3   Their desire to die must be enduring, persistent and completely voluntary.
4   They must convince two physicians that they have met the first three criteria.[3]

Such criteria exclude many, if not most, seriously ill patients and in effect, 'skim off the top', selecting only the easier cases. The difficult cases – the seriously demented and those too physically debilitated either to commit suicide or demand euthanasia – are shunted aside. In fact, the Royal Dutch Medical Association and the Dutch Commission for the Acceptability of Life Terminating Action recently rejected euthanasia for the severely demented except where the patient also suffered grave *physical* illness and had signed a living will.[4] Current and proposed guidelines for physician-assisted suicide also deny help to previously competent persons who signed an advance directive while still competent; nor can a proxy named in that directive act on the patient's behalf. As one Dutch doctor put it, 'If they cannot speak, they cannot die':[5] the fact of having spoken in the past is of no avail in their present dilemma.

Even those officially opposed to euthanasia have noted the incongruities of current proposals, as indicated in a recent statement by a panel of 13 Jewish and Christian theologians, philosophers, and legal scholars:

> ... if the warrant for euthanasia is to relieve suffering, why should we be able to relieve the suffering only of those who are self-determining and competent to give their consent? Why not euthanasia for the suffering who can no longer speak for themselves?[6]

Ironically, the people who meet the current stringent criteria are those in the best position to help themselves (without physician assistance) because their cognitive capacity is intact. They may, for example, obtain lethal drugs on the black market, commit suicide in any number of other ways as their condition permits, or persuade a friend or relative to help them die. The 'protective' limits, on the other hand, may seriously harm the most helpless patients who have been deliberately excluded and, in addition, create fears in everyone else that they too may fall into a helpless state. Of course, 'passive' aid in dying, such as withholding or withdrawing life-sustaining treatments, is legally available to the incapacitated, but this approach may increase their suffering as it delays their death. We will return to this topic later.

To date, social scientists (including sociologists, anthropologists, historians, psychologists and economists, among others) have contributed relatively little to debates on death control, defined as 'deliberate behavior that causes a quicker death for a person suffering from an incurable condition, or complex of conditions, including the degenerative symptoms of old age'.[7] Their record compares poorly, for example, with the multitude of books and articles produced in recent years by ethicists, lawyers, and physicians; when social scientists mention these issues at all, euthanasia and physician-assisted suicide are quickly dismissed.

Yet insights from the social sciences can and should have a place in formulating policies and changing the laws with respect to death control. In particular, evidence from the social sciences clearly indicates that current guidelines on physician-assisted suicide and other forms of euthanasia are too limited and that they are contrary to what most people value. The discussion in this chapter is meant to be indicative rather than exhaustive. Although much of what is said applies to patients of any age, the primary focus is on the aged because the incidence of death in advanced industrial societies is concentrated in the older age groups, making the elderly the single largest population affected by changes in the law.

Sociology

Sociology is the scientific study of human society and human social behaviour. Its focus is on the group – whether the group consists of two persons or many – not the individual. The discipline's underlying premise is that humans are *social* beings, that contact with others is essential if we are to survive and be fully human. We derive our outlook, identity, hopes, fears, and satisfactions from interactions with other people; human beings do not thrive in isolation and extended solitude is avoided except under certain special circumstances. Where does the irretrievably incompetent person fit here? The answer is suggested by two interrelated concepts: biographical life and quality of life.

First, the sociological perspective fits well with the universal distinction made implicitly or explicitly by people everywhere: that is, the distinction between having a life (a biographical concept) and being alive (a biological notion).[8] Having a life encompasses an awareness of oneself as a unique individual, with the ability to love, learn and laugh, remember yesterday and plan for tomorrow, have hopes and dreams, and interact with others. While to have a life in the biographical sense obviously requires life in the biological sense, the reverse is not true. If one's biographical life is over, there is no point in having a biological life. Biographical life requires, above all else, mental alertness. By emphasizing the extension of biological life, the medical establishment has often given short shrift to life's social dimension – the biographical component that differentiates human beings from other life forms.

Second, it follows from the foregoing statement that quality of life must be broadly defined to incorporate 'the more complete social and psychological being', encompassing the individual's social roles, mental alertness, sense of well-being, and relationships with others. Moreover, decisions about medical treatment are *social* decisions, guided by social values; they are not based solely on objective scientific criteria but encompass more subjective social judgements.[9] The absence of mental alertness and the consequent inability to interact with others already trigger treatment cessation for the incompetent, indicating the lack of value placed on their continued existence. But nowhere in the world, under current law, is euthanasia allowed for such individuals; if they are physically strong, they must linger on until the onset of illness provides an opportunity to withhold treatment.

Social influences affect the definition of a 'good' death and the 'right' time to die. Decisions about death and dying typically extend beyond the individual to involve negotiations with relatives, the medical establishment and wider society. Only the individual dies, of course, but dying is inevitably also a social act; every death affects others and is affected by them. Others' needs and opinions inevitably play an important role in end-of-life decisions for the incompetent. In this context it is telling that, when a recent public opinion poll questioned Americans about the appropriateness of administering lethal drugs to the terminally ill, approval was greater (68 per cent) for mentally incapacitated patients than for others (60 per cent) – provided they had signed an advance directive while still competent.[10] This is an indication of the low valuation placed on the maintenance of mere biological life for the mentally incapacitated. Another important indicator is the fact that those who kill suffering, but incapacitated, friends or relatives are seldom indicted and, if they are, juries rarely convict, notwithstanding the letter of the law and judges' instructions.

Anthropology

Anthropological research amplifies the sociological perspective by describing human values and behaviour in comparative perspective, across time and place, with the emphasis traditionally on societies that are small, remote, isolated, preliterate and 'primitive'. In societies at every stage of development, important distinctions have been drawn between biological life and biographical life, between the intact and the decrepit, between those who are alert and aware and those who have 'lost their marbles'.[11]

Families and communities have also invariably recognized that people who are merely old differ from those who are decrepit. The later are not just old, but too ill, too weak or too senile to engage in normal social roles; further, their continued existence may constitute a threat to kin or community well-being.[12] Though sometimes tolerated, they have been neither respected nor deferred to, although some superstitious tribes may have feared their supposed supernatural powers.[13] Continued support for such individuals seems pointless or even counterproductive, and unreciprocated and unacknowledged assistance eventually breeds indifference and resentment on the part of the carer.[14] This helps to explain why the decrepit have often been singled out for special, negative treatments, many of which have served to hasten death directly or indirectly. Such people are treated in sharp contrast to valued members of the community for whom desperate efforts are made to avert death with every available means: the decrepit suffer non-supportive treatment ranging from ridicule and derision to the withholding of food and water, abandonment and outright killing.[15] The hastening of death has been approved, and openly practised, in many societies, often at the suggestion of, and with the active cooperation of, the 'victim'. Suicide has also been encouraged.[16] The biological occurrence of death itself is, in fact, anticlimactic, since the individual was already socially dead by reason of having lived beyond his or her capacity for productive involvement in social affairs.[17] Deliberate choices for earlier death have thus been made in many instances where the option of waiting for nature to take its course was clearly available.

In past non-industrial societies death occurred relatively quickly. No antibiotics staved off pneumonia or other infections, no respirators mechanically maintained breathing, no 'Code Blue' brought doctors and nurses running with special equipment when a heart stopped, no courts or ethics committees endlessly debated the issues. Significantly, decisions to hasten death have often been made in social contexts in which frail elders were only a negligible proportion of the population and where long-term care of the scope and duration commonly undertaken today was medically impossible, making frail elders, at worst, only a short-term burden.[18] More importantly, passivity worked: no one need actively kill an incapacitated elder, since simply waiting would accomplish that end in a relatively short time, especially if the person was unable to eat and drink independently. However, some groups did not hesitate to expedite death by the use of violence (stabbing, strangling, or pushing an elder off a cliff, for example). Thus 'primitive' peoples clearly made important distinctions among different categories of old people, set limits on care provision to the 'over-aged', and deliberately hastened death when the culture so directed.

These distinctions continue today, although we are prohibited from acting openly on them. Avoidance of demented patients occurs in nursing homes, for example, as the more intact patients shun the less intact. Like members of the most primitive tribes, more intact residents physically recoil from those who are senile, highly debilitated, or actively dying, in addition to distancing themselves psychologically. They object strongly to any forced mixing with such patients, although they may express sympathy with their plight.[19] Medical professionals at all levels engage in the same behaviour. Moreover, it is the oldest and most helpless patients, especially the mentally impaired, who are most likely to be victimized in institutions, and are equally likely to be neglected and abused by their families. Her work experiences inside US nursing homes led anthropologist Maria Vesperi to conclude, for instance, that staff members were likely to wish wholeheartedly for the death of incontinent and other troublesome residents.[20]

History

History, the study of past societies, reinforces the findings of anthropologists, especially as regards the distinction between a 'green old age' on the one hand and decrepitude and prolonged dependency on the other.[21] History shows us repeated instances of intolerance and lack of support for old people no longer able to actively contribute to group welfare.

Every society must deal with dependency: infants and children, the handicapped, the sick and injured are always present. But the dependency and burden of caring for very frail old people is a special case. Since the elderly have already lived long lives, since their condition is expected only to worsen and their ability to make positive contributions only to decline, and since the burdens of providing care will only increase, elder dependence is less easily tolerated than that of other groups. The weight of the historical evidence indicates limited tolerance for decrepitude and prolonged dependency in old age, with non-contributing elders perceived as burdensome and their needs treated as low priority. Incompetent elders were neither respected nor deferred to, whether by relatives or the larger community, and were often victimized.[22]

There is a long history of inadequate social institutions and grudging provision of funds to meet the long-term care needs of dependent elders, in terms of either quality or quantity. Historically, the chronic care facilities where many elders were consigned operated 'on an inevitably lowest-cost-per-day basis', plagued by 'constrained budgets, an almshouse heritage, and the dispiriting awareness that the brave new weapons of medical science were of little use in treating the victims of degenerative ills'.[23]

This is not to suggest that the plight of the most vulnerable has been of no concern to philanthropists or policy-makers, for concern has been expressed in a wide variety of historical contexts. Indeed, reams of idealistic words have been written about care, love, duty, filial piety and the deservingness of the vulnerable old. Prescriptions for improvement have not been lacking either, but sufficient and effective *action* has been rare. Our collective behaviour towards incapacitated elders has meshed very poorly with our noble words, reflecting doubts about their social worth and considerable ambivalence about their continued survival. This long history of inadequacies (of funds, of personnel, of time, of physical facilities) for meeting the long-term care needs of growing numbers of incompetent elders continues; both quality and quantity are lacking now, as in the past. Everywhere, other social groups are deemed more worthy, other needs more compelling, scarce resources better spent than on the non-productive old. Hence the conclusion that human communities, explicitly or implicitly, continue a long tradition of disvaluing those whose biographical potential has ceased to exist.

Psychology

Additional indicators of the significance of biographical life and the relative unimportance attached to biological life in its absence come from the discipline of psychology. Prolonged dying has increased long-term care burdens for individuals, their families, and health-care workers. What can we learn from each of these groups regarding appropriate treatment for permanently incompetent patients and the desirability of extending their lives?

Individuals

Many people are terrified of dying slowly, as helpless victims attached to tubes and machines, with no-one listening or caring about their suffering. They envision a scenario wherein their weakness makes it impossible for them to ask for assistance in ending their suffering, let alone act independently. Most individuals wish to avoid a dying process that is undignified, 'degrading' or 'disgusting' and to spare their friends and relatives from watching it.[24] Lingering deaths, delayed beyond the point where a meaningful biographical life is possible, are particularly dreaded. Because of its long duration and the loss of personhood its victims experience, Alzheimer's disease has come to epitomize a bad death.[25]

These apprehensions reflect far more than anxiety about physical pain; they encompass psychological fears such as a sense of helplessness, dependency and being a burden to others, and provide rationales for requests for aid in dying. Likewise, loss of mental faculties and being a burden on the family (two problems that are closely related) are the most important criteria underlying treatment cessation – these are equally important to patients and proxy decision-makers.[26]

Families

Family members dread having to watch the slow downhill course of an incapacitated relative. The pain of watching helplessly as a loved one deteriorates is sometimes so severe that families must be discouraged from visiting an institutionalized relative.[27] Families clearly distinguish competent from incompetent elders and treat them differently. Recent empirical work in the USA, for example, shows that an elder's health status is relevant for his or her relationships with kin: the 'vulnerable' aged in the community had *less* contact with children (though presumably they needed *more*) than the 'non-vulnerable'. Institutionalized elders had the least contact; family visits taper off and relatives withdraw as a patient's condition deteriorates in a nursing home setting.[28] Many question the sacrifices entailed in providing care that seems to yield no appreciable benefits to the patient or anyone else, despite the effort expended. Caring for the demented is particularly stressful, since they may not be able to appreciate the care provided or even recognize the care giver; in addition, they may be hostile or uncooperative.[29]

Although few families today literally abandon or kill frail relatives, their sense of burden and limited tolerance for one-way support manifests itself in more subtle ways, such as abuse and neglect. Elders in poor health are three to four times more likely to be abused.[30] Neglect, a more prevalent form of mistreatment than abuse, tends to be concentrated among the oldest and most impaired elderly and is closely related to care giver stress and sense of burden, especially when the patient is demented.[31] Both abuse and neglect are indirect forms of death-hastening directed at particular elders – the most helpless, dependent and disvalued.

Health-care workers

Like workers everywhere, medical professionals want to go home at the end of the day feeling good about themselves and their accomplishments, and to sleep well at night. Practitioners want what they do to make sense, to behave morally as well as legally, and to have the approval of colleagues and the general public. Care that is futile may deprive doctors of sleep, short-change other patients whose needs may be compelling, and result in stress, frustration and depression: understandably, therefore, workers strive to protect themselves by minimizing their involvement with patients who seem to gain nothing from the encounter.[32]

Health-care professionals distinguish between 'treatable' patients – those capable of resuming social roles – and 'non-treatable' patients, rejecting the latter and devoting minimal time and energy to their care.[33] Practitioners also tend to hold very negative attitudes about the frail aged, especially the demented, and view chronic care as tedious, uninteresting, an inefficient use of their time and talents, and ultimately futile. Doctors frequently use strongly pejorative terms such as 'turkey', 'crock' or 'brain stem preparation' for patients who are beyond medical help, especially those with diminished mental capacity.

Physicians obviously believe that such people would be better off dead. But the patients do not die, so doctors try to 'get rid of' them in other ways, as detailed in recent descriptions of medical training and practice: for example, they may transfer them to another department or to a different hospital where staff, in their turn, try to move them elsewhere or back to the first institution.[34] In a novel based on his experiences as an intern, Samuel Shem refers frequently to the frustration, burden and depression associated with caring for patients who cannot get well, referred to as 'gomers' by staff. The term, an acronym for 'Get Out of My Emergency Room', refers to 'a human being who has lost – often through age – what goes into being a human being'. The designation is typically accompanied by treatment that ranges from indifference to outright cruelty.[35]

For their part, nurses tend not to linger in the rooms of patients who are feeble, confused or unaware of their surroundings, exiting as soon as their tasks allow; although time pressures are often blamed for impeding better care, nurses who have free time on the job do not use it to intensify contact with such patients.[36]

The advanced decrepitude and cognitive incapacity of some patients are significant causes of stress and burn-out for professional care givers. Attempts to manage chronic, but not life-threatening, illnesses such as dementia are enormously frustrating.[37] Trained to cure, or at least to alleviate, suffering, practitioners are confronted with incurable diseases of long duration that require a wide variety of supportive services. But those services may yield no biographically meaningful improvement in the recipient's quality of life; instead they seem merely to prolong the dying process.

Burn-out is 'a reaction to chronic, job-related stress ... characterized by physical, emotional, and mental exhaustion' and having many deleterious effects, such as sleeplessness, depression, substance abuse, marital conflict, and feelings of powerlessness.[38] Further, 'most standard medical textbooks attribute anywhere from 50 to 80 percent of all diseases to stress-related origins', and medical evidence links stress to changes in the body's ability to fight disease.[39] Significantly, burn-out affects workers who question their effectiveness in their jobs and the value of the jobs themselves.[40]

Cognitive dissonance is a term used to describe a conflict between roles or ideas which are mutually inconsistent and which the person must consequently attempt to deny or reconcile. Physicians are coming to realize that they are currently 'practicing in an age of cognitive dissonance', treating incompetent (but not terminally ill) patients 'who cannot speak for themselves and who exist in a state [the physician] considers not worth living'.[41] Their inability to resolve the dissonance between what they are 'supposed' to do and their feelings of futility on doing it produce frustration, stress and burn-out. On the other hand, the desire to imbue their care-giving efforts with meaning can lead health-care professionals to bizarre rationalizations as they attempt to reduce dissonance. For instance, in one prominent US case nurses convinced themselves that they 'loved' a young patient and regarded her as a member of their family. Yet Nancy Cruzan, the patient in question, had been in a persistent vegetative state for eight years and the nurses never knew her before her accident.[42]

As with sociology, history and anthropology, psychological responses expose people's *real* feelings as to the relative significance of biographical and biological life: although care givers may talk idealistically about care giving and go through the motions of providing care, few seem convinced of the utility of their actions with respect to patients whose biographical potential has come to an end. As for patients and potential patients, although few would opt to continue long in such a non-human state, current restrictions on aid in dying provide no encouragement.

Economics

Finally, we turn to economics, the study of human activities relating to the production, consumption and distribution of goods and services. The major lesson of economics is that whereas resources (money, time, human energy, materials) are limited, wants are infinite; thus choices must be made. Very high public costs are associated with long-term care, whether provided in the client's home, the community or an institution. Spending decisions have consequences for the wider society and raise issues of distributive justice. Evidence of poverty, neglect and preventable suffering is all around us – from drug-infested inner-city streets to unemployment to deteriorating housing stock, schools and transportation systems. Resources devoted to one set of problems limit those that can be devoted to other problems. However, it is not the financial outlay *per se* that explains the typically low priority assigned to long-term care, although a minimally adequate system would require substantial sums. What matters most is that the expenditures seem unlikely to yield commensurate benefits in terms of improvements in recipients' biographical potential: their quality of life remains low. Thus long-term care is minimally funded because decision-makers anticipate greater returns from alternative uses of resources and because advocates have been unable to make a convincing case.

Certain categories of people are implicitly considered (and treated) as low priority when spending decisions are made. Again and again, decisions are based on biographical potential, using similar, if unarticulated, criteria. The demented, the decrepit and others who have outlived their capacity for meaningful social interaction are all low priority. Public attitudes toward death and dying in old age suggest the persistence of age-old views that death is natural in old age, that social loss is minimal when an elder dies, and that scarce resources are more appropriately directed towards the young. Mass media appeals for contributions to the care of senile or disabled elders, analogous to those we often see for a sick child, are inconceivable. Many believe, with ethicist Paul Menzel, that extending the lives of severely demented and senescent patients should have very low priority even if they are not terminally ill.[43]

Foregoing curing in favour of caring, as some have recommended, is unlikely to lower costs; many frail elders will require both expensive acute-care services and expensive long-term custodial care before they die. The growing prevalence of dementia alone, as populations age, will ensure that long-term care is required for years, even decades, by people who are mentally compromised but physically robust. Ever greater commitments of funds will be needed. It is unlikely that taxpayers anywhere will agree that the gain is worth the cost.

Care provision has opportunity costs, both for care giving kin and professionals. Family care givers often provide care involuntarily, because there are no acceptable or affordable public alternatives. Presumably, many would be engaged in other productive pursuits if care giving requirements were reduced – pursuits which would be more to their liking or where their talents could be more efficiently utilized. There is no doubt that carers' productivity, health and morale are negatively affected by long-term care provision, as worry, competing responsibilities and exhaustion take their toll. The effects on the national welfare of compulsory care giving by family members have not yet been the focus of scholarly interest or governmental concern. Indeed, the aim of many governments is to encourage *more* family care giving, not less, as one way to control public costs. As we have seen, professional care givers too are prone to stress and burn-out, with all their associated personal and social costs, when they try to do the impossible.

Taxpayers are entitled to ask what better uses there might be for their hard-earned tax payments than expending them on futile or unwanted care for permanently incompetent old people. We need to distinguish between public willingness to provide expensive programmes that enable competent old people to enjoy a decent standard of living in their final years from willingness to finance expensive programmes that merely extend biological life when biographical capacity has been lost. The lessons of economics now, as throughout history, show that limited resources are only grudgingly conveyed to incompetent elders; they are redefined as less than human and their deaths are subtly, if not overtly, hastened. Thus, economic decision-making conveys important latent messages about the appropriateness of aid in dying for those who become irretrievably incompetent.

Risks of Barring Aid in Dying for the Incompetent

As Alzheimer's disease slowly destroyed his wife's mind, 79 year-old Hans Florian cared for her at home, with the help of his son. Together, they 'bathed Johanna, prised open her mouth at feeding time, woke to her screams, picked her up when she stumbled and changed her clothes five or six times a day as she wet and soiled them'. For nearly two years, unless she was heavily sedated, Johanna screamed almost constantly, using only two words, the German words for 'fire' and 'pain'. Finally, Hans moved her to a nursing home. There the screaming grew worse, terrifying other patients, and he was asked to remove her.[44]

Johanna's dilemma illustrates the fact that, in circumstances under which most people would prefer death, they are often least capable of directing their fate. Such patients can neither help themselves nor ask someone else to assist them but must rely on the compassion of others to release them from their suffering. In this case, seeing no recourse, Hans shot his wife to death. A grand jury refused to indict him.[45]

The costs of excluding incompetent patients like Johanna Florian from eligibility for euthanasia are considerable. First, the assaults to human dignity and the denial of a 'good' death are obvious. Unnecessary suffering, victimization of the most helpless and waste of scarce resources on futile care also result from law-makers' unwillingness to act. Moreover, we know that fears of dementing illnesses and institutionalization, not just physical ailments, can lead to suicide among older adults. The mere possibility of being institutionalized is enough to cause some people to take their lives prematurely because, once they are bedridden and helpless, they will be unable to act.[46] It is also extremely difficult to commit suicide or help someone end his or her life in an institutional setting, where the constant presence of staff can forestall such an attempt, and medical workers can prevent a death if it is attempted.

Dementia, of course, makes self-deliverance difficult or impossible. Studies of suicide attempts among the aged have found that dementia interferes with a patient's coordination, planning, determination to act and awareness of reality.[47] Similarly, patients who are extremely forgetful or confused are unable to persuade others to help them. To die on their own terms, patients must act *before* they become too incapacitated. Hence individuals may be driven to end their lives prematurely, while they still can, lest their health declines to the point where it becomes impossible to implement their decision.

Uncertainty plays a large role in premature death. In the words of a prominent ethicist, no one can 'count on being lucky enough to have adequate warning of deterioration and enough time in which to deliberate while still free of impairment'.[48] As Percy Bridgman, a Nobel Prize winner in physics, wrote in his suicide note at age 80, after his doctor refused to help him die: 'Probably this is the last day I will be able to do it myself.'[49] It follows that if people were confident that help would be available when and if it was needed, they would undoubtedly choose to live longer; moreover, the quality of their remaining time might well be improved as their fears of helplessness subside.

Millions of people who are already incompetent, like the two women described in this chapter, are left to suffer because the law has failed to act. Moreover, since many people are reluctant to plan for their own demise, we may anticipate that many will become incompetent without having left any instructions about their final wishes; they too will be left to endure their fate until a crisis intervenes and treatment may be lawfully withheld. Those who are willing to plan, ironically, are thwarted because nowhere do current or proposed guidelines respect advance directives requesting euthanasia.

Why are passive approaches, wherein the individual is 'allowed' to die when treatment is withheld or withdrawn, insufficient? As illustrated by the case of the journalist's mother, passive approaches may entail allowing the incapacitated to endure their suffering for months or years, until a life-threatening physical crisis occurs and treatment can legally cease. While a suitable crisis is awaited, palliative care, intended to keep patients comfortable and pain-free, presumably alleviates suffering. But palliation is extremely limited when it comes to patients such as those described here.

The palliative approach does not always preclude aggressive medical interventions either. Invasive procedures (including amputations), radiation therapy, and chemotherapy may be used to relieve symptoms or prevent their development. Whether cognitively impaired or too physically frail to protest effectively, the patient may be subjected to anxiety, discomfort, indignity and pain.[50]

Nor does death always occur quickly when treatment is withheld or withdrawn. For example, it may take a week or more for a patient to die after a feeding tube is removed. Although the decision to allow death has been made in such cases, the passive way in which that choice is implemented is repugnant to many. Additionally, families and society suffer as scarce resources are consumed to no good end.

With euthanasia forbidden, the relatives and friends of incapacitated patients may find themselves in a difficult situation. They may suffer severe emotional trauma if they provide the help that doctors refuse, out of fear of the law: however, there may be equally severe guilt feelings if they have to live with the knowledge that their loved one would not have wanted biological life on the only terms available. And, of course, there is still the risk of prosecution associated with illegal acts, however merciful the intent. Family care givers may also be severely harmed by the day-to-day distress of trying to cope with unrelievable suffering, providing care that merely prolongs dying, and making numerous personal sacrifices to do so.

There is also a risk of harm to non-family care givers, such as the day-to-day distress of health-care workers who must cope with difficult, incurable patients or risk their career to end another's suffering. Long death watches create considerable stress for professional care givers, including those with special training in dealing with the dying, such as hospice workers. As a patient lingers, staff stress inevitably heightens, creating discomfort over the patient's inability to let go and subsequent grief over a difficult death. Other stressors include feelings of helplessness and anger over inadequate symptom control.[51] Are these sorts of trauma necessary or humane? Care givers want to do their best for a patient. They need to know that if they assist a patient's death out of compassionate motives, they will not suffer for it.

Conclusion

Human values, attitudes, and behaviour do not develop in a vacuum, but are largely shaped by social institutions, such as the family, age cohorts and the school system. Because one lives in a particular society at a particular time, one behaves according to that society's rules and is rewarded for compliance and punished for deviance. Most people take their social world for granted, rarely questioning its assumptions and customs. But this is not a totally rigid system: innovators are constantly challenging the status quo as new problems demand innovative solutions. The modern death control movement is already having a substantial impact on both thinking and behaviour.[52] A social science perspective assures us that change is possible. Moreover, when the opinion of more than half the population is taking a particular direction, it is far more likely that the rest of the population will follow than that a minority will sway the majority. If authority figures and authoritative institutions take the lead, social change will be facilitated.

Hence the current situation – with aid in dying so narrowly defined that help is denied to the worst-off patients – is surely temporary. A few writers are already calling for euthanasia to be permitted for the permanently incompetent if they have previously signed an advance directive to that effect.[53] Euthanasia in such circumstances is already being granted in the Netherlands.[54] Life termination without the explicit request of the patient also occurs there. Patients in these cases are 'near death and clearly suffering grievously', according to the Remmelink Study, and their cases are adding a new dimension to the Dutch euthanasia debate.[55]

If meaningful possibilities for biographical life have ceased to exist, there is no point in preserving biological life. Nothing is lost by euthanasia in such cases, but much is gained by providing a dignified end for those unable to help themselves. Gentle means of aiding death are at hand, but that option is unavailable to many because the law has failed to act. Risks cannot be entirely eliminated in exercising the right to die, but the present system is full of abuses, and the advantages of euthanasia are too appealing to simply go away. The risks can be minimized: good legislation can anticipate problems, guard against abuses and punish those who violate the rules. A social science perspective suggests that families, care-giving professionals, judges and juries, and ordinary citizens, can distinguish between biographical and biological life, between compassionate aid in dying and wilful murder. It remains for the law to catch up.

Endnote

The term 'euthanasia' as used in the text always refers to a deliberate act, such as a lethal injection, intended to end a patient's life quickly and painlessly. In line with current usage in the Netherlands, euthanasia does *not* encompass the cessation of medically useless treatment, the withholding or withdrawal of treatment at the explicit request of the patient, nor the use of medication in such high doses to alleviate suffering that it inadvertently shortens the patient's life.[56]

Notes

1   Otten, A.L. (1986), 'Can't We Put My Mother To Sleep?' in Humphrey, D. (ed.), *Compassionate Crimes, Broken Taboos*, Los Angeles: Hemlock Society.
2   For further discussion, see Chapter 5.
3   Gomez, C.F. (1991), *Regulating Death: Euthanasia and the Case of the Netherlands*, New York: Free Press, p. 62.
4   Docker, C.G. (1993), 'National and international outreach', *VESS Newsletter*, September.
5   Quoted in Gomez, *op. cit.*, note 3 above, at p. 118.
6   Arkes, H. *et al.* (1991), 'Always to care, never to kill', *Wall Street Journal*, 27 November.
7   Logue, B. (1993), *Last Rights: Death Control and the Elderly in America*, New York: Lexington Books/Macmillan, p. 1.
8   Rachels, J. (1986), *The End of Life: Euthanasia and Morality*, Oxford: Oxford University Press, pp. 5, 26–7, 32–3.
9   Levine, S. (1987), 'The changing terrains in medical sociology: emergent concern with quality of life', *Journal of Health and Social Behavior*, **28**, (1).
10 Logue, *op. cit.*, note 7 above, at p. 82.
11 Ibid., pp. 20–39.
12 Counts, D.A. and Counts, D.R. (1985), 'Introduction: linking concepts, aging and gender, aging and death' in D.A. Counts and D.R. Counts (eds), *Aging and Its Transformations*, Lanham, MD: University Press of America; Nason, J.D. (1981), 'Respected elder or old person: aging in a Micronesian community', in P.T. Amos and S. Harrell (eds), *Other Ways of Growing Old: Anthropological Perspectives*, Stanford CA: Stanford University Press.
13 Lepowsky, M. (1985), 'Gender, aging and dying in an egalitarian society' in Counts and Counts, *op. cit*, note 12 above.
14 Colson, E. and Scudder, T. (1981), 'Old age in Gwembe District, Zambia' in Amoss and Harrell, *op. cit.*, note 12 above.
15 Glascock, A.P. (1990), 'By any other name, it is still killing: a comparison of the treatment of the elderly in America and other societies' in J. Sokolovsky (ed.), *The Cultural Context of Aging: Worldwide Perspectives*, New York: Bergin & Garvey.

16 Simmons, L. (1946), 'Attitudes toward aging and the aged: primitive societies', *Journal of Gerontology*, **1**, (1).

17 McKellin, W.H. (1985), 'Passing away and loss of life: aging and death among the Managalase of Papua New Guinea' in Counts and Counts, *op. cit.*, note 12 above.

18 Logue, *op. cit.*, note 7 above, at pp. 26–7.

19 Gubrium, J. (1975), *Living and Dying at Murray Manor*, New York: St Martin's Press, *passim*.

20 Vesperi, M. (1990), 'The reluctant consumer: nursing home residents in the post-Bergman era' in Sokolovsky, *op. cit.*, note 15 above.

21 Achenbaum, W.A. (1978), *Old Age in the New Land: The American Experience Since 1790*, Baltimore: Johns Hopkins University Press, p. 3.

22 Haber, C. (1983), *Beyond Sixty-Five: The Dilemma of Old Age in America's Past*, Cambridge: Cambridge University Press; Johnson, C.L. (1987), 'The institutional segregation of the aged' in P. Silverman (ed.), *The Elderly as Modern Pioneers*, Bloomington: Indiana University Press; Quadagno, J.S. (1982), *Aging in Early Industrial Society: Work, Family, and Social Policy in Nineteenth-Century England*, New York: Academic Press; Stearns, P.N. (1976), *Old Age in European Society: The Case of France*, New York: Holmes and Meier; Stearns, P.N. (ed.), (1982), *Old Age in Preindustrial Society*, New York: Holmes and Meier; Van Tassel, D. and Stearns, P.N. (eds) (1986), *Old Age in a Bureaucratic Society: The Elderly, the Experts, and the State in American History*, Westport CT: Greenwood Press.

23 Rosenberg, C.E. (1987), *The Care of Strangers: The Rise of America's Hospital System*, New York: Basic Books, p. 306.

24 Beckwith, B.P. (1979), 'On the right to suicide by the dying', *Dissent*, **26**.

25 Kearl, M.C. (1989), *Endings: A Sociology of Death and Dying*, New York: Oxford University Press, pp. 121–3, 126.

26 Zweibel, N.R. and Cassel, C.K. (1989), 'Treatment choices at the end of life: a comparison of decisions by older patients and their physician-selected proxies', *Gerontologist*, **29**, (5).

27 Tobin, S. (1987), 'A structural approach to families' in T.H. Brubaker (ed.), *Aging, Health and Family: Long-Term Care*, Newbury Park, CA: Sage.

28 Kotlikoff, L.J. and Morris, J.N. (1989), 'How much care do the aging receive from their children?' in D.A. Wise (ed.), *The Economics of Aging*, Chicago: University of Chicago Press.

29 Doty, P. (1986), 'Family care of the elderly: the role of public policy', *Milbank Quarterly*, **64**, (1).

30 Pillemer, K. and Finkelhor, D.A. (1988), 'The prevalence of elder abuse: a random sample survey', *Gerontologist*, **28**, (1).

31 Cicirelli, V.G. (1986), 'The helping relationship and family neglect in later life' in K.A. Pillemer and R.S. Wolf (eds), *Elder Abuse: Conflict in the Family*, Dover, MA: Auburn House; Wolf, R.S. (1986), 'Major findings from three model projects of elderly abuse' in ibid.

32 Conrad, P. (1988), 'Learning to doctor: reflections on recent accounts of the medical school years', *Journal of Health and Social Behavior*, **29**, (4); Light, D.W. (1988), 'Toward a new sociology of medical education', *Journal of Health and Social Behavior*, **28**, (4); Munley, A. (1983), *The Hospice Alternative: A New Context for Death and Dying*, New York: Basic Books, p. 16.

33 Crane, D. (1975), *The Sanctity of Social Life: Physicians' Treatment of Critically Ill Patients*, New York: Russell Sage Foundation, pp. 8, 11, 206.

34 Leiderman, D.B. and Grisso, J. (1985), 'The gomer phenomenon', *Journal of Health and Social Behavior*, **26**, (2).

35 Shem, S. (1978), *The House of God*, New York: Dell, esp. p. 424.

36   Preston, R.P. (1979), *The Dilemmas of Care: Social and Nursing Adaptions to the Deformed, the Disabled, and the Aged*, New York: Elsevier-North Holland, pp. 139, 162.

37   Everitt, D.E., *et al.* (1991), 'Resident behavior and staff distress in the nursing home', *Journal of the American Geriatrics Society*, **39**, (4).

38   Ray, E.B., Nichols, M.R. and Perritt, L.J. (1987), 'A model of job stress and burnout', in L.F. Paradis (ed.), *Stress and Burnout Among Providers Caring for the Terminally Ill and Their Families*, New York: Haworth Press.

39   Humphrey, J.H. (1988), *Stress in the Nursing Profession*, Springfield IL: Charles C. Thomas, p. 28; Sommers, T. *et al.* (1987), *Women Take Care: The Consequences of Caregiving in Today's Society*, Gainesville FL: Triad Publishing Company, pp. 54–5.

40   Ray, *et al.*, *op. cit.*, note 38 above.

41   Niemira, D. (1993), 'Life on the slippery slope: a bedside view of treating incompetent elderly patients', *Hastings Center Report*, **23**, (3).

42   Anon (1990), 'Sad farewells for young women starting on road to death', *New York Times*, 16 December.

43   Menzel, P. (1990), *Strong Medicine: The Ethical Rationing of Health Care*, New York: Oxford University Press, p. 200.

44   Anon (1986), 'Jury refuses to indict man in mercy killing of wife' in D. Humphry, *op. cit.*, note 1 above.

45   Ibid.

46   Loebel, J.P. *et al.* (1991), 'Anticipation of nursing home placement may be a precipitant of suicide among the elderly', *Journal of the American Geriatrics Society*, **39**, (4); Beckwith, *op cit.*, note 24 above.

47   Osgood, N.J. and McIntosh, J.L. (1990), 'The vulnerable suicidal elderly' in Z. Harel *et al.* (eds), *The Vulnerable Aged: People, Services and Policies*, New York: Springer.

48   Prado, C.G. (1990), *The Last Choice: Preemptive Suicide in Advanced Age*, Westport, CT: Greenwood Press.

49   Osgood, N.J. (1985), *Suicide in the Elderly: A Practitioner's Guide to Diagnosis and Mental Health Intervention*, Rockville, MD: Aspen Systems Corporation, at p. xxxix.

50   Besdine, R. (1985), 'Decisions to withhold treatment from nursing home residents', in M.B. Knapp *et al.* (eds), *Legal and Ethical Aspects of Health Care for the Elderly*, Ann Arbor, MI: Health Administration Press; Zimmerman, J.M. (1986), *Hospice: Complete Care for the Terminally Ill*, Baltimore: Urban and Schwarzenberg, pp. 54–5, 282.

51   Ray, *et al.*, *op. cit.*, note 38 above; Munley, *op. cit.*, note 32 above, at p. 199.

52   Logue, B.J., *op. cit.*, note 7 above.

53   Battin, M.P. (1992), 'Euthanasia in Alzheimer's disease?' in R.H. Binstock, *et al.* (ed.), *Dementia and Aging: Ethics, Values, and Policy Choices*, Baltimore: Johns Hopkins University Press; Helme, T. (1992), 'Proposals for formalising euthanasia', *VESS Newsletter*, September.

54   Ibid.

55   van Delden, J.M., *et al.* (1993), 'The Remmelink Study: two years later', *Hastings Center Report*, **23**, (6).

56   See Admiraal, P., Chapter 7 in this volume.

7 Voluntary Euthanasia: The Dutch Way

PIETER ADMIRAAL

The title of this chapter suggests that there are different ways to practise voluntary euthanasia, and that the Dutch way is one of these. This chapter will seek to establish that the situation in the Netherlands represents the best option.

In an opinion poll carried out in the Netherlands in January 1993 one of the questions asked was: 'Do you think that someone always has the right to have their life terminated when they are in an unacceptable position without any prospects?' (*Vindt u dat iemand die in een voor hem of haar onaanvaardbare, uitzichtloze noodsituatie verkeert, altijd het recht heeft om dan beeindiging van zijn of haar eigen leven te vragen?*) The outcome was as might have been expected: 78 per cent said 'yes', 10 per cent said 'no' and 12 per cent had no opinion. When divided into separate groups by religion, the percentage of those who agreed was 93 per cent for those who professed no religious faith, 74 per cent for Roman Catholics, 60 per cent for members of the Reformed Church, and 48 per cent of the group who professed another religion. In 1991 van der Maas published the results of an investigation, performed at the request of the Ministry of Justice concerning euthanasia and other medical decisions concerning the end of life.[1] Dependent on the region in the Netherlands, 40–60 per cent of doctors admitted to having carried out euthanasia.

The official definition of euthanasia appears in the Report of the Dutch Government Commission on Euthanasia, published in 1985.[2] Euthanasia is

> A deliberate termination of an individual's life at that individual's request, by another. Or, in medical practice, the active and deliberate termination of a patient's life, on that patient's request, by a doctor.

Article 293 of the Dutch Criminal Code says:

> Anyone who takes the life of another at that person's express and serious request, will be punished with a prison sentence of a maximum of twelve years or a category five fine.

So, active euthanasia, despite the fact that it is practised on a relatively wide scale in the Netherlands, remains a criminal offence. How are we to reconcile this apparent contradiction?

In 1972 the Royal Dutch Medical Association issued a provisional statement on euthanasia. In their view:

> ... legally euthanasia should remain a crime, but if a physician after having considered all the aspects of the case, shortens the life of a patient who is incurably ill and in the process of dying, the court will have to judge whether there was a conflict of duties which could justify the act of the physician.[3]

Over recent years jurisprudence in the Netherlands has developed to the extent that the legal view now is that, although euthanasia is not a part of regular or routine medical care, a physician will be judged to be guilty but not culpable if he performs euthanasia or assists suicide in the correct way. This legal decision is based on the concept of the state of emergency within which the physician acts. This state is thought to be applicable because the physician is confronted with conflicting obligations – towards his patient as a care giver and a health professional, and towards the law as a civilian. His professional obligations force him to act against the formal statements of the law, but in accordance with principles developed in medical ethics and in congruence with the explicit wish of his patient.

The current position is that most doctors practising euthanasia are not prosecuted if they have met the substantive requirements published by the Royal Dutch Medical Association in 1984, which have also been confirmed by court decisions. These requirements are as follows:

1   the patient makes a voluntary request;
2   the request must be well considered;
3   the wish for death is durable;
4   the patient is in unacceptable suffering;
5   the physician has consulted with a colleague who agrees the proposed course of action.

In 1990 the Royal Dutch Medical Association and the Ministry of Justice agreed upon a notification procedure which contains the following elements:

1   the physician performing euthanasia or assisted suicide does not issue a declaration of a natural death, but informs the local medical examiner of the circumstances by filling in an extensive questionnaire;
2   the medical examiner reports to the district attorney; and
3   the district attorney then decides whether or not a prosecution should be instituted.

This notification procedure has been laid down in regulations under the Burial Act and acquired formal legal status, in 1994.[4]

It should be noted that, in common with other jurisdictions, the following practices in respect of terminally ill patients are not regarded as euthanasia, but rather as good and acceptable medical practice: stopping senseless or futile treatment; stopping or not commencing treatment on request of the patient him/herself; using analgesic medication in high doses to alleviate suffering even though it may also shorten life (the principle of double effect). The term 'passive euthanasia' is not one which is used in the Netherlands, as will be explained below.

In discussing voluntary euthanasia it must be borne in mind that this is not possible without also considering the right of autonomy or self-determination. In the Netherlands, the patient is informed from the beginning of the diagnosis and prognosis of his/her condition and about therapeutic possibilities, and all other relevant information is provided. As a result of this, the patient is frequently put in the position of having to decide, together with his or her doctor, what course of action is appropriate and should be taken.

Other than the stark question about whether to opt for life or death, the central question is whether life under the known circumstances will be acceptable to the patient. Social development in the Netherlands over the last decades has led to an increase in the value placed on shared decision-making and openness, leading to a situation where patients now have a legal right of access to their health records. The right of self-determination has also been respected. In other words, in the Netherlands every patient has the right to the most advanced treatment, the right to refuse even that treatment and the indisputable right to judge his or her own suffering and to request euthanasia. In these ways, it may be thought that the Netherlands is considerably ahead of other countries where the medical profession remains paternalistic in respect of its patients.

One of the legal requirements of lawfully carrying out euthanasia is that the person must be in a situation where the suffering is unbearable, thus posing the question, 'What is suffering, and what makes it unbearable?' The *Oxford English Dictionary* defines the word 'suffer' as 'To have (something painful, distressing or injurious) inflicted or imposed upon one' and 'suffering' as 'The bearing or under-going of pain, distress or tribulation'. Suffering is specific for each human being and to each species – an animal does not, for example, suffer pain in the sense used here. An animal *feels* pain, a human being *suffers* it. Only someone who is conscious and capable of delib-erative retrospective and prospective contemplation can suffer. The person who suffers compares, weighs and evaluates life in the past and in the future. Suffering, therefore, also includes grief, depres-sion, concern and anxiety. But, fortunately, it may also include the essentially human characteristics of hope, acquiescence and accept-ance. Thus, the suffering of a human being is strictly individual and is determined by the psychological tensions and inner resources of the individual in enduring the condition.

However, the suffering of others is largely outside our comprehen-sion and is consequently difficult for us to weigh and judge. We can try to understand the suffering of another, based upon our observa-tions and leaving aside our own emotions, but this has proved to be very difficult. It takes long years of experience with palliative care to be as fair as possible in our judgement. In any event, we must seri-ously ask ourselves from where comes the authority to judge the suffering of another to be bearable when the individual him or her-self tells us that it is not. But what factors may cause suffering to be unbearable?

Objective considerations lead us to distinguish physical and psycho-logical causes which are nonetheless closely related to each other.[5] There are a number of physical causes, release from which depends on the diagnostic and therapeutic skills of the doctors and nurses. The most important of these would generally be:

1 *Loss of strength*. Cachectic patients, in particular, experience a seri-ous loss of strength. As a result, the patient in the terminal phase is no longer capable of any physical exertion, making him or her totally dependent on nursing care, both day and night. Almost always, this is accompanied by extreme fatigue which cannot be alleviated in any way and is experienced as exhausting.
2 *Shortness of breath*. An increasing shortness of breath often occurs in the terminal phase as a result of specific lung aberrations, cardial decompensation or diminished oxygenation of the blood, and will be a serious problem.
3 *Nausea and vomiting*. These can be side-effects of opioid analge-sics, cytotoxic drugs or a total blockage of the stomach or intes-tines. Vomiting is, in most cases, very exhausting for the patient.
4 *Incontinence*. Being incontinent with respect to either urine or faeces is experienced by the human being as degrading.

5   *Pain*. Until recently, pain was the most important cause of physical and psychological suffering.

The hospice movement has placed great emphasis on pain and its treatment. A study at St Christopher's Hospice in 1978 showed that pain was reported as a problem in 76 per cent of patients on admission.[6] In 1987 Higginson found that pain was the most common main symptom, occurring in 41 per cent of the patients, at referral to a district terminal care support team.[7] Nowadays, pain can be adequately controlled without the normal psychological functions of the patient being adversely affected in almost 95 per cent of cases. Examples of pain control include the use of opioid analgesics, psychopharmaca, continuous epidural or spinal application of opioids, and the fixed blocking of the sympathetic nervous system.

Emotional distress as a result of psychological causes is complex, but was very well described by Cassidy in 1986.[8] Speaking about fear, she says:

It is important to find out what a patient is afraid of. Simple reassurance that pain can be controlled, that he is not going to choke to death or go mad, can reduce distress to manageable proportions. The truth is virtually always easier to face than the terrors of the unknown.[9]

About loss, she comments:

One of the major losses in an incurable illness that often goes unacknowledged is the loss of a person's role [in life]. Loss of that role, can be a source of enormous pain and leave the person concerned with a sense of futility and worthlessness.[10]

She reminds us also that terminally ill patients who are going to die are uncomfortable companions and are easily left alone by their friends or even their medical care givers.

Practically every patient is plagued by anxiety during the course of the illness. Anxieties about pain and suffering are frequently based on information from lay persons, which is seldom encouraging. But many doctors also could improve the information they give to patients. When, for example, will we stop promulgating the view that pain associated with cancer is necessarily worse than other pain? Much more difficult to combat or refute is the anxiety about spiritual and physical decay and deformation. After all, we cannot protect the patient against these. The same thing holds for the anxiety about needing total nursing care and becoming totally dependent on others.

Loneliness and isolation are also threats especially during long wakeful nights, alone with one's fears and hopeless expectations.

Anxiety about dying itself can have various causes. In dying, there comes, of course, the inevitable parting from this life, the world in which one has lived and worked, and from all beloved relatives and friends. But there can also be anxiety about the moment of dying – the anxiety that 'something' will happen which is unpleasant and threatening, without the person having any real idea of what that might be. Thinking about what comes after death is culturally and religiously determined and can vary from a vague anxiety about the unknown to a literal fear of punishment, perhaps even for eternity. Fortunately, many persons also die in the firm conviction of another, blessed life, united with those who went before. Today, there are many patients who, in consequence of the present Western cultural pattern, no longer believe in a hereafter and do not have any anxiety about this. In the Netherlands, it is estimated that half of the population is areligious.

Grief is an important part of emotional distress. However much we realize that death is unbreakably linked to life, the certainty of the approaching end of our lives makes us sorrowful. Grief can be about the loss of family and friends, but it may also be about the loss of earthly things, the possession of which has now become useless. Grief will become worse the less that it can be expressed. Especially in the beginning, it is not uncommon that the patient, the family and friends conceal their grief from each other and are not open to the grief of the other. Grief is bottled up and becomes genuine sorrow. It would be preferable to listen to each other and to give vent to one's feelings. Mutual understanding makes sorrow less – grief can be unbearable when the patient is emotionally or spiritually isolated. On the other hand, grief can become bitter when the patient poses the question as to why it has happened to him or her – a person who does not deserve this suffering – or why this has happened at this stage in his or her life. Such grief can easily turn to rancour, revolt and aggression. Grief may also be about the emotional pain of others or about what will happen to those left behind. Such grief depresses the patient.

Every person, and especially every patient with a terminal disease, has his or her own feelings about human dignity. Again, these feelings are very individual and again may be influenced by society, culture and even religion. In a civilized world, we all try our best to protect and respect the human dignity of others, and we see this respect as being a natural human right. We see it also as a right to judge for ourselves our own human dignity and expect others to respect that. As competent persons, we do not expect others to decide about our own dignity. The same is true of our feelings about our own lives and our own feelings of suffering. We can inform others about our feelings, but we cannot oblige others to share our ideas.

These above-mentioned physical and psychological problems can be overcome by the patient, or they may become unbearable and trigger a request for euthanasia. Undoubtedly, the best way of dealing with these situations is by the provision of supportive and adequate palliative care by a team of dedicated nursing, medical and spiritual care givers.

In 1961, after specializing in anaesthetics, I began the study of pain and its treatment. For this reason, I had regular contact with cancer patients and with their pain. For this reason also, I visited the newly opened St Christopher Hospice in the late 1960s to speak about the treatment of pain and the care of the terminally ill. In 1973, whilst working in a hospital in Delft, we officially started a Terminal Care Team. So much has been written, and so much experience gained, about palliative care that it is not necessary to describe here the principles underlying terminal care. However, a number of publications on this subject merit consideration. Most notably, these are *The Guide to Symptom Relief in Advanced Cancer*, by Regnard and Davies,[11] *The Management of Terminal Malignant Disease*, edited by Dame Cicely Saunders[12] and the excellent article on nursing care by Tiffany,[13] which contains the important statement: 'The change in emphasis is summarized by saying that now we are caring for Mr Smith who happens to have leukaemia rather than a leukaemia case who happens to be Mr Smith.';[14]

Everyone will surely agree with the following statement:

It is important that doctors, and everyone else who is involved with the care of the terminally ill, appreciate the need to communicate with their dying patients. Doctors need to be able to discuss the fears of the dying patient with them. They need to be able to discuss terminal care openly so that patients can see that they will not be abandoned and left helpless in the face of terminal disease. We believe that high standards of palliative care and support for the patient and their family should be the focus of care for the dying patient. It is our view that doctors need not and should not take extraordinary measures to preserve life in all circumstances.[15]

However, it is sad to realize that, after so many years of experience and so many publications, especially in the UK, this statement was made only recently by the British Medical Association in a Briefing Paper. Perhaps what Walsh and West wrote in 1988 is still true:

Many doctors (including oncologists) have received no training in caring for dying patients. Some feel helpless and inadequate, with predictable effects on the care of the patient. Dying patients are still commonly ignored on ward rounds or placed in a side room.[16]

Nevertheless, it is clear that palliative care offers the best way of alleviating the suffering of the terminally ill patient. But the question remains, how is this care best organized – in hospices, in general hospitals, in nursing homes, at home or anywhere else? To find an answer at the hospital with which I was involved, members of the Terminal Care Team visited St Christopher Hospice in 1976. Our conclusion was that we could integrate the care into our general hospital. At about the same time, the project 'Care for the terminal patient' was started in a nursing home in Rotterdam. After seven years it was concluded that this type of care in a separate unit had more disadvantages than advantages within the context of the Dutch system of health care.[17] At present it is interesting to note that, in the Netherlands, 40 per cent of cancer patients die in a general hospital, 10 per cent in a nursing home and 50 per cent die at home. The National Organization for Voluntary Terminal Care supports about 90 local groups.

Thus, the statement of the British Medical Association in a Working Party Report in 1988 that 'The hospice movement in the Netherlands is quite unlike that which exists in Britain ...' is correct, but the rest of the sentence '... and the development of palliative care is not as advanced ...' is unfair.[18] In fact, one thing is abundantly clear – one cannot practise euthanasia without terminal care. Euthanasia can only be the last dignified act of terminal care. However, it is equally true that one cannot practise terminal care without the *possibility* of euthanasia. In the debate surrounding euthanasia an important question must be asked: 'Can we stop all of the suffering of a terminally ill patient?' The answer is 'No, we cannot'. The next question must be: 'Can we make unbearable suffering bearable?', again, the answer must be, 'No'.

Speaking of spiritual pain, Dame Cicely Saunders said, 'Sometimes unrealistic fears can be explained and eased, but a good deal of suffering has to be lived through. The very pain itself may lead to resolution or a new vision, as came to Job' and, further, that 'Our vision is of God's sharing with us all in the deeper way still, with all the solidarity of His sacrificial and forgiving love and the strength of His powerlessness'.[19] Of course, these words reflect her Christian view of life, death and suffering. We must certainly respect that view, but she also must be aware that there are a lot of terminally ill patients with different views which must also be respected. In the Netherlands, for example, about 8 per cent of terminally ill cancer patients judge their suffering to be unbearable and ask for euthanasia. This means that, of the total number of euthanasia cases, 80 per cent are suffering from cancer.

The question must now be asked, what are the principal reasons for a euthanasia request? In answering this, reliance will be placed on the investigations of van der Maas,[20] the thesis of van der Wal,[21] and my own observations.[22] The most important factors seem to be: loss of human dignity (57–59 per cent), loss of strength and fatigue (85 per cent) and complete dependence (33–74 per cent). It is noteworthy that pain was the sole reason for the request in only 5 per cent of all cases.

Many patients, in fact, see their suffering as senseless – they see no reason to continue to live in their own specific circumstances. Moreover, many patients who have arrived at the point of total acceptance and acquiescence in their fate may no longer attach any value to their life, their relatives and friends and their world. In other words, they reach a state of total detachment – something that is especially difficult for relatives and caregivers to understand or to accept. But these patients long for an early, gentle death. They regard any hesitation from others in fulfilling their wishes as unjustified and a denial of their last wish. Indeed, arguably, this longing to die is also a part of normal human life. Interestingly, in the work referred to, there seemed to be no relation between age, sex, religion or social status.

Some doctors may well say that the above-mentioned reasons for requesting euthanasia must be the result of a depression, and will prescribe anti-depressant drugs. However, in my opinion, these doctors are unobservant and seem to be more preoccupied with their own concerns than with serving the needs of patients. To send a terminally ill patient to a psychiatrist is an insult.

As has been said, in the Netherlands the autonomy of patients is respected and their rights to self-determination is valued. We have learned to accept and not to deny the fact that we cannot make all suffering bearable, and most doctors are willing to carry out active euthanasia or to assist suicide under strict rules. The Dutch position has compassionate supporters and vehement opponents all over the world. Some of these are well informed and have witnessed what is going on, whilst others have gathered their information from hearsay or tendentious articles written by opponents of the Dutch system. Twycross, for example, does not seem to have realised that much of the evidence used in his 1990 article in the *Lancet* was based on what I believe to be inaccurate information.[23] This belief is based on the fact that an approach to the Prosecutor to try to force the author of the anecdotal evidence to prove its truth resulted in a failure so to do. Indeed, reference might usefully have been made to the 'Letters to the Editor' in the next issue of the Hastings Center Report by several alarmed scientists.[24] Nonetheless, we must all respect Twycross's belief that 'it would be a disaster for the medical profession to be permitted to use pharmacological means to precipitate death deliberately and specifically'.[25]

In a much discussed article in the *New England Journal of Medicine* by Wanzer *et al.* it is concluded that, even with the best palliative care,

... occasionally all fails. The doctor, the nurse, the family, and the patient may have done everything possible to relieve the distress occasioned by a terminal illness, and yet the patient perceives the situation as intolerable and seeks assistance in bringing about death.[26]

Opponents of euthanasia raise three main problems in accepting it: the slippery slope argument; the potential for abuse; and the effect on the relationship between doctor and patient.

Borst-Eilers, Dutch Minister of Health, says:

The fear that legalization of euthanasia gradually leads to a policy of involuntary termination of patients' lives has also been expressed during the political debate. Doctors too are anxious to lift the veil of ignorance and to establish, by actual fact-finding, if there is any ground for the accusation that some Dutch doctors are indeed on the slippery slope from euthanasia to involuntary termination of life. Some people might argue that the small number of severely defective newborns whose lives have been actively terminated – when they did not die spontaneously from their disorders and they seemed to suffer very much – are already proof that things have gone too far. In view of the very careful procedure of decision making in these cases, involving the medical team, the nurses, the parents, and the pastor or psycho-social worker, I do not agree with that conclusion.[27]

The then Bishop of Durham, David Jenkins, said:

If we decide responsibly to re-define proper medical care to include providing an easier death, and if we work out agreed conditions for permitting this and safeguards surrounding it, we are neither inserting a wedge which will split up the curing, caring and comforting vocation of doctors, nor are we encouraging doctors or relatives generally to bring pressure to bear for the early removal of difficult patients. We are working together at the next stage of humanizing our mutual care for one another from conception to death.[28]

In the Netherlands, after many years, there is no evidence which would support the slippery slope argument. On the contrary, euthanasia has improved relationships between doctor and patient. It must be remembered that there is a traditional and unique relationship between doctors and their patients. As to the question of abuse, it should be remembered that every citizen has the constitutional obligation to report a crime to the Prosecutor. During the last two decades, at least 30 000 patients have died as a result of active euthanasia, yet not one single case has been so reported. And this is so despite the fact that the opponents of euthanasia are singularly alert and that excellent social control also exists in the Netherlands.

The slippery slope argument is, of course, familiar from the example of abortion when it was legalized in the Netherlands in 1984. However, currently the Netherlands has the lowest abortion rate in the world – a figure of 5.6 per 1,000 pregnancies – thanks to a sophisticated sex education programme and good relations between the family doctor and the patient. The rate in the UK, for example, is more than twice as high. Perhaps it might be argued, then, that the Dutch are peculiarly interested in suicide. Again, this is not borne out by the figures which show the Dutch rate of suicide – 120 per 100,000 inhabitants – as the lowest in Western Europe.

However, a study conducted by van der Maas *et al.*,[29] has shown that in 0.8 per cent of all deaths in the Netherlands, life was terminated without the explicit request of the patient, and this has disturbed many opponents of euthanasia. In the most recent publication on this issue, Pijnenborg gives the following results: in 59 per cent of these cases the doctor had information about the patient's wishes, albeit short of a specific request; in all other cases discussion with the patient was no longer possible; in 2 per cent of cases the doctor had made the decision without discussing it with anyone. This 2 per cent represents two doctors. Clearly, no one agrees with such behaviour.

But it is also clear that a doctor, who has treated a patient for many years and sees that the patient is suffering and will die within a short time but is unable to express his or her wishes, may consider it as a duty to shorten the patient's life. I would therefore support the conclusion

> … that open discussion, starting from the premise that medical decisions concerning the end of life have to be made in any country with high standards of medical care, will contribute to a better quality care for the dying. Such discussion may reduce the incidence of life-terminating acts without the explicit request of the patient and will improve decision-making in those cases that, inevitably, remain.[30]

To turn now to 'passive euthanasia'. This can be defined as 'the conscious decision by a doctor either to discontinue an existing treatment or not to initiate treatment, as a result of which the patient dies after a shorter or longer period'. It also implies that in most cases the life of the patient will be shorter. But does it also imply that there will be less suffering during that shorter period? Manifestly, it does not inevitably mean this. Let us face the facts honestly and objectively.

We stop treatment, or we do not begin it, in the conviction that treatment is senseless or futile and will prolong suffering. Thus, the patient will die as a direct consequence of the condition from which he or she suffers. Of course, we continue support and palliation until the end, but this has nothing to do with euthanasia. Under these circumstances, the word 'euthanasia' is completely inappropriate. Its use gives the false impression that passivity has something to do with euthanasia, but passive euthanasia is no more than abstention. It is a hypocritical euphemism and not in the interests of the patient in the terminal phase of an illness. Twycross supports this view, saying, 'As it does not involve deliberate death acceleration it should not be described as euthanasia. Moreover the care of the dying should not be thought of as simply a passive pursuit, that is, simply a matter of omissions.'[31] Indeed, in the Netherlands, the distinction between active and passive euthanasia has been dropped in official documents. In the eyes of the law acts of omission and commission directed at a hastening of death are the same. Therefore, when we speak of euthanasia we mean active euthanasia.

Of course, after abstention it is possible to make dying easier in various ways. But if this occurs with opioids or psychopharmaceuticals in such high doses that life may be shortened, then there is arguably no difference between this and active euthanasia. Passive euthanasia merely becomes a cover for active euthanasia which is not allowed. The distinction between directly intended and merely foreseen consequences of treatment has, of course, led to serious philosophical and ethical discussion. However, as Kuhse has said:

> Stripped of all other differences, what remains if we look at killing and letting die is a difference that has no moral significance. In active euthanasia, the doctor initiates a course of events that will lead to the patient's death. In letting die, the agent stands back and lets nature take her sometimes cruel course. Is letting die morally better than helping to die, or active euthanasia? I think not. Very often it is much worse.[32]

Further, Brody says:

> In the most difficult and compelling cases, the ethical rights, duties, and consequences seem fairly evenly balanced on both sides of the argument … . We cannot resolve these moral tensions by making one side of the tension disappear. Instead, we must learn to live with these tensions within a pluralistic society. This requires more reliance on negotiation, compromise and practical reasoning, and less on abstract ethical theory.[33]

In recent years, the Royal Dutch Medical Association has published preliminary reports about the care of the severely handicapped newborn, patients in persistent vegetative state and demented patients. There is an ongoing discussion with experts, including those who oppose euthanasia, and these reports engender a certain confidence.

Conclusions

In the situation within which I work, the decision to carry out euthanasia is the result of a multidisciplinary discussion by two doctors, a nurse and a spiritual care giver. We have a Protestant, a Roman Catholic and a Humanist pastor, and we are all equal in the decision-making process. After a request for euthanasia we will try to improve the care available, in order to avoid the need for euthanasia because none of us likes to become involved in the act. We will always hesitate – decision-making is never a process of hours, but always of days. The principles which guide this process are respect for the humanity of both life and death, respect for the self-determination and self-responsibility of the patient. Respect for the conscience of every care giver and respect for the law. In this hospital, euthanasia is seen as the last dignified act of terminal care.[34]

Until now, the emotions of everyone involved in the decision-making process have not been mentioned, but they are important. It is extremely difficult for all of us to reach the decision to terminate the life of another person. Yet, moments of carrying out euthanasia have been the most decent and the most emotional moments in my life as a doctor. These patients have become my personal friends during the long days and nights of their terminal weeks. After the act of euthanasia, I am always both sad and satisfied. Sad about the fact that I have lost a friend and satisfied that I was able to stop the unbearable suffering of that friend. Should I be asked, 'Do you think that it is right for a doctor to end the life of a patient, from a medical and an ethical point of view?', I would counter with another question, 'Do you think it is right for a doctor to allow a patient to die in unbearable suffering?'

In 1989 the *British Medical Journal* published a commentary on the British Medical Association Report on euthanasia. The first sentence was 'The United Kingdom and the Netherlands are separated by a narrow stretch of sea, but in terms of an understanding of euthanasia they seem to be lightyears apart'.[35] Hopefully, this chapter will have helped to bridge at least part of that gap.

Notes

1   van der Maas, P.J., *et al.* (1992), 'Euthanasia and other medical decisions concerning the end of life: an investigation performed upon request of the Commission of Inquiry into Medical Practice concerning Euthanasia', *Health Policy*, **22** (special issue).
2   *Staatscommissie Euthanasie. Rapport inzake euthanasie*, Staatsuitgeverij, den Haag, 1985.
3   De Wachter, M.A.M. (1989), 'Active Euthanasia in the Netherlands', *Journal of the American Medical Association*, **262**, p. 3316.

4   Royal Dutch Medical Association (1993), *Euthanasia in the Netherlands: The State of the Debate*, Utrecht.
5   Admiraal, P.V. (1988), 'Justifiable euthanasia', *Issues in Law and Medicine*, **3**, p. 361.
6   Haram, B.J. (1978), 'Facts and figures' in C.M. Saunders (ed.), *The Management of Terminal Malignant Disease*, (1978), London: Edward Arnold, pp. 12–18.
7   Higginson, I. *et al.*, 'Measuring symptoms in terminal cancer: are pain and dyspnoea controlled?', *Journal of the Royal Society of Medicine*, **82**, p. 264.
8   Cassidy, S. (1986), 'Emotional distress in terminal cancer', *Journal of the Royal Society of Medicine*, Discussion paper, **79**, p. 717.
9   Ibid.
10   Ibid., at p. 718.
11   Regnard, C.F.B. and Davies, A. (1986), *A Guide to Symptom Relief in Advanced Cancer*, Manchester: Haigh and Hockland Ltd.
12   Saunders, Dame Cicely (ed.) (1984), *The Management of Terminal Malignant Disease*, (2nd edn), London: Edward Arnold.
13   Tiffany, R. (1980), 'Emotional support for cancer patients in hospital', *Journal of the Royal Society of Medicine*, **73**, p. 214.
14   Ibid., at p. 214.
15   British Medical Association, Briefing Paper, November 1992.
16   Walsh, T.D. and West, T.S. (1988), 'Controlling symptoms in advanced cancer', *British Medical Journal*, **296**, p. 477.
17   Bruning, H. (1986), Omgaan met sterven, Part 1, 2 and 3, Leiden; Zorn.
18   *Euthanasia*, Report of the Working Party to review the British Medical Association's guidance on euthanasia, London: BMA, 1988, p. 49.
19   Saunders, C.S. (1988), 'Spiritual pain', *Journal of Palliative Care*, **4**, (29), at p. 31.
20   *Op. cit.*, note 1 above.
21   van der Wal, G. (1992), 'Euthanasie en hulp bij zelfdoding door huisartsen', Thesis, Rotterdam: WIJT.
22   Admiraal, P.V. (1991), 'Is there a place for euthanasia?', *Bioethics News*, **10**, pp. 10–22.
23   Twycross, R.G. (1990), 'Assisted death: a reply', *Lancet*, **336**, p. 796.
24   Aartsen, J.G.M. *et al.*, (1989), Letter, *Hastings Center Report*, 1989, 47.
25   Twycross, *op. cit.*, note 23 above, at p. 796.
26   Wanzer, S.H., *et al.* (1989), 'The physician's responsibility towards hopelessly ill patients', *New England Journal of Medicine*, **320**, at p. 847.
27   Borst-Eilers, E. (1992), 'Euthanasia in the Netherlands: brief historical review and present situation' in R. Misbin (ed.), *Euthanasia*, Frederich, Maryland: University Publications Group International.
28   Jenkins, D.A., 'Why Not Choose Death – In the End', *Care of the Critically Ill*, 1991, **7**, 6, at p. 6.
29   van der Maas, P.J. *et al.* (1991), 'Euthanasia and other medical decisions concerning the end of life', *Lancet*, **338**, p. 669.
30   Pijnenborg, L., *et al.* (1991), 'Life-terminating acts without explicit request of the patient', *Lancet*, **341**, p. 1196.
31   Twycross, R.G. (1980), 'Euthanasia – a physician's viewpoint', Lecture to an International Conference on Voluntary Euthanasia and Suicide, Oxford, 12–14 September.
32   Kuhse, H. (1987), 'The case for active voluntary euthanasia', *Law, Medicine and Healthcare*, **14**, 145, at p. 147.
33   Brody, H. (1992), 'Assisted death – a compassionate response to a medical failure', *New England Journal of Medicine*, **327**, p. 1384.
34   Admiraal, P.V. (1990), 'Euthanasia in a general hospital' in *Right to Self-Determi-*

nation, Proceedings of the 8th World Conference of Right to Die Societies, Maastricht, Amsterdam: VU University Press.

35   Rigter, H., *et al.* (1989), 'Euthanasia across the North Sea', *British Medical Journal*, **50**, p. 97.

8 The Way Forward?

CHRISTOPHER DOCKER

Executive Secretary, Voluntary Euthanasia Society of Scotland

'Ω θάνατε, Παιὰν, μόνοσ ἰατρὸσ τῶν ἀνηκέστων κακῶν (Death, the Great Healer, thou alone art the physician of unendurable sorrows). Aeschylus

Introduction

After examining so many well argued and diverse viewpoints, and from such illustrious scholars and experts, it might be prudent to ask if it is realistic to summarize and talk about *the* way forward, and whether a 'way forward' can be posited without engaging in over-optimistic oratory?

In attempting to answer the question, it is proposed to consider the problem from two angles. The first is a probable way forward such as might be extrapolated from the contemporary situation – a result largely of prevailing momentum or inertia. The best results that can perhaps be anticipated along this road are practical, but somewhat circumscribed, changes, both good and bad. The second viewpoint takes ideals and strives to relate them back to the present with a holistic view on a wide range of problems.

In Chapters 4 and 6, Sheila McLean and Barbara Logue have both, in different ways, ably demonstrated the validity of looking at a broader picture, whereas other chapters in this volume have examined specific applications. One might be tempted to criticize the former approach as being too far-reaching to evoke the consensus of support needed to effect widespread reform or, as McLean observed on another occasion, sufficient 'public involvement in community morality' to allow democratic change.[1]

If the criticism were to hold true, however, and the US experience might seem to suggest such a narrowly pragmatic approach,[2] it is argued here that it is not sufficient justification for allowing ideals to be subjugated to the more immediate but partial applications, such as advance directives, guidelines on PVS, or a bill allowing the limited prescription of lethal drugs.

It is only by retaining an internally consistent approach that we can hope to take small steps without going astray. Cheryl Smith's immediate involvement has been in the practicalities of devising a bill that could, primarily, stand a chance of being passed, but her experience in this field was in the somewhat broader context of co-drafting the Model Aid in Dying Act[3] – a comprehensive framework on many aspects of dying which, rather than a bill that would be passed in its entirety, was intended as an ideal to work from for particular, narrow pieces of reform. There seems a great difference between this piecemeal yet (one hopes) internally sound approach in Oregon, and the lamentably inconsistent piecemeal development of the law in the UK.

One of the opportunities this book may proffer is hopefully to place the small steps very firmly in the context of a bigger picture. As we consider an ideal situation, however, there is of course the problem that there may be disagreements about where we ideally want to go. The multiplicity of sincerely held but differing views in today's world can make identification of shared values a difficult task, but a task which nevertheless demands our attention. It can be argued that there are certain basic ethical principles common to all jurisdictions of Western society, such as autonomy, non-maleficence and beneficence, and justice, which govern medical decision-making; society uses the law as one of the means of translating these values into policies, and we may strive to reflect these ethical principles in legal principles.[4] An increasing danger seems to be of developing simplistic dichotomies that would bog us down, and, for this reason, this chapter will argue the viability of a middle course rather than the case for or against euthanasia. The opposing arguments have been well rehearsed elsewhere[5] without bringing us any nearer to a solution. Perhaps one clue should be taken from Brooks who says:

> ... it is the failure to respect the intellectual integrity of other moral approaches and to understand the levels on which these differ fundamentally from the utilitarian approach that generates much of the heat in ethical controversy within the profession, whilst failing to illuminate the issues clearly.[6]

Once public debate has aired an issue, reform generally only proceeds from centrist arguments that are accessible to a broad populace; that juncture may quite probably have been reached on a number of the issues here under discussion, and so the diatribes of 'pro-life' or 'right to die' campaigners become tangential and anachronistic, fuelling the debate but not the reform.

The courts will be hesitant to advocate principles that are still contentious. As Lord Browne-Wilkinson said in the *Bland* case:

> Where a case raises wholly new moral and social issues, in my judgement it is not for judges to seek to develop new, all embracing principles of law in a way which reflects the individual judges' moral stance when society as a whole is substantially divided on the relevant moral issues.[7]

Political and sociological perspectives may be more important than overreliance on the ability of the law to enable, effect or enforce change; a further problem that can arise when there is too hasty recourse to making laws is that a bill intended to protect patient options may effectively be little more than paper, or even result in infringing those options,[8] and, to use Logue's analogy, effectively 'skim off' the easy cases and disadvantages those who may previously have been protected by common law.

This is a further reason not to look at specific areas in isolation. The interlocking areas of the debate might include decision-making involving competent adults, competent minors, incompetent adults but with previously expressed decisions or wishes, incompetent adults without such prior anticipatory decisions, neonates, and the terminally ill and non-terminally ill in all of these categories.

Justification of certain actions, which might be provided by moral arguments in favour of euthanasia, for instance, needs to be separated from justification of legislative or policy reform that would allow such actions, and some coherence between the two arguments obtained before proceeding.[9] Enactment of a law, or adoption of a liberal professional code, changes the circumstances under which such actions take place.[10] Even if there is no evidence to show that abuse or a slippery slope will occur, the theoretical possibility is introduced and must be admitted; and if developments cannot be predicted with certainty, the need for a consensual approach is emphasized:

a) to maximize the chances of reform being implemented;
b) to spread the burden of responsibility for reform as equally as possible within the society to which it applies; and
c) to minimize any instability following implementation.

The difficulty of devising effective reform is hardly an answer to the growing debate and discontent with the present situation,[11] especially as we have no way of knowing for certain if the alternative of continuing with the present situation will be worse. Common frames of reference from which to proceed are urgently needed.[12]

> We develop theories to illuminate experience and to determine what we ought to do, but we also use experience to test, corroborate, and revise theories. If a theory yields conclusions at odds with our considered judgements ... we have reason to be suspicious of the theory and to modify it or seek an alternative theory.[13]

If reform measures are undertaken, perhaps not infallible in themselves, but subject to amendment against a background of commonly held principles, then a process of gradual improvement may be initiated. The use of case law in the Netherlands is often seen as a way of clarifying existing practice and the conditions under which a doctor will not be found criminally liable: the interpretation of the conditions is thus subject to constant refinement.[14] (The fact that some commentators from outside the Netherlands find the Dutch practice unacceptable is irrelevant to the fact that the Dutch have found a way that is generally acceptable within their own country.) In the USA, Oregon drafters have learnt from the experiences of Washington and California to amend their remit until a proposal with a chance of general acceptance is formulated. In the UK common ground has established a successful foothold in the living will document of the Terrence Higgins Trust and Kings College[15] which contains options for requesting continued treatment as long as possible as well as the more usual living will refusal-of-treatment options.[16]

This is not to deny, however, the role of champions of more polarized positions:

> The history of rights movements shows that sympathy, even of enlightened people, moves the public conscience or at least custom and legal institutions only slowly when there is not supporting motivation from protests, nonviolent noncooperation, and sometimes violent action.[17]

A background theme in this chapter is that protests, opinion polls, eloquent arguments in favour of euthanasia or the more strident demands of voluntary euthanasia societies may provide *supporting motivation* for change, but the main instruments of reform are likely to be agreements between opposing factions, commonly held values such as compassion, practical caring, shared emotional responses to specific dilemmas and the insights these generate.[18]

The Present Situation

To examine and comprehend a way forward – or backward – we need first to map out where we are now, and that, hopefully, could be the least contentious of objectives. In so doing, we must distinguish between ascertainable facts, practices and processes on the one hand, and those which are subject to interpretation on the other. With persistent enquiry we may be able to place an increasing number in the former category,[19] but nevertheless we need to accept that the concepts of some will remain governed by semantics or current definitions – even the definition of death itself.[20] In sketching out some of the pertinent areas of concern, the next section will examine briefly in turn, persistent vegetative state, assisted suicide and active euthanasia, palliative care, resource allocation and advance directives.

Persistent Vegetative State

Jennett's analysis demonstrates that, in the UK, the Lords' handling of *Airedale NHS Trust* v. *Bland* seemed to give temporary respite in the area of withdrawing treatment of a PVS patient, yet was inconsistent and failed, as did the Government Select Committee, satisfactorily to answer basic, pressing problems. At the time of writing, the UK is considerably behind other countries. The *Bland* case highlighted many legal anomalies which were becoming self-evident. Anthony Bland could be starved to death, but could not be injected to die swiftly and painlessly. Considering the patient's dilemma, Dworkin observed that:

> … the law produces the apparently irrational result that people can choose to die lingering deaths by refusing to eat, by refusing treatment that keeps them alive, or by being disconnected from respirators and suffocating, but they cannot choose a quick, painless death that their doctors could easily provide.[21]

On the other hand, Ogden has summarized some of the problems for the medical profession, stressing that '[t]he present legal climate, with its inconsistencies and confusion about killing versus allowing to die, imposes a barrier that precludes any accountability for justified killing'.[22] These examples perhaps highlight the shortcomings of ignoring a broader, more internally consistent picture.[23]

Assisted Suicide and Active Euthanasia

The UK government declared early in 1994 that assisted suicide and active euthanasia would remain illegal. Two weeks later, the *British*

Medical Journal reported on the not insignificant number of doctors that have, at some stage, practised euthanasia.[24] One might be tempted to debate the empirical reliability of significance, or even the relevance (if any), of the age of the doctors involved, but such digressionary analysis should not be allowed to subvert the main issue: what *is* clear is that the active assisting of death is going on[25] – even though it is against the law. Such other data that are available suggest similar practices occurring elsewhere and do so in no uncertain terms. In Ciesielski-Carlucci's study, 27 per cent of doctors had assisted in a suicide at least once.[26] Some would wish that this be facilitated and others that it be stopped, but what if neither is possible in the present climate? Some sort of consistency and safeguards for what is going on now would seem to be eminently desirable as a minimum measure. The UK is frequently compared with her continental neighbour, but it might be disingenuous to suggest that euthanasia never occurred in the Netherlands before the practice became openly accepted – for all we know there could have been a lot more of it going on, so it is actually impossible to know whether the slope has been upwards or downwards,[27] or even whether it is 'slippery'.[28] This is not to criticize or advocate the Dutch approach; the underlying practice is a separate issue to the way in which we choose to deal with that practice. In asking whether legislation is an effective way to control euthanasia, one might be tempted to observe that, in the Netherlands where there is one of the most permissive of abortion laws, there is also the lowest incidence of abortion in Europe. This does not mean that legislation against euthanasia is necessarily ineffective, but we should not assume that something can necessarily be best controlled by simply outlawing it. The Dutch have attempted to deal with the problem openly, and the British, typically, with repression and resultant secrecy.[29]

Logue, mentioned above, draws our attention to the needless dying involved when individuals may be driven to end their lives prematurely, while they still can, lest no one be there to help when they become helpless. The relatives who assist, she said, suffer trauma – and might not these doctors who are now assisting be suffering trauma also? One might examine, in this context, the heart-searching of people like American hospice veteran Dr Timothy Quill before assisting a suicide[30] or, at another extreme, people who have witnessed the torment when a terminally ill person *fails* in a suicide attempt.

Doctors are losing out on the sounding-board opportunity of conferring with colleagues, patients are losing out on the opportunity of counselling,[31] and the illegality, while arguably providing *some* deterrent, basically *prevents* what we would term control or 'safeguards'.[32] One hardly visualizes the doctors who are currently carrying out euthanasia in the UK going through a checklist of safeguards such as the one included in the Oregon law, and the public does not even have the comfort of knowing that the euthanasia is being carried out appropriately and efficiently.

Palliative Care

The Netherlands does not have a hospice system akin to that which exists, for example, in the UK but this is perhaps largely because the high standards of palliative care are run within Dutch hospitals or, as from British hospices, through a well funded outpatient service. The *quality* of palliative care was underlined by Admiraal's own typical experience – one reinforced by government statistics – that pain is far from being the most frequent cause of a request for euthanasia.[33]

In the UK, we occasionally hear that all pain is controllable, but an advertisement to this effect by the hospices in *The Guardian* resulted in a stream of complaints until the Advertising Standards Authority took action to prevent its reappearance.[34] One of the complainants quoted the Royal College of Surgeons Symposium (11 May 1990) that had stated that 25 per cent of cancer patients in the UK die without pain relief, and pointed out that although there were 3000 hospice beds (in 1992) – all very well-funded compared to NHS beds – there were approximately 100 000 cancer patients dying a year. The UK is a nation of limited resources, and helping a chosen few does not absolve society of moral responsibility to those it did not help or those it could not help.

A comforting reaction is to call for greater funding for hospices. The practicality of such a noble desire is not always beyond question however, as for instance when the *Bulletin of Medical Ethics* that year pointed out that, if the rate of increase of support for hospices (then officially at £32 million a year) was maintained, they would require the entire NHS budget in ten years' time.[35]

Sommerville considered that levels of palliative care may, in many ways, be getting worse not better. But to put the question of palliative care into context, we could turn to philosopher Janet Radcliffe Richards, who said:

> If we could reliably make everyone's life worth living, no one would want to die, and laws preventing assistance would have no purpose. Conversely, to the extent that they have a purpose, precisely what they achieve is to force continuing life on people whose suffering we have not managed to prevent. The claim that we should prevent suffering is being used to defend a law whose main effect is to perpetuate it.[36]

To argue that better palliative care would eliminate the need for euthanasia is merely to fudge the issue. We should recognize that improved pain control is generally attractive yet extraneous to the argument over assisted suicide or voluntary euthanasia (just as were the sanctity of life arguments exposed in the *Bland* case) – emotive, and usable for arguing the case for or against, but essentially unable to progress dialectically one way or the other.

Resource Allocation

The question of resource allocation is all too often avoided. It matters little that we want the best possible care for everyone if there is no way to produce it. Supply not only outstrips demand, but increasingly costly technological innovation seems to guarantee that the gulf will widen. The expanding elderly population (as more people survive into old age) means that, in the resultant dilemmas, a swiftly increasing number of people will be affected. Concern is frequently expressed in the view that talk about futility is in reality a convenient 'code' for talking about rationing and cost containment; if this is the case it is manipulative and unethical to disguise economic matters in such a fashion, especially as the different phrases display distinct meanings and ethical norms.[37] Logue has faced the economic issues squarely – answers must be found *within the context of our present financial situation as a nation*. Pace has reinforced the reality by presenting it in a specific application.

If there is confusion over resource allocation, it is easy to see the prospect of euthanasia as one which could include abuse or fear of abuse.[38] Yet if the objective is to avoid a type of death that is not in accordance with the best interests of the individual, Logue has pointed out that 'Restriction or denial of medical care may also encourage suicide among the elderly of both sexes if they are left to choose between deprivation and death'.[39] 'Bad' deaths result from confused policies, not simply from specific types of policy that either allow, on the one hand, individuals to seek and obtain assisted or accelerated dying or, on the other hand, that outlaw such options. High technology threatens not only funding for more basic-care medicine but also generates a fear of overuse. While it can be argued that this is a more justifiable worry in the USA,[40] the treatment biases prevalent in the UK suggest it cannot be discounted.[41] Hence the very pressing need for adequate guidelines on allocation of such services and the resources involved.

Resource allocation is a separate problem to the rights and wrongs of euthanasia, and one which needs a separate answer. It is interesting to note that no one answer has been consistently applied within the NHS.[42] Fear of 'non-voluntary' euthanasia could be just as much a reality as fear of not getting the best cancer treatment or best consultant. The problem lies not with the practice, its availability or lack of it, but with the lack of guidelines, regulations or procedural transparency.

Advance Directives

As has been seen, the House of Lords Select Committee has encouraged the use of advance directives (or living wills) without giving them any legal force. There often exists confusion over the legal status of the advance directive, and medical and legal journals have recently attested to that in a flurry of articles either saying that living wills are legally binding or saying that they are not.[43] They are certainly a legally valid way for a patient to express wishes about future non-treatment; and the doctor who in good faith feels obliged to apply medical treatment in contra-indication to those wishes might be found culpable in the eyes of the law.[44] As long as basic conditions are fulfilled (that the directive is clearly established and applicable in the circumstances), their force at common law seems secure: but that the advance decision *was clearly established and applicable in the circumstances*, means, for instance, that the patient clearly understood the result of refusing treatment, was capable of making a directive on the basis of such information, and that the instructions clearly coincide with circumstances in incompetence about which the patient had previously only hypothesized.[45] That gives us sufficient ground to work out that they are *persuasive* legally – as long as the basic conditions are not challenged by medical opinion, or other evidence. The Law Commission observed that a decision which was based on false assumption, for instance, would be vitiated and, likewise, that a doctor would be entitled to proceed with treatment if there was evidence which cast doubt on whether a directive was a true expression of a patient's wishes.[46] In cases of doubt, English courts

> ... are not slow, the moment there is the slightest doubt as to a patient's views, to fall back on the 'best interests' tests with a dash of *Bolam* thrown in for good measure. This may reflect the tendency towards paternalism and 'doctor knows best' which is endemic in English medical law.[47]

The case known as *Re C*,[48] hailed by some as an important step forward for advance directives, was in fact only a step forward for advance decisions, and in a lower court at that. The court was able to establish that, for a competent[49] patient, the decision was clearly established and applicable in the circumstances, and so make the decision binding – this facility is not the case for advance directives.

Whether this is an acceptable state of affairs is another matter, but given the current momentum for the increased use of living wills, both, as Sommerville observed, by the young with AIDS[50] and by the momentum given by the House of Lords Select Committee's require-ment for guidelines and their subsequent development,[51] it is impor-tant for health-care workers to know where they stand. As Lord Staughton said:

> The surgeon will be liable in damages if he operates when there is a valid refusal of consent, and liable in damages if he fails to operate in accordance with the principle of necessity when there was no valid decision by the patient.[52]

As with euthanasia, the law seems to disadvantage both doctor and patient.

Ways Forward

Re-examining some of the areas in turn, and within our 'broader context', we may ask what interventions might be possible to im-prove developments, and the likelihood, if any, of success.

Looking Forward: Persistent Vegetative State

There seems some agreement that statutory provision and guidelines on treatment of the persistent vegetative state could ease the imple-mentation of what is now accepted procedure in such cases so, as Jennett stated, we could avoid the necessity of court hearings in the UK.

At about the time of *Airedale NHS Trust* v. *Bland*, another case, in South Africa,[53] also tried to find a legally acceptable way of withdraw-ing treatment from a PVS patient. This second case was perhaps aided by the fact that the gentleman in question had made a living will. But the majority of people who make living wills are elderly, as was Mr Clarke; many patients in PVS are young, as was Anthony Bland, and attempts to rely on the often missing device of a living will in cases that can and should be decided on other grounds are quite unrealistic. A New Zealand judge who said that it might be timely to look at new ways of defining death was probably on a closer track, and it is inter-esting to apply Logue's distinction between biological and biographi-cal life, not only to PVS, but to the slightly more difficult area of the 'locked-in' state in that New Zealand case.[54]

Familiar paradigms can be seen with a different lens. Current ideas of death or of 'best interests' or 'substituted judgement' can, potentially, be usefully developed into something more comprehensive and less results-oriented.[55]

Looking Forward: Assisted Suicide and Active Euthanasia

I have suggested that the question of euthanasia is not one of for or against, but of how to manage an existing practice. On the one hand there is a need for regulation when it is performed by doctors, for ethical awareness over personal moral values or the differing moral values of another, for consistency of approach and patient safeguards. On the other hand, in controlling the assisted suicides that do not involve medical assistance, we have nothing less than a backstreet situation – comparable to the days of backstreet abortion – that needs to be put on a more humane and civilized level.[56] We are not going to prevent suicides by outlawing them – but we can hope to use our expertise to minimize the suffering. We are also in a situation where non-voluntary euthanasia for various situations is tolerated by the law, but voluntary euthanasia is outlawed.[57]

The language may cause us to view the arguments in an unhelpful manner; phrases such as 'assisting a suicide' are elusive to analysis[58] and may highlight the insufficiencies of working on a specific area instead of looking with a more comprehensive approach. As a society, we are seeking humane and responsible solutions to problems that are comparatively recent; more appropriate (and less confrontational) language may be needed. It is interesting to note that, after the protracted debates about how and when to let Anthony Bland die, his death was recorded as 'kidney failure', yet an 87 year-old woman who killed herself rather than suffer the indignity of progressive Alzheimer's disease had the wishes in her suicide note respected when a coroner recorded a verdict of 'euthanasia'.[59] In both cases the arguably inappropriate language reflects the dissatisfaction with available terminology.

Proposals for extensive enabling legislation, such as have been put forward by McLean, offer, it can be argued, perhaps the most comprehensive and caring of solutions, but the political divisiveness that plagues the question may mean that the type of narrow proposal being tested in a number of US states might be a more practical step in damage control and in confronting unpalatable truths. The more comprehensive solutions come into their own more as a guiding light. However, enabling or permissive legislation, *permitting* an exception to the rule, has the advantage of not challenging the validity of that rule (such as the 'rule against killing').[60] Or as Brody put it:

> I argue here that an adjudication of assisted death might follow from viewing it as a compassionate response to one sort of medical failure,

rather than as something to be prohibited outright or as something to be established as a standard policy.[61]

The need for clarity in the theory of the law,[62] especially in an area that entertains wide divergences from one jurisdiction to another[63] is clear from the practical inadequacies exposed, for instance, in the case of Dr Cox. Dr Cox administered a lethal injection of potassium chloride to a woman who was suffering indescribable agony, had a very short time – possibly less than an hour – to live, and who had repeatedly asked him for death. The injection gave her a few moments of calm before she died, but was undoubtedly lethal in itself. Many high-dose levels of painkilling drugs, routinely administered to dying patients, would also be lethal if given to non-terminal people, but not in smaller doses. Potassium is not, however, on such a list of accepted painkillers. The court felt that Cox intended to kill his patient, for whatever noble motives. But as the death *might* have been due to natural causes, Cox had only been charged with attempted murder rather than murder (thus also saving the embarrassment of being forced to put a doctor in prison when the public consensus was that he had acted beneficently). The principle of double effect (which was considered by a jury in Michigan shortly afterwards in acquitting Dr Kevorkian of using carbon monoxide to relieve suffering by administering death) was predictably used *against* Dr Cox and he was found guilty. The difficulty of presenting such a case in a context of antiquated and ill-equipped laws was evident:

> It is submitted that the line to be drawn between a primary purpose to alleviate pain, which may, or even will, incidentally cause death, and, on the other hand, a purpose to kill which may – for however short a time – incidentally alleviate suffering, is so finely and subtly drawn as to be incapable of sensible application by any doctor confronted with this particular situation.[64]

Euthanasia is illegal in the UK – as it is in the Netherlands – but in the UK there is no freedom from prosecution for following guidelines. Whereas, in the Netherlands, there are numerous court actions if there is doubt, in the UK the covert nature of the practice means that, with the exception of Dr Cox, cases are not brought to light.

Of course, the cultural differences between the two countries limit the ready transferability of such a system to the UK,[65] even if there were sufficient support to effect the transformation. In the USA the option of assisted suicide is being pursued with the awareness that this seems to be a less drastic step than decriminalization of active euthanasia.

As has been observed, the only hard information on euthanasia in the UK indicated that 32 per cent of doctors surveyed, who had faced a request for euthanasia, had complied with such a request. Quite apart from the alarming number of doctors who assisted, also striking is the fact that 68 per cent did *not* comply. Data from other countries suggest that many such patients whose request had been refused would attempt, maladroitly, to end their own lives or end their own lives with the help of a friend. Ogden's recently published study[66] of assisted suicides in Canada has shown that many such attempts fail horribly, producing even further suffering and indignity to the patient in his or her final days. With an increasingly elderly population, and a less than elderly population affected by diseases such as AIDS, we can expect this trend to grow.

Admiraal has indicated that it is not necessarily so easy to kill yourself as reading off a dose of barbiturates from *Final Exit.*[67] What may seem like a very simple thing can have many wrong turnings, and a prescribing bill, such as the Oregon one, would engender a need to look anew at the pharmacology of inducing death.

Looking Forward: Palliative Care

Palliative care, including not only pain alleviation but psychological support, may be an area that could throw light on other problems in unexpected ways. The active versus passive euthanasia distinction revolves unfairly, as Pace explained, around an erroneous notion of acts versus omissions that still has much support in law in many countries.[68] Yet it is dispensable, for instance, when the doctor has a duty to act.[69]

So how can a health-care team legally respect the wishes of a patient who wishes to end his or her life? One option has been found in some US hospices. Evidence has been surfacing that death from starvation and dehydration in conscious, dying persons is not necessarily painful as widely believed, especially when symptoms can be adequately attended to. This means that a patient can elect to die, have the full cooperation of the medical team, yet not involve them in any acts that carry a legal penalty – after all, he or she is only *refusing* a certain treatment – food and water – and the right to refuse treatment is well established in law. The data on starvation was slow in asserting itself partly, as the researchers noted, because it ran contrary to a culturally established emotional bias about the 'goodness' of providing food to the sick.[70]

Other traditional biases may need to be re-examined. In one survey,[71] age alone was found to be a reason why a considerable number of nurses would prefer to die.[72]

There is a sharp need in the area of palliative care to recognize unpalatable facts about the limitations of pain and symptom control, and also differing patient values. Armed with a clear picture of current capabilities, the hospice movement can help to continue leading the way in palliative care. As Australian hospice pioneer Roger Hunt said:

> Unrealistically high expectations about what palliative care can achieve may cause stress among hospice workers, and may lead to a loss of credibility with clients. The rhetoric–reality mismatch, between an ideal of care and the reality of limitations, can add fuel to the process of burnout. If the limitations of palliative care and the virtual inevitability of residual suffering are not acknowledged, then palliative carers may be spurred on to try harder and harder to relieve patients' distress, only to be further disillusioned by their efforts and filled with a sense of failure.[73]

Hunt suggests that palliative care and passive euthanasia are closely linked, preferring to use such terminology rather than rely on the 'principle of double effect' which he describes as a 'psychological defence mechanism'[74] which encourages what Dr Pace has referred to as 'moral dishonesty.' On the other hand, the practice of relieving symptoms as a patient refuses food and water – with the cooperation of the health-care staff – could, whatever the words used, herald a step forward that offends neither voluntary euthanasia campaigners nor 'pro-lifers.'

Looking Forward: Resource Allocation

The importance of keeping in mind the 'broader picture' is perhaps nowhere more apparent than when considering the question of resource allocation. The perennial bogey-fears of abuse regarding laws allowing assisted suicide or euthanasia, or even the introduction of statutory living will provisions,[75] must be met, yet much of the muddy water concerns not these issues but the issue of resource allocation. Without clear guidelines, understood by public and professionals alike, fears of not getting the treatment one would have wished will be compounded.

The British NHS has largely left this difficult area to develop as it will, often with the result that 'first-come-first-served' or localized age criteria predominate. The *Economist* observed that '… 20% of the UK's coronary care units and 40% of consultants administering thrombolytic therapy have age-related admission policies, some with age thresholds as low as 60'.[76]

Preservation of choice, rejection of a fixed age of death,[77] and public awareness are mentioned by Battin[78] as three essential protections in a resource allocation policy to discourage abuse. There are a number of features in the Dutch health-care system that would seem to encourage certain advantages. As Wal says:

Almost all patients (99.4%) have health care insurance, and 100% of the population is insured for the cost of protracted illness. There are no financial incentives for hospitals, physicians, or family members to stop the care of patients. Moreover, the legal right of patients to health care on the basis of their insurance will override budget and other financial agreements.[79]

Wal also points out that: 'Many patients (40%) die at home, especially patients with cancer (48% of all cancer deaths)'.[80] We thus have an example first of public awareness and, second – remembering that most patients in the UK would prefer to die at home but do not – respect for patient autonomy.

Balancing various systems is a hazardous task, and equally difficult, from the point of view of this chapter, is the question of transparency: whatever system is adopted it should be clear and open, so that fears of being unfairly treated are minimized. An attempt to achieve a workable consensus position has been put forward by Kilner, who suggests a basic approach to the selection of recipients of limited life-saving medical resources, which claims to be based on common ground identified within various systems:

1. Only patients who satisfy the medical-benefit and willingness-to-accept-treatment criteria are to be considered eligible.
2. Available resources are to be given first to eligible patients who satisfy the imminent-death criterion, and next to eligible patients who satisfy the special-responsibilities criterion or resource-required criterion.
3. If resources are still available, recipients are to be randomly selected, generally by lottery, from among the remaining eligible patients.[81]

Kilner suggests his proposals could be modified, if necessary, to garner necessary popular support – for instance, by replacing the 'lottery' provision with a 'first-come-first-served' provision. Until a system that has broad consensual support has been adopted, however, the resource-allocation arguments are likely to spill over into the death and dying debates, producing apparently sustainable arguments against allowing people to die with the help of a physician (although the large part of such arguments may be the real fear of abuse rather than any actual abuse). Aspects of health care do not operate in isolation any more than aspects of health care ethics, and a broad approach perhaps offers the most reliable way of ensuring that individual aspects avoid, first, becoming unmanageable or, second, disadvantaging patients in another part of the spectrum.

Looking Forward: Advance Directives

Finally, looking at the place of advance directives – or whether there is a place for advance directives – the trend now has its own momentum. Government endorsement was taken up by the BMA to develop a code of practice, even though serious questions about the living will's effectiveness in promoting patient autonomy have not fully been answered. In the immediate future, doctors will need to be conversant with the concept of a living will when such a document is presented, as well as with the relevant underlying principles and laws. The Law Commission has proposed that legislation should provide for the scope and legal effect of anticipatory decisions and that a judicial forum might make a declaration as to whether or not an apparent decision by the patient concerned meets the requirements of being 'clearly established' and 'applicable in the circumstances'.[82] Statutory provision would also have the effect of publicizing the issue and making patients and health-care staff more aware of their options to make advance directives.

We have behind us the experiments of the USA and Denmark, and can perhaps avoid potential pitfalls of a 'living wills on admission policy' or a user-friendly national register that is nevertheless underconsulted by doctors.[83]

A possibility that is arguably worrying is the potential mentioned by Sommerville for extending the durable power of attorney so that a third person can be empowered to make health-care decisions on behalf of a person when that person becomes incompetent. Even though Sommerville argues that finding a sufficient number of proxies could in itself prove quite a problem, it is an attractive notion to extend existing law rather than devise a new one, especially as UK jurisprudence seems almost unique in its lack of even basic provisions that would make such proxy decisions legally binding. It may also seem quicker and more straightforward to discuss treatment options with a competent proxy than to attempt to interpret a complicated written living will in the midst of a dilemma on a busy ward. Patients also seem to favour the idea. Unfortunately, several large studies in the USA, which paired proxies and patients and asked them to make hypothetical decisions, produced the vexatious conclusion that proxies, however confident, are generally unable or unwilling to make the choices that the patient would have made. As Emanuel and Emanuel noted:

> Only half of the patients who designated a proxy in a written document have discussed with that person their preferences regarding specific interventions, such as mechanical breathing or artificial feeding and fluids. [And:] ... potential proxies are more hesitant to with-

> draw or terminate life-sustaining treatment than patients are. The
> burden of decision making is heavy, and produces much greater reluc-
> tance to withhold care from a loved one than from oneself.' [Also:]… of
> the proxies who do manage accurately to judge patients' wishes, less
> than two-thirds will be emotionally capable of carrying them out.[84]

Even if we were not convinced by a mass of sociological and
empirical evidence,[85] one only has to recall the not uncommon scenario painted by Dr Pace, of relatives insisting on all available treatment being administered.[86] Proxies can be an unreliable way of protecting prior choice.[87] Autonomy in the sense of choosing who makes
the medical decisions, yes, but not in the sense of having one's preferences for accepting or refusing treatment carried into incompetence. Unless the procedure is radically improved to allow for better
patient–proxy communication and less proxy emotional bias, of one
sort or another, then this durable power of attorney for health care
seems like the sort of piecemeal change that has *not* had the benefit
of being in the context of a more comprehensive ideal structure. Yet *if*
the proxy's ability accurately to second-guess patient choices can be
radically improved, and sufficient doctor–patient and doctor–proxy
communication developed, at least one study has indicated that:
'Detailed advance directives with a supportive proxy, coupled with
physician-patient discussion, furnish the most reliable medical directives.'[88] One should also distinguish correcting anomalies or shortcomings in the law (suggested by the lack of effective proxy provisions), from the likely *effectiveness* of that legal for a specific purpose.
Eagerness to correct the legal vacuum should perhaps be tempered
with consideration of the difficulties in ensuring that the vehicle will
be properly used by patients that are, on the evidence, ill-informed.

Returning briefly to living wills as directives, rather than the proxy
type of instruction, excellent motives are again apparent, but a clearer
analysis of the underlying problems and how to solve them could
perhaps take us further forward in the implementation of autonomy
and good medicine. We don't want to end up with mere window
dressing in response to the current demands for development.[89]

Living wills, since their initial appearance in the late 1960s,[90] have,
it can be said, evolved through three observable phases (apart from
the three 'legal' generations already described by Sommerville).[91]
Initially, we saw a simple statement about how, if there was no
prospect of improvement from an intolerable condition, one should
be allowed to die naturally and not be kept alive by artificial means.
As the limitations and particularly the legal ambiguity of such simple documents became apparent, this phase gave way to the 'checklist' or 'laundry list' style which mentions very specific medical treatments and specific illnesses. Recognizing that these checklists focus

the patient's decisions on methods of treatment, rather than on the goal of a peaceful life-ending, documents emphasizing the patient's underlying life-values have now begun to appear.[92] As Roe observed:

> A clear indication of the patient's goals for therapy is probably more important than an exhaustive checklist; the latter may indicate preferences that change with slight changes in the medical situation.[93]

They suggest a practical change of attitude from the all-too-common medicalization of life choices, and are more dialogue-based, acknowledging a need to move away from documents that seem theoretically sound perhaps but largely unworkable in practice.[94] Whatever type of directive is presented, however, a physician has the opportunity, when confronted with one, of acquainting the patient with potential benefits and burdens of treatments that might be called for in the future. We can attempt to maximize the usefulness of living wills, without overstating their usefulness,[95] their effectiveness,[96] their applicability[97] or thinking that they address more than a tiny part of the overall problem.[98] It is also important to look at the area of decision-making that might, it could be argued, ideally be covered by a living will, but where no such document has been completed. Rather than rely on arbitrary standards, best interests or the decision of a (possible ill-informed) relative, a default possibility has been suggested:

> Patients' choices for care in the event of terminal illness relate to an intricate set of demographic, educational, and cultural factors. These results should not be used as a shortcut to determine patient preferences for care, but may provide new insights into the basis for patients' preferences.[99]

A system that caters only for those patients who happen to have made a living will before becoming incompetent necessarily puts a strain on the overall principles, possibly at the expense of patients without living wills and for whom no release from suffering is countenanced by law. A default system would make the world of living wills more like that of ordinary wills. However, a system of specific default decision-makers (usually relatives in a descending precedence), as suggested in a number of Canadian jurisdictions, carries the same problems discussed already under proxies and has less to recommend it than the improvement suggested, other than ease of drafting.

Comment

So how realistic is it to talk of a 'way forward'? Changes will be inevitable, and in that sense we are *propelled* forward. A *way* forward may depend on how far we allow ourselves to be driven by events at the expense of trying to follow a clear map. Until we have the latter, perhaps we cannot realistically know whether we are going forwards or backwards. Principles need to precede practice, not to be reinterpreted to fit existing practices. Broad principles need to underlie a consistent approach in overlapping areas, and if the exigencies of the situation require that change is enacted in one area alone, then it should be with reference to the whole. Developments in living wills and treatment decisions for those in a persistent vegetative state have, for too long, been made in isolation instead of as part of a comprehensive approach to death and dying; they are like the wheels of a car acting independently and endangering overall safe progress when they turn at different speeds. Nevertheless this chapter has hopefully demonstrated that a way forward may depend more on shared understanding than battles fought or won, and, in some small way, the present volume may be seen or used in the attempt to further such a way forward.

Notes

1   McLean, S. (1993), 'To treat or not to treat? Dilemmas of the hopelessly ill', talk given at the *Royal Society of Edinburgh International Conference*, 24 February. The ten points enumerated by McLean as prerequisites in relation to the euthanasia question were:

    1   the recognition of patients' rights;
    2   public involvement in community morality;
    3   certainty of outcome, once a decision had been made,
    4   compassion as the overriding cause of the decision,
    5   accountability of decision-makers,
    6   transparency of decision-making (the need for clear rules),
    7   an appropriate forum for decision making policy;
    8   consistency or formal justice;
    9   the need to allay public fears against inappropriate cases being considered for euthanasia;
    10 the need to allay professional fears concerning the law (no sanctions against doctors).

2   The data supplied by Cheryl Smith (see Chapter 5 above) and the Oregon campaign are not unique. On the choice to limit benefits to terminal patients, for instance: Ciesielski-Carlucci noted that 'Respondents were more likely to assist (defined as prescribing or administering) a patient who is suffering from a terminal illness than one who is in chronic pain. This trend would remain the same if medically assisted suicide were made legal': Ciesielski-Carlucci C. (1993), 'Physician attitudes and experiences with assisted suicide: results of a

small opinion survey', *Cambridge Quarterly of Healthcare Ethics*, **2**, pp. 39–44, at p. 43.

3   C.K. Smith (1989), Model Aid in Dying Act 75 *Iowa Law Review*, **75**, pp. 139–215.

4   Giesen, D. (1990), 'Law and ethical dilemmas at life's end' (Section B, Ethical and Legal Framework), a talk given as part of the proceedings of the *20th Colloquy on European Law: Law and Moral Dilemmas Affecting Life and Death*, Glasgow: Council of Europe.

5   For example in: House of Lords Select Committee on Medical Ethics (1994), *HL Paper 21–I. 21–II, 21–III*, London: HMSO, Parts II & III. For a basic overview of principal philosophical autonomy arguments from which much of the debate devolves, see, for instance Gillon, R. (1992), *Philosophical Medical Ethics*, Chichester: Wiley & Sons, especially pp. 60–5.

6   Brooks, A. (1984), 'Dignity and cost-effectiveness: a rejection of the utilitarian approach to death', *Journal of Medical Ethics*, **10**, pp. 148–151, at p. 148.

7   *Airedale NHS Trust* v. *Bland* [1993] 1 All E.R. 821, 879.

8   Stevens, C. and Hassan, R. (1994), 'Management of death, dying and euthanasia: attitudes and practices of medical practitioners in South Australia', *Journal of Medical Ethics*, **20**, pp. 41–6, at p. 45: 'These and previous findings suggest, firstly, that alteration or clarification of the law would not necessarily change the practices of individual medical practitioners, and secondly, that questions of legality are currently not the principal considerations used when making decisions to withhold or withdraw treatment to terminate the lives of patients.' Note also in: McLean, S. (1989), *A Patient's Right to Know – Information Disclosure, the Doctor and the Law*, Aldershot: Dartmouth, p. 169: 'The ease with which any jurisdiction is capable of vindicating patients' rights depends on its history and jurisprudence as much as it does on willingness to make appropriate modifications or enthusiasm for change.' See also: Annas G. (1985), 'When procedures limit rights: from Quinlan to Conroy', *Hastings Center Report* April, pp. 24–26, at p. 26: '... the "New Jersey approach" of declaring broad-ranging substantive rights, and then attempting procedurally to restrict their application to very narrow categories of patients, creates a "Catch 22" effect that fails to promote the autonomy of once-competent patients.'

9   Beauchamp, T. and Childress, J. (1994), *Principles of Biomedical Ethics* (4th edn), Oxford: Oxford University Press, p. 228: 'We believe that sufficient moral reasons exist in some cases to justify mercy killing and assist suicide, but these reasons are not necessarily sufficient to support revisions in either codes of ethics or public policies. In addressing whether we should retain or modify some current prohibitions, we therefore need to be clear about whether the topic of discussion is the moral justification of individual acts or the justification of institutional rules and public laws governing practices.'

10   Ibid., p. 10: '... the thesis that active euthanasia is morally justified if patients face uncontrollable pain and suffering and request death is consistent with the thesis that the government should legally prohibit active euthanasia because it would not be possible to control abuses if it were legalized. We are not here defending particular moral judgements about the justifiability of such acts. We are maintaining only that the connections between moral action-guides and judgements about policy or law or legal enforcement are complicated and that a judgement about the morality of acts does not entail a particular judgement about law and policy. Factors such as the symbolic value of the law, the costs of a program and its enforcement, and the demands of competing programs must also be considered.' The stalemate has been reached in various forms by the Law Reform Commission of Canada, the Supreme Court of Canada in *Rodriguez* v. *British Colombia (Attorney General)* (1993) 82 BCLR (2d) 273 (Can Sup Ct), and the House of Lords Select Committee on Medical Ethics.

11   Mason, J. and McCall Smith, A. (1994), *Law and Medical Ethics* (4th edn), Edinburgh: Butterworths, p. 338: 'To say that legislation will be difficult is not, however, to say that it should not be attempted and we now believe that some form of statutory law regulating "controlled death" is inevitable, and needed, in the United Kingdom.'

12   In the UK, the Abortion Act 1967, whatever its shortcomings, largely stemmed from the need to limit the deaths of women undergoing backstreet abortions and contained provisions in the wake of the thalidomide disaster that even religious opponents could concede. In contrast to comparatively quiet UK developments, the USA reforms, based on court decisions involving *rights* have involved ongoing contention which has reached such violent levels that it is becoming increasingly difficult and dangerous to perform or undergo lawful abortion. The reactions of opposing factions appear to be unrelated to the marked drop in neonatal homicide following the landmark legal decision on abortion in *Roe* v. *Wade 410 US*, 113, (1973) 35 L Ed 2d 147, 93 S Ct 705; figures from the National Center for Health Statistics are reproduced in *Journal of Medical Ethics*, **267**, (22), 1992, p. 3027.

13   Beauchamp, and Childress, *op. cit.*, note 9 above, p. 23.

14   Smith II, G. (1993), 'Reviving the swan, extending the curse of Methuselah, or adhering to the Kevorkian ethic?', *Cambridge Quarterly of Healthcare Ethics*, **2**, pp. 49–56, at p. 53: 'The goal of the Royal Dutch Medical Association (KNMG) has long been to control this area rather than to seek to prohibit it simply because the Association realized that rigid prohibitions, once established, could not be enforced uniformly or verified.' Note, however, that religious opposition is not such a considerable factor in the Netherlands as in many countries: Kimsma, G. and Leeuwen, E. (1993), 'Dutch euthanasia: background, practice, and present justifications', *Cambridge Quarterly of Healthcare Ethics*, **2**, pp. 19–35, at p. 22: 'In 1972 … the Dutch Reformed Church published a pastoral writing in which voluntary euthanasia was conditionally accepted as a humane way of dying.'

15   Reproduced in Kennedy, I. and Grubb, A. (1994), *Medical Law, Text With Materials* (2nd edn), London: Butterworths, pp. 1365–8.

16   This approach is not new. In 1985 a law was passed in Indiana that included a 'life prolonging procedures declaration' as an option to the refusal-of-treatment declaration in the same bill. The move won the support of the Roman Catholic Church in Indiana. The current bill still contains such provisions (*Indiana Living Wills and Life-Prolonging Procedures Act*, Ind. Code Ann. 16–8–11–1 to –22 (Burns 1990). At the opposite end of the scale: '… since they [living wills] are written on the Voluntary Euthanasia Society's headed notepaper, they often alarm doctors who receive them': Rodger J. (1994), 'Living wills', *Summons* (The journal for the Medical and Dental Defence Union of Scotland members), Spring, p. 2.

17   Brandt, R. (1983), 'The concept of a moral right and its function', *Journal of Philosophy*, **80**, pp. 29–45, at p. 45.

18   Beauchamp and Childress, *op. cit.*, note 9 above, p. 87–90, and especially at p. 88: 'As long as principles allow room for discretionary and contextual judgement, the ethics of care need not dispense with principles. However, like many proponents of virtue theory, defenders of the ethics of care find principles often irrelevant, unproductive, ineffectual, or constrictive in the moral life. A defender of principle could say that *principles* of care, compassion, and kindness tutor our responses in caring, compassionate, and kind ways. But this claim seems hollow. Our moral experience suggests that our responses rely on our emotions, our capacity for sympathy, our sense of friendship, and our knowledge of how caring people behave.'

19   For example: 'Since trustworthy empirical data have not been available until recently, moral viewpoints have coloured the estimated numbers of cases of euthanasia (and assisted suicide) and the way in which it is practised. Recent reports, however, have diminished this empirical uncertainty': Wal, G., Dillman, R. (1994), 'Euthanasia in the Netherlands', *British Medical Journal*, **308**, pp. 1346–9, at p. 1346.

20   *Auckland Area Health Board* v. *Attorney-General* (NZ High Court) [1993] 4 Med. L.R. 239. Mr Justice Thomas at p. 246: 'The problem arises when life passes into death but obscurely. It is a problem made acute by the enormous advances made in technology and medical science in recent decades. With the use of sophisticated life-support systems, life may be perpetuated well beyond the reach of the natural disease. The process of living can become the process of dying so that it is unclear whether life is being sustained or death being deferred ... .' For a general discussion of the problem see: Brazier, M. (1992), 'Defining death' in *Medicine, Patients and the Law*, London: Penguin, Ch. 20.

21   Dworkin, R. (1993), *Life's Dominion – An Argument About Abortion and Euthanasia*, London: Harper Collins, p. 184.

22   Ogden, R. (1994), *Euthanasia, Assisted Suicide & AIDS*, British Columbia: Perreault Goedman Publishing, p. 102.

23   Cf. Savulescu, J. (1994), 'Treatment limitation decisions under uncertainty: the value of subsequent euthanasia', *Bioethics*, **8**, (1), pp. 49–73, at p. 49: 'With treatment, a patient may recover such that he no longer requires life-supporting treatment. However, his life may be not worth living. If active euthanasia of "non-terminal" patients is prohibited, the option of dying will no longer be available.' And at p. 52: 'Paradoxically, patients are allowed to die when they are (or would be) very uncertain about the nature of the final outcomes of treatment, but are not allowed to die when it becomes clearer what the nature of their options are.' And ibid: 'Critically ill patients are allowed to die because it is believed that future disabled life is not in their interests. However, there may be considerable uncertainty about the nature of outcomes. While this may be the best guess of what life will be like in the future, it may also be a blind guess. It is likely that some patients are allowed to die when there is some objective chance of a worthwhile future life.' And at p. 72: 'Paradoxically, it is only with the possibility of death that we can rationally save more worthwhile lives.'

24   Ward, B. and Tate, P. (1994), 'Attitudes among NHS doctors to requests for euthanasia', *British Medical Journal*, **308**, pp. 1332–4, at p. 1333: '... 32% of doctors who had faced a request for active euthanasia reported that they had complied with such a request. This proportion is comparable to the 29% of doctors in an Australian study who said that they had taken active steps to end a patient's life.'

25   Wells states: 'It has been estimated that there could be 10,000 cases of assisted euthanasia in the United Kingdom each year'. Wells, C. (1994), 'Patients, consent and criminal law', *Journal of Social Welfare and Family Law*, **1**, pp. 65–78, at p. 65. Cf. Quill, T., Cassel, C. and Meier, D. (1992), 'Care of the hopelessly ill – proposed clinical criteria for physician assisted suicide', *New England Journal of Medicine*, **327**, (19), pp. 1380–4, at p. 1381: 'Approximately 6000 deaths per day in the United States are said to be in some way planned or indirectly assisted, probably through the "double effect" of pain-relieving medications that may at the same time hasten death or the discontinuation of or failure to start potentially life-prolonging treatments.'

26   Ciesielski-Carlucci, C., *op. cit.*, note 2 above, p. 42.

27   'To demonstrate a slippery slope one would need to show that something changed after introducing a certain practice and for this at least two investiga-

tions would be required. Even then it is doubtful that this would yield conclusive proof either for or against' Delden, J., Pijnenborg, L., and Maas, P. (1993), 'Dances with data', *Bioethics*, 7, pp. 323–9, at p. 327. See also Delden, J., Pijnenborg, L. and Maas, P. (1993), 'The Remmelink Study: two years later', *Hastings Center Report*, 23, (6), pp. 24–7, at p. 26: '… the impression may have arisen that the Dutch began by hastening the end of life on request and ended up with life-terminating acts that the patient had not explicitly requested. This, however, is not necessarily true. First of all, we simply do not know whether unrequested life-terminating acts occurred less or more often in the past. To demonstrate a slippery slope one would need to show that something changed after introducing a certain practice, and for this at least two investigations would be required.'

28 'Although there are slippery-slope arguments that are sound and convincing, typical formulations of the Nazi-invoking arguments are found to be seriously deficient both in logical rigour and in the social history and psychology required as a scholarly underpinning'. Burgess, J. (1993), 'The great slippery-slope argument', *Journal of Medical Ethics*, 19, pp. 169–74, at p. 169. See also Delden, *op. cit.*, note 27 above, p. 26: 'We conclude that no empirical data can be marshalled to support the slippery slope argument against the Dutch.'

29 '… there is more risk for vulnerable patients and for the integrity of the profession in such hidden practices, however, well intended, than there would be in a more open process restricted to competent patients who met carefully defined criteria'. Quill, *op. cit.*, note 25 above, p. 1383.

30 Quill, T. (1991), 'Death and dignity – a case of individualized decision making', *New England Journal of Medicine*, 324, (10), p. 691–4. Case scenarios are presented in Quill, T. (1993), 'Doctor, I want to die. Will you help me?', *Journal of the American Medical Association*, 270, (7), pp. 870–3. A counter-argument to Quill is presented in Pellegrino, E. (1993), 'Compassion needs reason too', *Journal of the American Medical Association*, 270, (7), pp. 874–5.

31 '… the current law on euthanasia is not satisfactory for patients. Patients may be aware that, although they may request active euthanasia, doctors cannot provide it legally; indeed, to raise this issue may be thought to compromise their relationship with the doctor. Conversely, remaining silent may also affect this relationship. A doctor may think that he or she cannot raise the issue for personal, professional, or legal reasons, and so communication between doctors and patients may be blocked', Ward, B. *op. cit., supra*, note 24 above, p. 1334.

32 'Physicians who respond to requests for assisted suicide from such patients do so at substantial professional and legal peril, often acting in secret without the benefit and support from colleagues. This covert practice discourages open and honest communication among physicians, their colleagues, and their dying patients. Decisions often depend more on the physician's values and willingness to take risks than on the compelling nature of the patient's request. There may be more risk of abuse and idiosyncratic decision making with such secret practices than with a more open, carefully defined practice. Finally, terminally ill patients who do not choose to take their own lives often die alone so as not to place their families or caregivers in legal jeopardy.' Quill *op. cit., supra*, note 25 above, p. 1383.

33 Statistics are provided in Maas, P., Delden, J. and Pijnenborg, L. (1992), 'Euthanasia and other medical decisions concerning the end of life – an investigation performed upon the request of the Commission of Inquiry into the Medical Practice concerning Euthanasia', *Health Policy* (special issue), 22, (1 and 2), Amsterdam: Elsevier. Note also the economic context: Kimsma, *op. cit.*, note 14, above, p. 23: 'The Dutch healthcare system, unlike that of other countries, provides care for all citizens at a highly advanced level, without exceptions.'

34   The *Guardian* advertisement appeared on 10 February 1992. Complaints to the ASA objected cogently to false claims concerning ability to provide total pain relief, or totally relieve bedsores and other distressing symptoms. The ASA took the matter up with the advertisers under the British Code of Advertising Practice and received the requested assurance that the advertisement would not be repeated.

35   *Bulletin of Medical Ethics*, **84**, 1992, p. 7. £32 million may be a very conservative estimate of the total resources: Goddard, M. (1992), 'Hospice care in the future: economic evaluation may be useful', *Cancer Topics*, **9**, (1), pp. 10–11, at p. 10: 'Hospices absorb a substantial amount of resources. Expenditure on services has been estimated at £54 million in 1988/89, excluding the costs of capital development which are likely to be large.' Total public funding is difficult to assess because of the variety of channels through which government money goes to the hospices, often by way of indirect grants.

36   Radcliffe Richards, J. (1994), 'Thinking straight and dying well', Voluntary Euthanasia Society of Scotland *Newsletter*, September, p. 21.

37   Jecker, N. and Schneiderman, L. (1993), 'Medical futility: the duty not to treat', *Cambridge Quarterly of Healthcare Ethics*, **2**, pp. 151–9, at p. 158. See also Lamm, R. (1994), 'Infinite needs – finite resources: the future of healthcare', *Cambridge Quarterly of Healthcare Ethics*, **3**, (1), pp. 83–98.

38   House of Lords Select Committee on Medical Ethics, *op. cit.*, note 5 above, HL Paper 21–I, p. 49: 'We are also concerned that vulnerable people – the elderly, lonely, sick or distressed – would feel pressure, whether real or imagined, to request early death.'

39   Logue, B. (1993), *Death Control and the Elderly in America*, New York: Lexington Books, p. 270.

40   For example, in regard to Alzheimer patients: 'Hospital level services including ICU stays and mechanical ventilation can reverse concurrent acute illnesses but have no beneficial effect on the underlying dementia and are frequently associated with superimposed delirium that exacerbate patient discomfort.' Cogen R., Patterson B., Chavin S. *et al.* (1992), 'Surrogate decision-maker preferences for medical care of severely demented nursing home patients', *Archives of Internal Medicine*, **152**, pp. 1885–8, at p. 1887.

41   Christakis, N. and Asch D. (1993), 'Biases in how physicians choose to withdraw life support', *Lancet*, **343**, pp. 642–6, at p. 645: 'The decision biases that we have identified here may, in some circumstances, prolong the period of dying, increase the suffering of patients and their families, and waste resources.'

42   British Medical Association (1994), *Medical Ethics Today*, London: BMJ Publishing Group, p. 309: 'In the absence of UK national guidelines on making rationing choices, decision-making on rationing is often inconsistent between district and regional NHS authorities and may not be based upon an adequate assessment of the local population's health care needs.' For a BMA discussion of various strategies, see: ibid., pp. 309–15. For a more detailed critique of the Dutch system, see: Van der Wilt, G. (1994), 'A report from the Netherlands – health care and the principle of fair equality of opportunity', *Bioæthics*, **8**, (4), pp. 329–49. For a critique of the USA system see Yarborough, M. (1994), 'The private health insurance industry: the real barrier to healthcare access?', *Cambridge Quarterly of Healthcare Ethics*, **3**, (1), pp. 99–107.

43   Dyer, C. (1993), 'High Court says advance directives are binding', *British Medical Journal*, **307**, p. 1023, which gave one message at the beginning of the article and a different one, by mentioning the enormous loopholes, at the end. See also: Day, M. (1994), 'An act of will', *Nursing Times*, **90**, (10), p. 14; also *BMA Statement on Advance Directives* (1944), London: BMA; also Jeffrey, D. (1994), 'Active euthanasia – time for a decision', *British Journal of General Practice*, **44**,

pp. 136–8, also Medical and Dental Defence Union of Scotland (1994), 'Living Wills', *Summons*, Spring, p. 2.

44 Meredith, S. (1994), 'A Testament of Intent', *Law Society Gazette*, 91 (15): 26–28, expands on this.

45 The basic conditions are delineated by Lord Donaldson in *In re T. (Adult: Refusal of Treatment)* [1992] WLR 782, particularly at 787, and expanded elsewhere in that case.

46 LCCP No. 29, *Mentally Incapacitated Adults and Decision Making*, London: HMSO, 1993, p. 32.

47 Kennedy, *op. cit.*, note 15 above, p. 1196. The reference to 'Bolam' is to *Bolam* v. *Friern Hospital Management Committee* [1957] 1 WLR 582, which held that '… a doctor who had acted in accordance with a practice accepted at the time as proper by a responsible body of medical opinion skilled in the particular form of treatment in question was not guilty of negligence merely because there was a body of competent professional opinion that might adopt a different technique'. The application of the principle outside of negligence cases is controversial: see *Airedale NHS Trust* v. *Bland, op. cit.*, note 7 above, at pp. 822, 845, 861 and 891. A criticism of the test in respect of patients' rights to given by McLean: 'The *Bolam Test* gives rise to the concern that the disinterested decision making, which can reasonably be expected in a court of law, will effectively be subject to control by the interested professional group, and that thereby the rights of the individual patient will take a poor second place to the protection of the doctor's exercise of clinical judgement. Whatever the motivation of the doctor, and no matter how potentially beneficial the therapy, the choice is that of the patient, and it is for the law to set a standard which clearly takes account of patients' rights. Clearly, the Bolam Test is more concerned with professional consensus and standards than it is with the rights of any patient.' McLean, S., *op. cit.*, note 8 above, p. 110.

48 *Re C. (Refusal of Medical Treatment)* [1994] I FLR 31.

49 The patient was, in fact, a schizophrenic. The court, however, was able to determine that his mental impairment did not extend to making him incompetent to make the particular medical decision in question.

50 Schlyter, C. (1992), *Advance Directives and AIDS – An Empirical Study of the Interest in Living Wills and Proxy Decision Making in the Context of HIV/AIDS Care*, London: Centre of Medical Ethics and Law, King's College. See also Emanuel, L., Barry, M., Stoeckle, J. *et al.* (1991), 'Advance directives for medical care – a case for greater use', *New England Journal of Medicine*, **324**, (13), pp. 889–95, at p. 889: '… most patients with the acquired immunodeficiency syndrome (AIDS) seem to want advance directives.'

51 House of Lords, *op. cit.*, note 5 above, HL Paper 21–I, p. 58.

52 *In re T. (Adult: Refusal of Treatment)* [1992] WLR 782, 805.

53 *Clarke* v. *Hurst and Others* [1994] 5 MLR 177. On 30 July 1988, while undergoing epidural treatment, Mr Clarke, then aged 63, went into cardiac arrest. Resuscitative measures were instituted but he suffered serious and irreversible brain damage. As a result he was in a persistent vegetative state with no prospect of any improvement in his condition and no possibility of recovery. Mr Clarke had made a 'living will' directing that if there was no reasonable expectation of his recovery from extreme physical or mental disability he be allowed to die and not be kept alive by artificial means. Judge Thirion granted the application for removing the feeding tube because 'the feeding of the patient did not serve the purpose of supporting human life as it was commonly known …'.

54 *Auckland Area Health Board* v. *Attorney-General* (NZ High Court) [1993] 4 Med. LR 239, 246: 'Whether or not ever-advancing technology and the maturity of thought which may be no more than the product of the passage of time will

lead to a further revision of the moment when a person can be accounted dead is an open issue. That is as it should be. It will ultimately be for the medical profession, sensitive to the values of the community and alert to the requirements of the law, to decide whether the irretrievable destruction of nerve tissues which are as imperative to breathing and heartbeat as are the "tissues" which constitute the brain stem, requires the definition of death to be revised.'

55   The Law Commission have considered ways of developing the 'best interests' criterion in: LCCP No. 29, *op. cit.*, note 46 above, p. 124. For a cross-disciplinary development see: Martyn, S. (1994), 'Substituted judgement, best interests, and the need for best respect', *Cambridge Quarterly of Healthcare Ethics*, **3** (2), pp. 195–208. For the development of such tests since *In the Matter of Claire Conroy (1985)*, 486 A 2d 1209 (NJ Sup Ct) and the relationship between UK and US law in this matter, see, for instance: Kennedy, *op. cit.*, note 15 above, pp. 1179–96.

56   Ogden, *op. cit.*, note 22 above, p. 90: 'Distressing images equal to those of deplorable back-alley abortions are conjured up by the appalling and torturous conditions amongst which some of the assisted deaths in this study took place. This may make a case for state regulation of euthanasia. The data indicate that individuals are involved in euthanasia and assisted suicide in a completely unregulated, underground environment.'

57   'There is an inherent paradox in our laws at the moment which can only serve to confuse and distress. On the one hand our law, using the professionally dominated model, seems to endorse what Jonathan Glover calls non-voluntary euthanasia (in respect of handicapped neonates) while simultaneously rejecting euthanasia in its least contentious, voluntary form'. McLean, S. (1994), 'Decisions about death and dying, memorandum to the House of Lords Select Committee on Medical Ethics' in *op. cit.*, note 5 above, HL Paper 21–II, p. 146.

58   '… when facts portray an active assistant and a passive suicidant, the assistant may be abusive by perpetrating a murder and subsequently disguising the crime as an assisted suicide. Second, the assistant may be abusive by eliminating opportunities for the suicidant to change his mind': Reno, J. (1992), 'A little help from my friends: the legal status of assisted suicide', *Creighton Law Review*, **25**, pp. 1151–83, at p. 1169.

59   'Coroner's euthanasia verdict sets landmark', *The Independent*, 7 October 1994.

60   McLean, S. *op. cit.*, note 57 above, pp. 144–6. Although McLean has, in this volume, demonstrated the flaws of such a rule, the popularity it commands gives it a pragmatic force that cannot be easily overridden.

61   Brody, H. (1992), 'Assisted death – a compassionate response to a medical failure', *New England Journal of Medicine*, **327**, (19), pp. 1384–8, at p. 1384.

62   Wells, *op. cit.*, note 25 above, p. 75: '… there is a need to expose the hidden relationship between motive and criminal culpability and to give critical thought to that between homicide, assisting suicide and euthanasia.'

63   German penal codes, for instance, consider motive in the evaluation of culpability, thus allowing for leniency in spite of the basic rigidity of the law; see Kottow, M. (1988), 'Euthanasia after the Holocaust – is it possible? A report from the Federal Republic of Germany', *Bioethics*, **2**, (1), pp. 58–69. Contrary to the USA and Canada, where motive is immaterial in evaluating legal culpability, the Swiss Penal Code considers the actor's motive as the essential factor in determining the actor's culpability; Ogden, *op. cit.*, note 22 above, pp.. 30–1.

64   *R.* v. *Cox*, [1994] 12 BMLR 38, 48.

65   The best analyses I have seen that demonstrate the lack of transferability of the Dutch system are by Margaret Battin (1994), for instance in her book, *The Least Worst Death*, New York: Oxford University Press, pp. 130–44, 'A dozen caveats concerning the discussion of euthanasia in the Netherlands'. An alternative to both the Dutch and (proposed) US systems is offered by Ogden, *op. cit.*, note 22

above, p. 99: 'A more suitable alternative (to the Dutch system) is to refer all such cases to a quasi-judicial tribunal that reviews applications for aid-in-dying. The onus would be on the patient to give evidence regarding his or her clinical condition, and consideration must be given to alternative treatments. The application would be completed with the assistance of a professionally trained aid-in-dying counsellor who would evaluate the applicant's ability to give informed consent and ensure that all relevant social, medical and psychiatric information was included. Approved applicants would be issued an aid-in-dying licence, which would allow for voluntary euthanasia to be administered under medical supervision, but not necessarily by a physician.' Despite the problems, half of the doctors surveyed said they would like UK law to be similar to that in the Netherlands ('GP calls for changes in the laws on euthanasia' (1994), *Pulse*, **54**, (21), 28 May 1994).

66 Ogden, *op. cit.*, note 22 above.

67 Humphry, D. (1991), *Final Exit*, Oregon: Hemlock Society. Popular manual with instructions on how to kill oneself. Translated into several languages but criticized for its lack of attention to depressive states. Sacks M. and Kemperman, I. (1992), *Final Exit* as a manual for suicide in depressed patients', *American Journal of Psychiatry* (Letters), **149**, (6), p. 842, on ease of availability, Chappell, P., King, R. and Enson M. (1992), '*Final Exit* and the risk of suicide', *Journal of the American Medical Association* (Letters), **267**, (22), p. 3027, or lack of scientific underpinning. The more recent *Departing Drugs* (Docker, C. and Smith C. (1993), Edinburgh: VESS, restricted availability) gives very different information on barbiturates and other drugs, based on extensive literature searches, worldwide consultation, evidence of failed suicides, and clinical trials of drugs in euthanasia in the Netherlands.

68 For an analysis of the legal position in the UK regarding acts and omissions, see Kennedy, *op. cit.*, note 15 above, pp. 1203–10.

69 'Doctors caring for patients are under a *duty* to care for their patients; any liability for their conduct will turn on whether they have breached this duty, *whether by act or omission*', *Id.* p. 1210.

70 Eddy, D. (1994), 'A conversation with my mother', *Journal of the American Medical Association*, **272**, (3), pp. 179–81. Sutcliffe, J. (1994), 'Dehydration: benefit or burden to the dying patient?', *Journal of Advanced Nursing*, **19**, pp. 71–6, (1994), 'Terminal dehydration', *Nursing Times*, **90**, (6), pp. 60–3. Phillips, P., *et al.*, (1984), 'Reduced thirst after water deprivation in healthy elderly men', *New England Journal of Medicine*, **311**, (12), pp. 753–9. Billings, J. (1985), 'Comfort measures for the terminally ill: is dehydration painful?', *Journal of the American Geriatrics Society*, **33**, (11), pp. 808–10. Printz, L. (1988), 'Is withholding hydration a valid comfort measure in the terminally ill?', *Geriatrics*, **43**, (11), pp. 84–7. Lover, D. (1984), 'Terminal dehydration', *Lancet* (Letters), 15 September p. 63. Collaud, T. and Rapin, C. (1991), 'Dehydration in dying patients: study with physicians in French-speaking Switzerland', *Journal of Pain and Symptom Management*, **6**, (4), pp. 230–40. Burge, F. (1993), 'Dehydration symptoms of palliative care in cancer patients', *Journal of Pain and Symptom Management*, **8**, (7) pp. 454–64. Lichter, I. and Hunt, E. (1990), 'The last 48 hours of life', *Journal of Palliative Care*, **6**, (4), pp. 7–15; Siegler, M. and Shiedermayer, D. (1987), 'Should fluid and nutritional support be withheld from terminally ill patients: tube feeding in hospice-settings', *American Journal of Hospice Care*, March–April, pp. 32–5, also Miller, R. and Albright, P. (1989), 'What is the role of nutritional support and hydration in terminal cancer-patients?', *American Journal of Hospice Care*, November–December, pp. 33–8. Printz, L. (1992), 'Terminal dehydration, a compassionate treatment', *Archives of Internal Medicine*, **152**, pp. 697–700. Andrews, M. and Levine A. (1989), 'Dehydration in the terminal patient: per-

ception of hospice nurses', *American Journal of Hospice Care*, January–February, pp. 31–4. Thomasma, D., Micetich, K. and Steinecker, P. (1986), 'Continuance of nutritional care in the terminally ill patient', *Critical Care Clinics*, **2**, (1), pp. 61–71. Bernat, J., Gert B. and Mogielnicki, R. (1993), 'Patient refusal of hydration and nutrition – an alternative to physician-assisted suicide or voluntary active euthanasia', *Archives of Internal Medicine*, **153**, pp. 2723–8. Frederick, G. (1993), 'An easy alternative to assisted suicide', *Globe & Mail*, 23 September; Ahronheim, J. and Gasner, M. (1990), 'The sloganism of starvation', *Lancet*, 3 February, p. 278.

71   Gillick, M., Hesse, K. and Mazzapica, N. (1993), 'Medical technology at the end of life – what would physicians and nurses want for themselves?', *Archives of Internal Medicine*, 22 November, **153**, pp. 2542–7, at p. 2542: 'We conclude that physicians and nurses, who have extensive exposure to hospitals and sick patients, are unlikely to wish aggressive treatment if they become terminally ill, demented, or are in a persistent vegetative state. Many would also decline aggressive care on the basis of age alone, especially in the presence of functional impairment.'

72   For an argument as to why the elderly have a unique claim to an ethical, unobstructed suicide, see Carpenter, B. (1993), 'A review and new look at ethical suicide in advanced age', *Gerontologist*, **33**, (3), pp. 359–65.

73   Hunt, R. (1994), 'Palliative Care – the rhetoric–reality gap' in H. Kuhse (ed.), *Willing to Listen, Wanting to Die*, Victoria, Australia: Penguin, p. 121. As an aid to assessing the realities, Hunt also provides a useful chart of the prevalence and severity of symptoms experienced by 100 cancer patients and the extent to which treatment helped (ibid., p. 120).

74   Ibid., p. 126.

75   For an example of abuse of living will provisions in connection with cost-cutting (living wills not being distinguished from DNR orders), see Stone, J. (1994), 'Advance directives, autonomy and unintended death', *Bioethics*, **8**, (3), pp. 223–46.

76   Mills, E. (1994), 'The greying of Europe – how can health systems cope?', *Economist*, 12 February, p. 24.

77   In other words, if age-based rationing is introduced in any form, it must be based on expected time left until death, not on a fixed cut-off age; even though resources are redirected to the individual at an earlier, rather than later, age in life.

78   Battin, M., *op. cit.*, note 65 above, pp. 74–6. See, also, arguing that a universal solution to rationing criteria is perhaps undesirable, Campbell, C. (1989), 'On James F. Childress: answering every person', *Second Opinion*, 11 July, pp. 118–44, pp. 133–4: 'The selection of ethically acceptable criteria for rationing conditions the adoption of an appropriate procedure. However, the choice of criteria will itself be constrained by the pluralism of contemporary society as well as by basic anthropological convictions.' Battin asserts (ibid., p. 77) that although '... there is a cogent argument for the moral preferability of a quite startling form of age rationing in a scarcity situation – voluntary but socially encouraged aged killing or self-killing of the elderly as their infirmities overcome them, in preference to the medical abandonment they would otherwise face – this is in no way a recommendation for the introduction of such practices in our present world.'

79   Wal and Dillman, *op. cit.*, note 19 above.

80   Ibid., p. 1346.

81   Kilner, J. (1990), *Who Lives? Who Dies? Ethical Criteria in Patient Selection*, New Haven: Yale University Press, p. 230. Kilner notes two exceptional circumstances to the proposals. On the occasions when a favoured group criterion is

legitimate, it is a prerequisite criterion – alongside of medical benefit and willingness to accept treatment – that must be satisfied by any recipient of the resource involved; limited applications of the ability-to-pay criterion, on the other hand, should not be made until a patient has actually been chosen according to the selection procedure outlined. On point (2) Kilner says: 'Patients preferred according to the latter two criteria can wait for priority consideration later, whereas those whose death is imminent cannot. Conflicts between the last two criteria are unlikely since the special-responsibilities criterion so rarely applies. Should a conflict arise in any particular case, priority is to be accorded wherever the greater number of lives is at stake. Ties are to be broken through a lottery'. (Ibid., p. 293).

82   LCCP No. 129, *op. cit.*, note 46 above, pp. 31 and 76.

83   For a fuller examination of living will legislation in other jurisdiction and its interconnection, see Docker, C. (1995), 'Advance directives/living wills' in S. McLean (ed.), *Contemporary Issues in Law, Medicine and Ethics*, Aldershot: Dartmouth (in press).

84   Emanuel, L. and Emanuel, E. (1993), 'Decisions at the end of life guided by communities of patients', *Hastings Center Report*, September–October, pp. 6–14, pp. 7–8.

85   Lynne, J. and Teno, J. (1993), 'After the patient self-determination act – the need for empirical research on formal advance directives', *Hastings Center Report*, January–February, pp. 20–4, p. 21: 'A flurry of articles has documented that surrogates (next of kin, usually) err substantially in predicting patient preferences.' See also Diamond, W., Jernigan, J., Moseley, R., Messina, V. and McKeown, R. (1989), 'Decision-making ability and advance directive preferences in nursing home patients and proxies', *Gerontologist*, **29**, (5), pp. 622–6, p. 625: '... patients with compromised decision making may be more likely to request aggressive therapeutic intervention. Discrepancies between stated preference and AD form signing, as well as between proxy and patient preferences, arose with sufficient frequency to merit concern.' Also, Hare, J., Pratt, C. and Nelson, C. (1992), 'Agreement between Patient and Their Self-Selected Surrogates on Difficult Medical Decisions', *Archives of Internal Medicine*, May, **152**, pp. 1049–54, p. 1049: '... within individual pairs, agreement on treatment occurred only 70% of the time even though surrogates were asked to base their treatment decisions on substituted judgement.' And '... physicians and spouses are no more accurate in predicting the treatment preferences of patients than would be expected by chance alone ...' And at p. 1053: 'Clearly confidence on the part of surrogates does not necessarily ensure the surrogates' accurate determination of patients' wishes.' And '... surrogates are often required to make emotion-laden decisions on the basis of an imperfect set of "facts"'. Also, Ouslander, J., Tymchuk, A. and Rahbar, B. (1989), 'Health care decisions among elderly long-term care residents and their potential proxies', *Archives of Internal Medicine*, **149**, pp. 1367–72, p. 1367: 'Comparisons were made between decisions made by the elderly participants and predictions of those decisions by potential proxies, including the participant's closest relative and a nurse, a social worker, and a physician in the facility. There was a low rate of agreement between decisions made by the elderly participant and the decisions the potential proxies thought they would make.' Also, Seckler, A., Meier, D. and Mulvihill, M. *et al.* (1991), 'Substituted judgement: how accurate are proxy predictions?', *Annals of Internal Medicine*, **115**, (2), pp. 92–8, at p. 92: 'Although patients predicted that both their physicians (90%) and family members (87%) would accurately predict their wishes, neither family members nor physicians, in fact, were able to accurately predict patients' wishes ...'. At p. 95 '... physicians did no better than chance alone in predicting the wishes of their patients...' and '...

most of the patients incorrectly believed that their designated family members and physicians would accurately predict their wishes'. And: 'Using hypothetical scenarios, the investigators found poor agreement between healthy elderly patients, their spouses, and their physicians concerning decisions for resuscitation.' See also Zweibel, N. and Cassel, C. (1989), 'Treatment choices at the end of life: a comparison of decisions by older patients and their physician-selected proxies', *Gerontologist*, **29**, (5), pp. 615–21, at p. 618: '... the proportion of pairs in which the patient would want the proxy to make a decision opposite the one the proxy reported she would make ranges from 24% for tube feeding up to 44% and 50% respectively for resuscitation and chemotherapy.' At p. 620: 'Our findings on preferences for resuscitation tend to support those of Uhlmann and colleagues in the only other study examining the ability of proxies to predict patient preferences for life-sustaining treatment. In both studies, proxies were often unable to accurately report patient treatment preferences.'

86   Bresnahan, J. (1993), 'Medical Futility or the Denial of Death?', *Cambridge Quarterly of Healthcare Ethics*, **2**, pp. 197–17, p. 215: '[relatives who] ... answer with the fatal words, "Do everything," because they translate the question as a challenge to prove their love for and fidelity to this person.'

87   Proxies should still be consulted however. As Lord Donaldson said in *Re T (op. cit.*, note 52 above, at p. 787): '... the next of kin has no legal right to consent or to refuse consent. This is not to say that it is an undesirable practice if the interests of the patient will not be adversely affected by the delay. I say this because contact with the next of kin may reveal that the patient has made an anticipatory choice which, if clearly established and applicable in the circumstances – two major "ifs" – would bind the practitioner.'

88   Mower, W. and Barraff, L. (1993), 'Advance directives – effect of directive on physicians' therapeutic decisions', *Archives of Internal Medicine*, 8 February, **53**, pp. 375–81, at p. 375. Also at p. 375: 'Respondents were more likely to withhold cardiopulmonary resuscitation when given a therapy-specific advance directive v. general-statement advance directive, 84% v. 73% respectively. With a therapy-specific advance directive that was supported by a proxy and prior patient–physician discussion, 100% of physicians were willing to withhold cardiopulmonary resuscitation.'

89   Diamond, for instance, observes: 'Presenting the AD form alone without interview and discussion may elicit inaccurate preferences.' Diamond, *op. cit., supra*, note 85 above, p. 626.

90   Annas, G. (1991), 'The health care proxy and the living will', *New England Journal of Medicine*, **324**, (17), pp. 1210–13, p. 1210: 'The term "living will" was coined by Luis Kutner in 1969 to describe a document in which a competent adult sets forth directions regarding medical treatment in the event of his or her future incapacitation. The document is a will in the sense that it spells out the person's directions. It is "living" because it takes effect before death.' See also Kutner, L. (1969), 'Due process of euthanasia: the living will, a proposal', *Indiana Law Journal*, pp. 539–54.

91   Kielstein, R. and Sass, H. (1993), 'Using stories to assess values and establish medical directives', *Kennedy Institute of Ethics Journal*, **3**, (3), pp. 303–25, in its entirety for a discussion of these phases. An example of a living will document by the present writer that includes both a medical directive and a values history can be found, for instance, in Barr, A., Biggar, J., Dalgleish, A. and Stevens, H. (1994), *Drafting Wills in Scotland*, Edinburgh: Butterworths/Law Society of Scotland, pp. 97–100. Values histories tend to be dialogue-, story- or scenario-based: an example of the first is published by the Center for Health Law and Ethics at the University of New Mexico, of the second in Kielstein, ibid., of the third in Schneiderman, note 92 below, Table 3.

92 For further information on the values history, see especially Schneiderman, L., Pearlman, R., Kaplan, R., Anderson, J. and Rosenberg, E. (1992), 'Relationship of general advance directive instructions to specific-life sustaining treatment preferences in patients with serious illness', *Archives of Internal Medicine*, **152**, pp. 2114–22. For instance, at p. 2120: 'Patients often are not equipped to make well-informed judgements on the basis of their limited medical knowledge, and asking them to complete a checklist of procedures may direct attention away from more important issues of values and goals.' And '... we suggest that advance directive instruments should be developed that enable patients to express their wishes in terms of quality of life under varying clinical states.' And 'The rationale is that patients are fully capable of knowing and expressing their wishes with respect to conditions under which they would prefer not to be kept alive and that physicians, through their training and experience, are best able to understand which treatments (or lack of treatments) best meet their patients' wishes.' A very extended example is provided in Lambert, P., Gibson, J. and Nathanson, P. (1990), 'The values history: an innovation in surrogate decision-making', *Law, Medicine & Health Care*, **18**, (3), pp. 202–12.

93 Roe, J., Goldstein, M., Massey, K. and Pascoe, D. (1992), 'Durable power of attorney for health care: a survey of senior center participants', *Archives of Internal Medicine*, **152**, pp. 292–6, at p. 295. See also Kielstein, *op. cit.*, note 91, above, p. 313: 'Many clinicians, lawyers and ethicists believe that traditional advance directive forms are largely ineffective in providing sufficient information on values, preferences, and guidance for medical intervention. Story-based value assessments and directives and other narrative methods that employ the development, evaluation, and integration of stories into a person's own life story are an alternative to traditional directives. Since story-based assessments and directives do not provide ready-made recipes for medical intervention, they challenge good clinical practice to integrate value assessment with medical assessment and improved physician-patient interaction into on-going stories of cure and care.'

94 Danis, for instance, noted: 'In an analysis of 96 outcome events (hospitalization or death in the nursing home), care was consistent with previously expressed wishes 75 percent of the time; however, the presence of the written advance directive in the medical record did not facilitate consistency.' And that 'The effectiveness of written advance directives is limited by inattention to them and by decisions to place priority on considerations other than the patient's autonomy.' Danis, M., Southerland, L. and Garrett, J. *et al.* (1991), 'A prospective study of advance directives for life-sustaining care', *New England Journal of Medicine*, **324**, (13), pp. 882–8, p. 882.

95 Molloy, D., Harrison, C., Farrugia, M. and Cunje, A. (1993), 'The Canadian experience with advance treatment directives', *Humane Medicine*, **9**, (1), pp. 70–6, at p. 72: 'Surveys of the attitudes of physicians and nurses to health care directives show support for their use; still, when confronted with them, a significant proportion of these professionals ignore the written directives and provide care incompatible with patients' choices.'

96 Patients who have been in PVS for more than twelve months, for instance, should not need recourse to a living will to have treatment discontinued – proper medical guidelines would generally be more appropriate.

97 It may be inadvisable to attempt to extend the use of living wills to cater for voluntary euthanasia. They also completely ignore the wide area of decision-making for competent patients. Similarly, their lack of prevalence, even among incompetent patients who could benefit from them, is such that other process mechanisms need to be investigated. These areas may be interrelated and a consistent approach is, I believe, called for. As living wills generally concen-

trate on life-prolonging treatment only, they may not even cover the most common and necessary areas of advance decision-making; as Ouslander observed: 'Decisions about cardiopulmonary resuscitation (CPR) among the extremely old and frail geriatric population, especially in nursing homes, may be viewed as moot because of the abysmal survival rate of CPR in this patient population. Decisions about eternal feeding, on the other hand, may be critical because more and more people are living to an age when self-feeding becomes problematic due to advanced dementia, stroke, Parkinson's disease or other conditions.' Ouslander, J., Tymchuk, A. and Krynski, M. (1993), 'Decisions about enteral tube feeding among the elderly', *Journal of the American Geriatrics Society*, **41**, pp. 70–7, at p. 73.

98   Garrett, J., Harris, R., Norburn, J., Patrick, D. and Danis, M. (1993), 'Life sustaining treatments during terminal illness: who wants what?', *Journal of General Internal Medicine*, 8 July, pp. 361–8, at p. 361.

99   Emanuel, E., and Emanuel, L. (1992), 'Proxy decision making for incompetent patients: an ethical and empirical analysis', *Journal of the American Medical Association*, **267**, (15), pp. 2067–71, p. 2070. And generally: Emanuel and Emanuel. *op. cit.*, note 84 above.

9 Death and Dying: One Step at a Time?

J.K. MASON
Honorary Fellow, Faculty of Law, University of Edinburgh

In so far as none of us has ever died, euthanasia is the one subject on which it is impossible to say that a given view is right or wrong. We have no way of knowing whether the pain of dying is any easier or worse than is the pain of existence, while for those who are theologically minded, death represents an unwitting choice between the extremes of happiness and misery as exemplified by heaven and hell. As Stevenson, L.J. put it when discussing the pros and cons of diminished life:

> Even if a court were competent to decide between the conflicting views of theologians and philosophers and assume an 'afterlife' or non-existence as the basis of the comparison [with a diminished life], how can a judge put a value on the one or the other, compare either alternative with the injured child's life in this world and determine that the child has lost anything without the means of knowing what, if anything, it has gained? … To measure loss of expectation of death would require a value judgment where a crucial factor lies altogether outside the range of human knowledge.[1]

It is, in fact, possible that this underpins the instinctive distinction which society makes between neonatal euthanasia – with which we have almost come to terms – and adult or geriatric euthanasia which is still the subject of intense debate. Whether or not one believes in life beyond the grave, it is inconceivable that an infant devoid of personality could be condemned for sins it has not committed. One major weight is therefore removed from the medico-legal balance between life and assisted death in the case of the neonate. Be that as it may, I believe that there *are* significant distinctions to be made between the management of the very young and of the old when the

161

value of continued life is in dispute; for the purposes of this chapter, I intend to concentrate almost entirely on the adult case.

This chapter will almost certainly represent a minority view and, so far as the volume is concerned, I see myself cast in the role of *advocatus diaboli*. This is, perhaps, not inappropriate. Coming, as I do, from a past generation of doctors, my intuitive training predates the current movement to apply broad-brush philosophical principles to the practice of medicine. This approach must run into difficulty in an ambience where every patient and every clinical situation is different. The principle of the patient's autonomy, for example, cannot be seen as an absolute. It can only exist within the overall framework of the individual case – a framework which includes the complementary autonomy of the individual health carers.[2] One cannot, in my view, say 'Euthanasia is a good thing' or 'Euthanasia is a bad thing'; the best that can be done is to decide whether euthanasia for a *given patient* is or is not an acceptable option.[3] If I distrust the adoption of broad principles in medicine, it follows that I am equally wary of legislation which should, I believe, be, at best, of an enabling nature. To be wary of a project is not, however, to exclude it as a possibility. The purpose of this chapter is not to condemn euthanasia outright but to suggest that we move slowly in our approach to the many problems it raises.

Activity and Passivity

Definitions are especially important in this area and I should outline my own terminology as a preliminary to discussion. Traditionally, euthanasia has been divided into active and passive components. The latter term is falling into disuse and is excluded from the Dutch definition of euthanasia. Arguably a preferable terminology is selective non-treatment. This will not be discussed here in any detail although it is difficult to avoid a comment on the appropriateness or otherwise of making the active/passive distinction. It almost goes without saying that, if the object of one's action or inaction is the death of one's patient, it is irrelevant as to intention whether one adopts passive or active means to that end. Transposed into the language of philosophical ethics:

> [W]hile there may be some social benefits in distinguishing between actively 'allowing to die' and painlessly killing ... there is, I believe, no other moral difference, and doctors who accept such 'allowing to die' ... should not deceive themselves into believing that there is such a difference.[4]

While this must, of course, be true in theory, it is difficult to accept in the everyday practice of medicine. There *is* a powerful psychological distinction to be made, which even the harshest critics of an unmodified sanctity of life doctrine find important,[5] and doctors may be grateful to an influential philosopher for his observation:

> We are, here, noting a deep human intuition which it might be unwise to tamper with in the name of logic.[6]

Moreover, one cannot ignore the distinction made by the law. There can be no clearer statement of the current position than that of Lord Browne-Wilkinson:

> [The] conclusion I have reached will appear to some to be almost irrational. How can it be lawful to allow a patient to die slowly …, but unlawful to produce his immediate death by a lethal injection …? I find it difficult to find a moral answer to that question. But it is undoubtedly the law and nothing I have said casts doubts on the proposition that the doing of a positive act with the intention of ending life is and remains murder.[7]

It follows that, illogical though it may be, the distinction must be made.

There can be few places where the subject of euthanasia has been so thoroughly discussed and refined as it has been in the Netherlands, and inevitably the Dutch attitudes are regarded as benchmarks from which to argue. A major terminological innovation was the coining of the phrase 'Medical Decisions Concerning the End of Life' (MDELs) to indicate a wide-ranging concept which includes the active administration of a drug, the withdrawal or withholding of treatment and the refusal of requests for euthanasia or assisted suicide.[8] MDELs are taken in some 34 per cent of all deaths in the Netherlands and, within that umbrella term, euthanasia, which is defined there as the intervention of an outside party with the specific intention of ending a person's life at the request of that person,[9] seems to be practised in 1.8 per cent of all deaths. The definition describes what most of us would call active voluntary euthanasia. The Dutch have, however, muddied the waters by introducing the sub-category of life-terminating activity *without* the explicit request of the patient.[10] It is difficult to see this as anything other than a euphemism for active *involuntary* euthanasia and it is, I suggest, such extensions of the ambit of euthanasia which underpin the opposition to the concept.

Euthanasia and the Doctor

It is my intention in this chapter to address the issue of active voluntary euthanasia and to do this, primarily, from the doctor's standpoint. In so doing, I am essentially posing two basic questions: first,
do we *want* legalized euthanasia and, second, do we want our doctors to be involved? With regard to the first question, such amor-
phous statements as 'almost three-quarters of a sample of the general
public agreed with the principle of euthanasia'[11] are unimpressive. It
is almost impossible to avoid selectivity in such surveys which are
also subject to the vagaries inherent in all public opinion polls. The
important attitudes to a service are those voiced by the likely users of
that service, and, in this particular context, it is the voices of the aged
and the ageing which need to be heard.[12] The attitudes of those
providing the service may also be determined by age. A recent major
survey of doctors' responses to the concept of euthanasia[13] either
found no significant association with age or was silent on the subject
according to the several questions asked. Nonetheless, one of my
most abiding memories is of the chilling words written as long ago
as 1980:

> How large a factor is age in deciding to relax therapeutic efforts seems
> to depend somewhat on the age of the physicians making the deci-
> sions.[14]

Age is, of course, not the only determinant of the quality of life. No
discussion of public attitudes to euthanasia should omit consideration of a study of tetraplegics undertaken in 1985.[15] A fit young
person can scarcely imagine a more terrible existence than that of
total paralysis. Yet, when 21 tetraplegics were asked whether, in the
event of further temporary ventilation becoming necessary, they
would prefer to be allowed to die, 18 replied 'No' and two were
undecided.

It is fully conceded that the foregoing discussion reaches no firm
conclusion. What it should do, however, is to promote considerable
caution before we find ourselves believing that euthanasia should be
legalized in the UK implicitly because *the public wants it*. And it
should be noted that this is not necessarily the case even in the very
liberal ambience of the western USA.[16]

Paternalism and Self-determination

Nevertheless there is little doubt that the pro-euthanasia lobby is
becoming steadily more articulate and that the pressures on the medical profession are increasing.[17] The definitive debate has been cata-

lysed by the collateral promotion of the right to refuse treatment as an integral aspect of the patient's autonomy. Patient autonomy has been elevated to the status of dogma over a relatively few years, and the fact that it has been developed very largely by lawyers and philosophers means that sight of the doctor's professional autonomy has been lost along the way. Whether this should be so is debatable at least, and there is perceptibly increasing academic support for recognition of the fact that autonomy and self-determination cannot be regarded as absolute rights.[18] The patient and his or her doctor form an inseparable therapeutic alliance, and to see the patient's right to refuse treatment as being written in stone is to nullify the doctor's intuition and training. Conflict as to the *choice* of treatment may well sharpen the doctor's intellectual approach and improve medical practice. Adulation of the patient's right to *refuse* treatment can have the opposite effect, and it is asking a great deal of the doctor to stand back and watch a treatable patient die. The prospect of legislation in the UK comparable to the Medical Treatment Act 1988 of Victoria, Australia is worrying in the absence of reports as to its true functioning. The Victorian Act not only provides a statutory basis for refusing treatment but also introduces the offence of medical trespass (s.6) which is committed by a doctor who gives treatment knowing that a relevant refusal-of-treatment certificate exists. Moreover, the doctor cannot rely on his ethical conscience in his or her defence.[19] We then reach the unenviable situation of which it has been said:

> A humane physician, just like a lay rescuer, may still have to proceed with life-saving or curative treatment even at the risk of incurring criminal penalty.[20]

Statute, perhaps, relieves the doctor of difficult decision-making but it may, at the same time, do significant harm to the Hippocratic ethos.

Even so, there is widespread academic disapproval when doctors protest and are supported by the courts in so doing.[21] I would not condone manifest involuntary treatment, nor would the great majority of medical practitioners. Nevertheless, just as there is scope to consider the capacity of a person to *consent* to treatment – and thus open the door to morally acceptable non-voluntary therapy – so there is room to consider the quality of *refusal* of treatment. I have far greater sympathy for the past Master of the Rolls, Lord Donaldson, in respect of many of his decisions – which were, in my view, designed essentially to avoid unnecessary waste of human life – than have the majority of commentators who saw such medico-legal paternalism as an affront to the doctrine of self-determination.[22] My principal concern with the latter view is that it conditions an insidi-ous change of attitude on the part of health carers. At the least, it fosters a tendency to perceive the option of death as preferable to treatment when there is doubt as to the course to be adopted;[23] at worst, it offers the tired doctor the opportunity to abrogate his or her responsibilities by leaving decision-making to the patient – and it must be remembered that many emergency decisions are taken by relatively junior doctors who are both young and subject to many extraneous pressures.

None of the above would be of great concern in the context of this chapter were it not for the fact that the issues of treatment refusal and suicide are very closely related. Certainly, suicide in its legal sense requires the intention to achieve one's own death, and this may not be so in the case of treatment refusal. In practice, however, the distinction can be very fine. It is all very well for Lord Donaldson to say of a dying woman who refuses a blood transfusion:

> There is no suggestion that Miss T wants to die … This appeal is about the 'right to choose how to live'. This is quite different, even if the choice, when made, may make an early death more likely.[24]

But the doctor in the intensive care unit is unlikely to appreciate such subtle shades of meaning. It is only a matter of time before any distinc-tion becomes blurred and an obligation not to treat in the presence of refusal is seen as an obligation not to interfere in what appears to be a case of uncompleted suicide. It is then only a further short step to regarding assisted or accelerated death, or life termination without the specific request of the patient, as not merely an option available to doctors but, rather, a service which it is their duty to provide – a progression which can be seen as an example of what Keown has called the 'logical slope'[25] or a change of attitude deriving from incre-mental changes in the interpretation of rules. Such pliancy makes for bad medicine, including a temptation to regard euthanasia as a *pre-ferred* option – a proposition which may well have underwritten the British Medical Association's opposition to change in the existing law.[26]

The Netherlands Experience

We can look to the Netherlands for indications as to whether such incremental changes operate in practice. Data from that source are difficult to analyse due to the extraordinary situation whereby the doctor who reports a euthanasia death – as he is legally expected to do – has no guarantee of immunity from criminal prosecution; conse-quently, the extent of physician-assisted death is almost certainly underreported.

Nevertheless, threading one's way through the statistics now available,[27] it seems that euthanasia, as defined, is responsible for one in 25 deaths occurring in the home in the Netherlands, where some 50 per cent of all deaths are domiciliary, and that about half the country's doctors do not report these deaths as is required by law. This figure becomes 2.6 per cent if van der Maas' prospective study of practice subsequent to an in-depth interview is considered alone. More important in the present context are the facts. First, in some 0.8 per cent of all deaths – that is, in about 1000 instances per year – the doctor prescribed a drug with the intended goal of shortening the patient's life but *without* an explicit request from the patient, and this decision was most commonly taken in hospital. The fact that life was shortened in the great majority of cases by less than a week makes the information even more disturbing. Why were these life-terminations, with all their associated emotional conflicts, carried out? It can hardly be said that they were designed to prevent *prolonged* suffering; indeed, the short expectation of life in two of the three exemplar cases is emphasized.[28] Concern for the future can hardly be avoided if one reads such data alongside any article describing the managerial advantages of a rapid turnover in bed occupancy in the UK National Health Service. Again, if van der Maas' prospective study is considered in isolation, the figure for non-voluntary euthanasia rises to 1.6 per cent – an increase of 100 per cent. The anomaly has been interpreted in different ways. Pijnenborg and her colleagues[29] considered it to be due to the grey area lying between life-terminating acts and the alleviation of pain with high doses of opiates, Keown,[30] on the other hand, suggests that the design of the prospective trial simply makes its results more reliable. It seems that one can bend the Dutch data in almost any direction one wishes.

Second, in some 2 per cent of all deaths, the distinction between voluntary, non-voluntary and involuntary ending of life was blurred. In short, there is always room for interpretation; there is an extensive grey area, as would almost certainly be the case in the UK in similar circumstances.

Third, and finally, there is the case of the Dutch doctor, who assisted the suicide of a woman who was neither physically nor mentally ill but who wanted to die.[31] The circumstances surrounding this case, as they have been reported in the UK literature, seem remarkable by any standards. The physician concerned could find no evidence of psychosis or of hysteria, personality disorder or depression that would respond to treatment; the patient's position was, therefore, that she was physically healthy, she was competent, she was suffering unbearably from the death of her two sons and she had a 'voluntary, well-considered and durable wish to die'.[32] Her doctor openly gave her a lethal preparation and reported the death to the

authorities. Local and appeal judges refused to prosecute; it was left
to the Solicitor General to take the matter as a test case to the Dutch
Supreme Court which confirmed that there was no legal distinction
to be made between mental and physical suffering – although, at the
same time, admitting that the definition of 'unbearable' was more
difficult in the former condition. The doctor concerned, Dr Chabot,
was eventually found guilty of assisting a suicide on the technicality
that his colleagues whom he consulted for further opinions did not
themselves see the patient! However, no penalty was imposed, and
Dr Chabot is now calling for a test case which would allow euthanasia for elderly people who, while currently healthy, wished to die
rather than suffer dependency on others. Battin[33] insists that any
abuse of legal voluntary euthanasia can be contained. But it is difficult to accept this with equanimity when the courts themselves are
applying the oil to an already smooth slope.

The Role of the Doctor

So we come to the second basic question: do we want our doctors to
be euthanasists? If my answer is to be 'no', it will be pointed out that
12 per cent of British doctors who answered a questionnaire admitted to having practised active voluntary euthanasia,[34] and the re-
markably sympathetic reaction to the prosecution and conviction of
Dr Cox[35] will be cited. But, as has already been said, questionnaires
are by no means ideal research tools, and I am one of the apparent
few who do not see Dr Cox as a martyr in the cause of beneficent
medicine. This is not the place to argue my reasons; in general, I
think that Dr Cox's public conduct bears comparison with that of Dr
Syme in Australia who announced his willingness to go to court to
defend the right to die an easy death.[36] But these are peripheral
issues. My central concern rests on what I see as the changing image
of medicine and on society's changing demands on the medical profession.

In my view, the Hippocratic ethos has taken enough hard knocks
in the last 50 years. It cannot take many more without the medical
profession undergoing a radical change in both practice and perspective; thus, the doctor's role in any form of legalized euthanasia is a
matter of major concern. Medical responsibility for diagnosis and
prognosis as to whether a condition is, say, incurable or terminal
cannot be avoided. A medical practitioner, even if not a qualified
psychiatrist, must ensure the validity of any request for termination
of life – always assuming that an unconstrained decision is *ever*
possible in the conditions envisaged. But whether doctors should be
involved in the actual euthanasic process is a different question.
Otlowski[37] has argued the case for medical involvement very force-

fully – even to the extent of supporting the concept of a specialism in the practice[38] (the true cynic might suggest a sub-specialty of geriatric medicine). None of the arguments against the exclusion of doctors seems to be insuperable, and we would do well to remember the words of Alexander Capron:

> I never want to have to wonder whether the physician coming into my hospital room is wearing the white coat of a healer ... or the black hood of the executioner. Trust between patient and physician is simply too important and too fragile to be subjected to the unnecessary strain.[39]

This statement, of course, describes *involuntary* euthanasia, and we have been discussing *voluntary* euthanasia. Nonetheless can we have the one without risking the rise of the other? It seems almost impossible to refine any relatively wide-ranging legislation which would not be susceptible to movement down Keown's 'practical slope', as exemplified by the case of Dr Chabot; nor would it be long before the ethical slope became crowded and non-voluntary euthanasia becomes condoned as it has been in Holland.

Yet, it has to be accepted that not everyone agrees with Capron's analysis. Otlowski, for example, suggests that concerns of this sort are largely unfounded and that the administration of active euthanasia at the patient's request can be seen as: 'a legitimate part of the doctor's role as health care professional'.[40] In saying this, she depends heavily on the reported experience in the Netherlands. Is it valid to do so? Admiraal, in Chapter 5 of this volume, tells us that, when discussing euthanasia with the patient and his or her relatives, he divests himself of his professional role and assumes that of a friend of the family. While in no way inferring that this is anything other than a totally sympathetic approach to a unique situation, I suggest that this role change is one that is determined by the circumstances. It may be that euthanasia *has* to be divorced from 'doctoring' if it is to be acceptable and that Capron is proved right by those who would deny his polemic. In the end, we should probably be relieved that the House of Lords Select Committee[41] did not recommend far-reaching and possibly precipitate legislation to legalize active voluntary euthanasia and that the government has accepted their view;[42] it is noteworthy that some of the more 'liberal' US states have also rejected the concept of doctor-assisted suicide.[43]

A Gradual Approach

However, that is not to say that *some* legislation, designed to clear up the fringes of the euthanasia debate and to adopt a cautious approach to the principal issues, should not be introduced. I suggest that Parliament could look first at the persistent vegetative state and then, in turn – and in ascending order of complexity – assisted suicide, voluntary active euthanasia and, finally, 'mercy killing' both within and without the medical arena. I propose here to discuss only the management of the persistent vegetative state. Nevertheless, the morality of all these procedures depends ultimately on a knowledge of the patient's wishes. It follows that the logical first step is to define the legal position of the advance directive or 'living will'.

The Status of the Advance Directive

Despite the apparent success of advance directives or 'living wills' in the USA where the majority of states now give statutory authority to such directives, it is still hard to see them as panaceas in the euthanasia debate. In the first place, it must be extremely difficult to draft an advance directive which will be unequivocal in any situation. It follows that, if a living will is to be regarded as a legally binding document, it must be prepared with legal precision and with the assistance of both a lawyer and a physician. Two extremes seem possible: the directive can be very narrow and deal only with specific issues, or it can be so general as to represent little more than an expression of the patient's overall views.[44] Both solutions have their advantages. Second, it is difficult to envisage any UK legislation in this field that did not include some form of 'opt-out' clause in deference to the doctor's professional conscience. Much would depend upon its terms, but it is probable that, at the least, it would enable the doctor to withdraw from any such agreement to limit his or her professional expertise; at most, it might empower a doctor to ignore an advance directive if he or she thought that it was in the patient's best interests to do so. In this way, the whole purpose of the directive would be compromised.

The greatest difficulty, however, lies in the possibility, or even probability, of a change of heart on the part of the patient which might, in the circumstances, be impossible for him or her to express; certainly, when I was in clinical practice, I was deeply impressed by the tenacity with which patients would strive for life when the watershed was reached. Inevitably, the responsible physician must wonder whether the directive was created in an unconstrained manner, since the pressures to complete a 'living will', like those to request euthanasia, can be subtle and varied in origin.[45] Even more importantly, he or she must question whether the prevailing conditions are precisely those previously anticipated and whether, in any event, the patient's stated intentions still apply. Lord Donaldson's comment on the situation:

> … what the doctors *cannot* do is to conclude that, if the patient still
> had the necessary capacity in the changed situation [he being now
> unable to communicate], he would have reversed his decision … what
> they *can* do is to consider whether at the time the decision was made it
> was intended by the patient to apply in the changed situation[46]

manages to do little more than demonstrate the complexity of the
doctor's dilemma. And, if that were not enough, we have Staughton,
L.J. saying:

> I cannot find authority that the decision of a doctor as to the existence
> or refusal of consent is sufficient protection, if the law subsequently
> decides otherwise. So the medical profession … must bear the respon-
> sibility unless it is possible to obtain a decision from the courts.[47]

Life for the doctor may be practically, if not ethically, easier in Victoria where, as we have seen, the Medical Treatment Act 1988 prohibits
him or her from questioning a non-treatment certificate!

There is, at present, some confusion as to the true legal status of
the advance directive. The only official statement appears to lie in a
practice note which reads:

> The views of the patient may have been previously expressed, either
> in writing or otherwise. The High Court exercising its inherent juris-
> diction may determine the effect of a purported advance directive as
> to future medical treatment … . In summary, the patient's expressed
> views, if any, will always be a very important component in the deci-
> sions of the doctors and the court.[48]

This is the view of the British Medical Association[49] and of the recent
House of Lords Select Committee.[50] The position has, however, been
confused by the obiter observations of Lords Keith and Goff in *Bland*.[51]
The former said:

> [I]t is unlawful, so as to constitute both a tort and the crime of battery,
> to administer medical treatment to an adult … without his consent … .
> Such a person is completely at liberty to decline to undergo treatment,
> even if the result of his doing so will be that he will die. This extends
> to the situation where the person, in anticipation of his … entering
> into a condition such as PVS, gives clear instructions that in such
> event he is not to be given medical care … designed to keep him alive.

Lord Goff spoke in much the same terms but qualified his statement:

> [I]n such circumstances especial care may be necessary to ensure that
> the prior refusal of consent is still properly to be regarded as appli-
> cable in the circumstances which have subsequently occurred.

Their Lordships clearly regarded an advance directive as binding, and this interpretation appears to have been followed in a later case at first instance in which is 'was common ground that a refusal can take the form of a declaration of intention never to consent in the future or never to consent in some future circumstances'.[52] Lord Goff, at least, however, was able to see the importance of some form of time limitation on the validity of the declaration.

Again, however, the living will focuses attention on death as something we should all be seeking; we seldom hear of an advance directive exhorting doctors to strive for one's life. There is, of course, no reason why such a directive should not be created (see Sommerville, Chapter 3 in this volume) and thus its rarity gives ground for some concern. Not only is death generally the easiest option when the question arises but, in the event of legislation giving legal authority to the advance directive, the fear of litigation for having given apparently unwanted treatment could be very considerable. The pressures on the doctor are therefore heavily biased in favour of non-intervention. I, myself, would hope that a frantic search for a living will is never added to the growing list of defensive measures which doctors have to take nowadays, and would hope even more fervently that the possession of a 'Treatment Card' never becomes a prerequisite for admission to the intensive care unit.

For all these reasons, I believe that the case against legislating for an imperative living will is stronger than that in its favour. There is, however, no reason why such a directive should not be called upon as a very useful aid to the clinician forced to make a treatment decision. In this respect, the alternative legislation – that is, to extend the compass of the Enduring Powers of Attorney Act 1985 (and the Law Reform (Miscellaneous Provisions) (Scotland) Act 1990, s.71) so as to include health-care decisions within the remit of the proxy – has much to commend it and already exists in Australia and the USA.[53] The function of proxies in such circumstances is seen as being advisory only – they should not, for example, be empowered to take a legally binding non-treatment decision on behalf of a principal. They could, however, be powerful advocates for the patient, basing their advice on a knowledge or interpretation of what the individual patient would want. Since the proxy would probably be in a relatively frequent contact with the principal, there would be an opportunity for the steady updating of changing attitudes. 'Substituted judgement' has far more affinity with the concept of patient self-determination than has the inherently paternalistic 'best interests test' and it should be, at least, admitted in evidence as representative of the patient's general views. It goes without saying that the appointed proxy would have to be a disinterested party. Much has been made in recent court decisions of the importance of consultation with the patient's relatives. It may be that this is designed for the protection of the health carers against later litigation; yet it is, indeed, arguable that psychogeriatric patients themselves have more to fear from their heirs than from their medical attendants.

The Persistent Vegetative State

I have isolated the treatment of the persistent vegetative state as constituting the ideal candidate for legislation in the field of euthanasia: the criteria for the diagnosis are clear; the condition is specific and widely understood; and it has been the subject of an exhaustive legal analysis. Moreover, several of their Lordships in *Bland*[54] called for parliamentary intervention.

As is well known, the *Bland* case concerned a request for a High Court declaration that, *inter alia*, the Hospital Trust might lawfully discontinue all life-sustaining treatment and medical support designed to keep the patient alive in a persistent vegetative state in which he had existed for more than three years. Effectively, this crystallized into the question of whether or not feeding by way of a nasogastric tube could be stopped. Many interesting arguments, both legal and moral, were put forward at all stages of the trial but, as an admitted oversimplification, it is suggested here that the case can be usefully regarded as representing little more than an aspect of non-voluntary treatment. In other words, once we regard assisted feeding as medical treatment, we can apply the common law principles which have evolved over a coherent series of legal therapeutic decisions. The justification of non-consensual therapy by way of necessity evaporates once its non-productivity is established; it is then justifiable – and indeed good medical practice – to discontinue that treatment.

Problems associated with medicalizing the *Bland*-type case can be overcome relatively easily. The US courts have had very little difficulty in accepting artificial feeding as treatment,[55] while the House of Lords in *Bland* was unanimously able to see it as, at least, an integral part of medical treatment. Moreover, the overall importance of the medical assessment was agreed. 'In the end', said Lord Goff, 'the decisions to be made in the individual cases must rest with the doctors themselves'.[56] Finally, members of both the Court of Appeal and of the House of Lords expressed the hope that involvement of the courts in these cases would be unnecessary in the future.

It ought, then, to be possible to say that withdrawal of artificial feeding in cases of PVS is now settled in the common law and that further legislation is superfluous. As Lord Browne-Wilkinson said in *Bland*:

In the past, doctors exercised their own discretion, in accordance with medical ethics, in cases such as these. To the great advantage of society, they took the responsibility of deciding whether the perpetuation of life was pointless.[57]

His Lordship, however, went on to say: 'there are now present amongst the medical and nursing staff of hospitals those who ... report doctors who take such decisions to the authorities with a view to prosecution for a criminal offence.' Moreover, it was stressed in a later case [58] that the courts in *Bland* had made plain that their decisions were to be understood as strictly applying to the specific situation – which was generally agreed to be relatively simple – and to no other. There is, therefore, a case to be made out for legislation in this relatively narrow field – legislation which, as noted above, was strongly urged by at least two of the Law Lords in *Bland*.

I would suggest the introduction of, say, a Medical Futility Bill which would be enabling in character and which would merely lay down the conditions under which the withdrawal of futile or non-productive treatment would not be unlawful. A possible framework, which would certainly need refinement, might run along the lines:

It will not be unlawful to withdraw treatment, including physiological replacement therapy such as artificial ventilation and feeding, when at least two independent registered medical practitioners, one of whom must be of consultant status in the relevant specialty, are of the opinion that, either

a) The patient has sustained such damage to the central nervous system that:
    i)   he cannot exist in the absence of continuous care
    ii)   he will never again be able to participate in human relationships or experiences
    iii) continued treatment cannot improve his condition and is, therefore, futile

or

b) The patient's condition is such that treatment would result in a life of such suffering as to render its provision inhumane and the patient is, himself, unable to express an opinion

and the patient's nearest relatives have been consulted.

Definitions – such as those of 'futile', 'treatment' in the various necessary circumstances and the like – could be incorporated within the bill or in a code of practice such as is now being considered by the government;[59] experience with the *Arthur* case[60] suggests that it would be well specifically to exclude uncomplicated mental defect as a reason for withdrawing physiological treatment. In my view, it would be necessary to include a clause enjoining consultation with relatives – one reason, additional to those already discussed, being that disagreement between the health carers and the next of kin would serve to delineate the complex cases which should still be subject to the scrutiny of the High Court.

Further Direction

That is, I believe, as far as we should go in the present climate of opinion. Clearly, however, there is room for expanding sub-paragraph (b) of my suggested clause above so as to include the express wishes of a competent patient and to move, from there, to legalizing physician-assisted suicide.[61] In my view, insufficient distinction has been made between euthanasia in the well-known conditions of terminal illness and intractable pain on the one hand and progressive neurological failure on the other. There are several conceptual differences which distinguish sufferers from the latter as a separate group for whom special considerations may apply. Battin[62] has proposed that the right to determine one's own mode of death is too fundamental for it to be suppressed without compelling reason and the suggestion must make us wonder whether we should be allowing what is, essentially, our fear of the maverick doctor to cloud our view of the problem as a whole. Maverick doctors can be controlled, but the difficulty is that major ethical issues in medicine tend to become politicized. Since politicians do not constitute the most dependable of groups, the problem can be contained by asking them to consider such matters one step at a time.

Envoi

Since this is the last chapter in this book, I feel entitled to end on a general note and to suggest that we stand back and consider the extent to which the euthanasia problem is of our own making. We are being constantly reminded – and are happy to accept – that we should forego many pleasures, that we should restrict our natural diet, that we should readily accept many irritating restrictions imposed for 'our benefit', and it is probable that, in the not-too-distant future, we will be breeding animals from which to replace our worn-out organs. All of this is done in the cause of 'saving lives' when what is meant is the postponement of the date of death. If we look at the reality, we are engaged in a quest for dementia.

McLean, in Chapter 4 of this volume, puts the meaning of euthanasia in the context of a 'good' or 'happy' death. In the earlier chapters, we have been confronted with the spectre of a lingering death – either painful or insentient – which is terminated as an act of mercy by a doctor. Compare this situation with that of the man who drops dead having sunk a long putt on the eighteenth green to win the match. No matter how well our psychogeriatric wards may be managed, I suggest that it is the latter man who has experienced true euthanasia.

Notes

1   In *McKay* v. *Essex Area Health Authority* [1982] QB 1166 at p. 1181.
2   An apparently reactionary view which is not without modern support. See, for example, Wells, C. [1994], 'Patients, consent and criminal law', *Journal of Social Welfare and Family Law*, **65**.
3   See Parker, M. (1990), 'Moral intuition, good death and ordinary practitioners', *Journal of Medical Ethics*, **16**, p. 28.
4   Gillon, R. (1986), 'Conclusion: the Arthur case revisited', *British Medical Journal*, **292**, p. 543. The fact that the author was discussing neonatal euthanasia at the time is, I think, irrelevant.
5   See Campbell, A.G.M. (1988), 'Ethical issues in child health and disease' in J.O. Forfar (ed.), *Child Health in a Changing Society*, Oxford University Press.
6   Downie, R.S. (1989), 'Modern paediatric practice: an ethical overview' in J.K. Mason (ed.), *Paediatric Forensic Medicine and Pathology*, London: Chapman and Hall.
7   In *Airedale NHS Trust* v. *Bland* (1993) 12 BMLR 64 at 131.
8   van der Maas, P.J., van Delden, J.J.M., Pijnenborg, L. and Looman, C.W.N. (1991), 'Euthanasia and other medical decisions concerning the end of life', *Lancet*, **338**, p. 669. This very wide-ranging survey is critically reviewed by Keown, J.(1994), 'Further reflections on euthanasia in the Netherlands in the light of the Remmelink, 'Report and the van der Maas survey' in L. Gormally (ed.), *Euthanasia, Clinical Practice and the Law*, London: Linacre Centre.
9   van der Wal, G. and Dillmann, R.J.M. (1994), 'Euthanasia in the Netherlands', *British Medical Journal*, **308**, p. 1346.
10 Pijnenborg, L., van der Maas, P.J., van Delden, J.J.M., Looman, C.W.N. (1993), 'Life-terminating acts without explicit request of patient', *Lancet*, **341**, p. 1196.
11 Dawson, J. (1986), 'Easeful death', *British Medical Journal*, **293**, p. 1187.
12 Dutch physicians report very few requests for euthanasia from older patients – the average age at request is 62 for men and 68 for women. See Battin, M. (1992), 'Voluntary euthanasia and the risks of abuse: can we learn anything from the Netherlands?', *Law, Medicine and Health Care*, **20**, p. 133.
13 Ward, B.J. and Tate, P.A. (1994), 'Attitudes among NHS doctors to requests for euthanasia', *British Medical Journal*, **308**, p. 1332.
14 Rhoads, J.E. (1980), 'The right to die and the chance to live', *Journal of Medical Ethics*, **6**, p. 53.
15 Gardner, B.P., Theocleous, F., Watt, J.H.T. and Krishnan, K.R. (1985), 'Ventilation or dignified death for patients with high tetraplegia', *British Medical Journal*, **291**, p. 1620.
16 Morris, M. (1991), 'Washington State rejects euthanasia', *British Medical Journal*, **303**, p. 1223. Rhein, R. (1992), 'California says no to euthanasia', *British Medical Journal*, **305**, p. 1175. The Oregon initiative is discussed in detail in Chapter 5 of this volume.

17 Smith, R. (1992), 'Euthanasia: time for a Royal Commission', *British Medical Journal*, **305**, p. 728. Dean, M. (1993), 'Euthanasia moves up in the medical agenda', *Lancet*, **341**, p. 482.

18 For example, Wells, *op. cit.*, note 2 above.

19 See Lanham, D. (1990), 'The right to choose to die with dignity', *Criminal Law Journal*, **14**, p. 401.

20 Mendelson, D. (1993), 'Medico-legal aspects of the "right to die" legislation in Australia', *Melbourne University Law Review*, **19**, p. 112.

21 See, for example, criticism of *Re R (a minor) (wardship: medical treatment)* (1991) 7 BMLR, 147 by Kennedy, I. (1992), 'Consent to treatment: the capable person' in C. Dyer (ed.), *Doctors, Patients and the Law*, Oxford: Blackwell.

22 Discussed in Mason, J.K. (1993), 'Master of the balancers: non-voluntary therapy under the mantle of Lord Donaldson', [1993], *Juridical Review*, p. 119.

23 The most recent example comes from the guidelines *Dying with Dignity* distributed to doctors in New South Wales: John, D. (1995), 'New South Wales gives guide to dying with dignity', *British Medical Journal*, **306**, p. 1363.

24 In *Re T (adult: refusal of medical treatment* (1992) 9 BMLR, 46 at 49.

25 Keown, J. (1992), 'Some reflections on euthanasia in the Netherlands' in L. Gormally (ed.), *The Dependent Elderly*, Cambridge University Press, ch. 6. Levin, B. (1989), 'Under patient's orders – to kill', *The Times*, 11 December, p. 12 discusses the 'fallacy of the altered standpoint'.

26 British Medical Association (1988), *The Euthanasia Report*, London: BMA.

27 See van der Wal and Dillmann, *op. cit.*, note 9 above, largely comparing their results with those of van der Maas *et al.*, *op. cit.*, note 8 above. See also ch. 5, above.

28 For immediate criticism of the case histories see Pollard, B. (1993), Letter in reply to 'Life terminating acts without explicit request of patient', *Lancet*, **341**, p. 1598.

29 Pijnenborg *et al.*, *op. cit.*, note 10 above.

30 van de Maas, *et al.*, *op. cit.*, note 8 above.

31 Spanjer, M. (1994), 'Mental suffering as justification for euthanasia in Netherlands', *Lancet*, **343**, p. 1630.

32 Sheldon, T. (1994), 'Judges make historic ruling on euthanasia', *British Medical Journal*, **309**, p. 7.

33 Battin, *op. cit.*, note 12 above.

34 Ward, B.J. and Tate, P.A. (1994), 'Attitudes among NHS doctors to requests for euthanasia', *British Medical Journal*, **308**, p. 1332.

35 *R v. Cox* (1992) 12 BMLR, 38.

36 See Ragg, M. (1992), 'Australia: for or against euthanasia?', *Lancet*, **339**, p. 800. Dr Syme publicly declared that he had practised euthanasia; no action was, however, taken either by the police or by the Australian Medical Association.

37 Otlowski, M. (1994), 'Active voluntary euthanasia: options for reform', *Medical Law Review*, **2**, p. 161.

38 See also Crisp, R. (1987), 'A good death: who is to bring it?', *Bioethics*, **1**, p. 74.

39 Capron, A.M. (1986), 'Legal and ethical problems in decisions for death', *Law, Medicine and Health Care*, **14**, p. 141.

40 Otlowski, *op. cit.*, note 37 above.

41 House of Lords Select Committee on Medical Ethics, HL Paper 21-1 (1994).

42 *Government Response to the Report of the Select Committee on Medical Ethics*, Cm 2553, 1994.

43 Greenberg, D.S. (1991), 'Dying, doctors, and politics', *Lancet*, **338**, p. 1446. Rhein, R. (1992), 'California says no to euthanasia', *British Medical Journal*, **305**, p. 1175. Whether or not the courts are moving faster than the legislatures is difficult to decide: see Roberts, J. (1994), 'Decisions in US say that doctors can assist

suicides', *British Medical Journal*, **308**, p. 1255. The acquittal of Dr Kevorkian in a criminal trial hardly makes a precedent, but see also Chapter 6 in this volume.

44   The route which commends itself to the British Medical Association: Sommerville, A. (1993), *Medical Ethics Today*, at p. 162.

45   Battin, *op. cit.*, note 12 above, has suggested that the economics of hospital management may lead to the compulsory completion of a living will before admission to hospital.

46   *Re T (adult: refusal of medical treatment)* (1992) 9 BMLR, 46 at 60.

47   *Re T*, note 46 above, at 68.

48   *Practice Note* [1994] 2 All ER, 413.

49   BMA *op. cit.*, note 26 above. Or, perhaps, was. There is evidence that the BMA is hardening its attitude. See Dyer, C. (1995), 'Doctors must honour living wills', *British Medical Journal*, **310**, p. 895.

50   House of Lords Select Committee on Medical Ethics, HL Paper 21–1 (1994).

51   *Op. cit.*, note 7 above at BMLR 105 and 112.

52   *Re C (mental patient: medical treatment)* (1993) 15 BMLR, 77 per Thorpe J at 82.

53   Such an option probably exists in Scotland through the appointment of a tutor-dative: Ward, A.D. (1987), 'Revival of tutors-dative', *Scots Law Times*, p. 69.

54   *Airedale National Health Service Trust* v. *Bland* (1993) 12 BMLR, 64.

55   See, in particular, *Re Hilda M Peter* 529 A 2d 419 (NJ, 1987): 'The assumption [that there are still some benefits to be derived from the continued existence of an incompetent patient] is not appropriate in the case of persistent vegetative patients.' For judicial analysis, see the various stages of *Re Claire C Conroy* 464 A 2d 303 (NJ, 1983); on appeal 486 A 2d 1209 (NJ, 1985).

56   At BMLR, 118. Lord Lowry, however, had reservations on the point (at 122).

57   At 12 BMLR, 126.

58   *Frenchay Healthcare NHS Trust* v. *S* (1994), 17 BMLR, 156 per Sir Thomas Bingham MR at 162.

59   Warden, J. (1994), 'Euthanasia remains illegal in Britain', *British Medical Journal*, **308**, p. 1255.

60   *R* v. *Arthur* (1981) 12 BMLR, 1.

61   Thus moving from the position in *Auckland Area Health Board* v. *Attorney-General* [1993] 1 NZLR 235, [1993] 4 Med LR, 239 (where the patient was unable to express his wishes) to that in *Nancy B* v. *Hôtel-Dieu de Québec* (1992) 86 DLR (4th) 385, (1992) 15 BMLR, 95 (where the patient, suffering from the same disease, was competent).

62   Battin, *op. cit.*, note 12 above.

Index

N.B. Page references to footnotes are suffixed by the letter 'n'.